POLITICIZING
SCIENCE

POLITICIZING SCIENCE

SCIENCE

The Alchemy of Policymaking

EDITED BY

MICHAEL GOUGH

HOOVER INSTITUTION PRESS   GEORGE C. MARSHALL INSTITUTE
Stanford University   Stanford, California   Washington, D.C.

Hoover Institution Press Publication No. 517

Copyright © 2003 by the Board of Trustees of the
    Leland Stanford Junior University

First printing 2003
09   08   07   06   9   8   7   6   5   4   3   2

Manufactured in the United States of America

The paper used in this publication meets the minimum requirements
of American National Standard for Information Sciences–Permanence
of Paper for Printed Library Materials, ANSI Z39.48-1984. ⊗

Library of Congress Cataloging-in-Publication Data

Politicizing science : the alchemy of policymaking /
edited by Michael Gough.
        p.   cm.
   Includes bibliographical references and index.
   ISBN 0-8179-3932-6 (alk. paper)
   1. Science–Political aspects.   I. Gough, Michael, 1939–
Q175.5.A42   2003
338.973′06–dc21   2003041732

Contents

Foreword

Politics and science are intrinsically related.

Politicians, like all citizens, welcome the improvements in the physical world that have come from science, and they also worry about unintended consequences that accompany some scientific advances. In their quest to improve society, politicians have embraced science and increased government funding for research. Use of the public largesse is accompanied by political judgment and even direction about which kinds of science should be pursued and which discouraged or ignored.

Scientists, eager to continue their research, are influenced to propose research that they judge is most likely to obtain government funding. Others elect to pursue funding from regulatory agencies, possibly thinking that results and conclusions that support instituting or expanding of regulations may be more likely to be rewarded with continued funding.

Political-scientific interactions are part of the modern world. There is no doubt that some such interactions have paid great dividends to society for improvements in the physical, biological, engineering, and technological world.

As the essays in this book illuminate, however, the interactions between politics and science do not always benefit society. Politicians can focus on scientific observations that provide support for a decision that they favor for other reasons. Scientists can tailor their research programs and, perhaps more often, slant their conclusions to encourage politicians to believe that great payoffs will follow from their research or that a lurking catastrophe can be detected or prevented only if funding for their research continues. At a more mundane level, when drawing conclusions from research into environmental risks, the scientist intent on continuing research and the government administrator intent on expanding the reach of his or her agency are likely to focus on results that favor their interests.

The essays in this book, written by scientists who have participated in or witnessed firsthand political-scientific interactions, provide descriptions of political manipulations of science and of political considerations. The essays describe excessive politicization—the misapplication or outright manipulation of the scientific record to advance policy agendas. Ultimately, actions such as those described have unintended consequences, the brunt of which are borne by everyday citizens, not those who politicize at the expense of objectivity.

Scholars of the Hoover Institution and the George C. Marshall Institute cooperated on this project to draw attention to the misgivings of politicization for citizens as well as for public policy. These essays are intended to offer important insights to society about the costs of misusing science for political ends that involve the nation's policymakers, interest groups, media, and scientists. Better policy decisions and efficient use of society's resources will come from an examination of all available science that is embarked upon in ways that encourage the public interest and discourage purely opportunistic behavior.

A number of individuals worked on various stages of this

project from its conception to its publication. This project started with conversations between Director John Raisian of the Hoover Institution and John Moore and Jeffrey Salmon of the George C. Marshall Institute. Mark Herlong of the Marshall Institute provided valuable assistance and Richard Sousa, Hoover's senior associate director, provided guidance and assistance through virtually all phases of the process.

JOHN RAISIAN
Director,
Hoover Institution

WILLIAM O'KEEFE
President,
George C. Marshall Institute

Contributors

BRUCE N. AMES is a Professor in the Graduate School of Biochemistry and Molecular Biology at the University of California, Berkeley, and Senior Scientist at the Children's Hospital Oakland Research Institute.

Dr. Ames was director of the National Institute of Environmental Health Sciences Center at U.C. Berkeley for twenty-three years, and he chaired the U.C. Berkeley Department of Biochemistry for six years, 1983–1989. Prior to that he was the Microbial Genetics section chief at the National Institutes of Health in Bethesda, Maryland, a National Science Foundation senior fellow in the laboratories of Frances Crick in Cambridge, England, and F. Jacob in Paris, France, and a biochemist with the National Institutes of Health, where he began his career.

Bruce Ames is the inventor of the Ames Test, which allows scientists to test chemicals to see whether they cause mutations in bacteria and perhaps cancer in humans. His research and testimony led to bans on such synthetic chemicals as Tris, the flame-retardant used in children's pajamas.

He is the author of numerous professional papers as well as

editorials and opinion pieces that have appeared in major newspapers and magazines and the recipient of nearly thirty professional honors and awards. A member of the National Academy of Sciences, Ames earned his Ph.D. in biochemistry and genetics at the California Institute of Technology.

ROGER BATE is the director of the International Policy Network in Washington, D.C., and an adjunct fellow at the Competitive Enterprise Institute (CEI), also in Washington. He was the founder of the Environment Unit at the Institute of Economic Affairs in 1993, and he co-founded the European Science and Environment Forum in 1994. He is a board member of the South African non-governmental organization Africa, fighting malaria. Bate's Ph.D. is from Cambridge University.

He has advised the South Africa government on water markets and his research interests focus on international environmental regulations. He is particularly interested in the effects of pressures from Western politicians and Green activists to impose first-world environmental policies on developing countries.

Dr. Bate is the editor of *What Risk?* (Butterworth-Heinneman, 1997), a collection of papers that critically assess the way risk is regulated in society, and the author of several scholarly papers about risk and policies in developing countries. In addition, he has published numerous articles about risk and politics in newspapers and magazines, including the *Wall Street Journal,* the *Financial Times, Accountancy,* and *LM.* His most recent book is *Life's Adventure: Virtual Risk in a Real World* (Butterworth-Heinemann, 2000).

BERNARD L. COHEN earned his D.Sc. in physics in 1950. He was a group leader in cyclotron research at the Oak Ridge National Laboratory from 1950 through 1958. From 1958 through 1994, he was professor of physics and an adjunct professor in four other departments at the University of Pittsburgh, and he is now professor emeritus at the university. He has received several awards from professional physics societies.

In addition to more that 300 papers published in professional journals, Dr. Cohen has written six books: *Heart of the Atom* (Doubleday, 1967), translated into French, German, Italian, and Japanese; *Concepts of Nuclear Physics* (McGraw-Hill, 1971), translated into Arabic and republished by Tata McGraw-Hill (India); *Nuclear Science and Society* (Doubleday, 1974); *Before It's Too Late: A Scientist's Case for Nuclear Power* (Plenum, 1983), translated into Turkish; *Radon* (Consumer Reports Books, 1987, and Avon Books, 1989); and *The Nuclear Energy Option, Alternative for the Nineties* (Plenum, 1990), translated into Japanese and Spanish. Dr. Cohen developed an inexpensive, accurate radon measurement device that has been used by thousands of homeowners.

LOIS SWIRSKY GOLD is director of the Carcinogenic Potency Project and a Senior Scientist, University of California, Berkeley, and Lawrence Berkeley National Laboratory. She has directed the Carcinogenic Potency Project for twenty-four years, and has been a member of the National Institute of Environmental Health Sciences Center at the University of California at Berkeley for fifteen years.

Dr. Gold has served on the Panel of Expert Reviewers for the National Toxicology Program and on the boards of the Harvard Center for Risk Analysis and the Annapolis Center; she was a member of the Harvard Risk Management Group and is at present a member of the Advisory Committee to the Director, National Center for Environmental Health, Centers for Disease Control and Prevention (CDC). She is among the most frequently cited scientists in her field and was awarded the Annapolis Center Prize for risk communication.

She is the author of 100 papers on the subjects of analyses of animal cancer tests and implications for human cancer prevention, interspecies extrapolation, risk assessment, and regulatory policy. Her Carcinogenic Potency Database (CPDB), which presents analyses of the results of 6,000 chronic, long-term cancer tests on 1,400 chemicals, was published as a CRC handbook and is available on the Worldwide Web at http://potency.berkeley.edu.

MICHAEL GOUGH, a consultant, earned a B.A. at Grinnell College, and a Ph.D. (biology) at Brown University. After a decade-long academic career at the University of Michigan, Baylor Medical School, and the State University of New York at Stony Brook, and two years at the National Institutes of Health, he joined the congressional Office of Technology Assessment in 1977. At OTA, he began work in health risk assessment and environmental health policy and directed and contributed to OTA reports on subjects ranging from environmental causes of cancer, occupational health and safety, and Love Canal through corn genetics and biotechnology to oil shale mining.

In the early 1980's, Gough directed OTA's congressionally mandated oversight of Executive Branch studies of cancer in veterans of atom bomb tests and of the health of Vietnam veterans. He chaired a Department of Veterans Affairs advisory committee (1987–90) about the possible health effects of herbicides used in Vietnam and the Department of Health and Human Services committee (1990–95) that advises the United States Air Force study of the health of Air Force personnel who sprayed Agent Orange in Vietnam. In September 2000, he accepted reappointment to the DHHS committee. In 1995, he served on the Environmental Protection Agency's Science Advisory Board committee that evaluated EPA's dioxin reassessment.

During his academic career, he was a Fulbright Lecturer in Peru and India, and published two dozen papers in molecular biology, genetics, and microbiology. He is the author of *Dioxin, Agent Orange* (Plenum, 1986), coeditor, with T. S. Glickman, of

Readings in Risk (Johns Hopkins University Press, 1990), and coauthor, with Steven J. Milloy, of *Silencing Science* (Cato, 1999). He is the author of more than forty papers about environmental and occupational health as well as numerous newspaper op-eds. He has testified about three dozen times before Congress. He is a fellow of the Society for Risk Analysis and was president of the International Society for Regulatory Toxicology and Pharmacology (2001–2002).

DR. WILLIAM HAPPER is a Professor in the Department of Physics at Princeton University. On August 5, 1991, with the consent of the Senate, he was appointed Director of Energy Research in the Department of Energy by President George H. W. Bush. He oversaw a basic research budget of some $3 billion, which included much of the federal funding for high energy and nuclear physics, materials science, magnetic confinement fusion, environmental science, biology, the human genome project, and other areas. He remained at the DOE until May 31, 1993, to help during the transition to the Clinton administration. He was reappointed Professor of Physics at Princeton University on June 1, 1993, and named Eugene Higgens Professor of Physics and Chair of the University Research Board in 1995. With an interest in applied as well as basic science, he has served as a consultant to numerous firms, charitable foundations, and government agencies. From 1987 to 1990 he served as chairman of the Steering Committee of JASON, a group of scientists and engineers who advise agencies of the federal government on matters of defense, intelligence, energy policy, and other technical problems. A Fellow of the American Physical Society and the American Association for the Advancement of Science, and a member of the American Academy of Arts and Sciences, the National Academy of Sciences, and the American Philosophical Society, he has published over 160 scientific papers. He is also a member of the Board of Directors of the George C. Marshall Institute.

JOSEPH P. MARTINO is a private consultant in the field of technology management. He is a Fellow or Associate Fellow of several professional organizations, including the Institute of Electrical and Electronics Engineers, the American Institute of Aeronautics & Astronautics, and the American Association for the Advancement of Science. Dr. Martino served for twenty-two years in the U.S. Air Force, retiring as a full colonel. He holds degrees in physics (A.B., Miami University), electrical engineering (M.S., Purdue University), and mathematics (Ph.D., Ohio State University). While on active duty, he was a member of the Plans Staff of both the Air Force Avionics Laboratory and the Air Force Office of Scientific Research and was also Chief of the Environmental Analysis Division of the Air Force Office of Research and Analysis. After leaving the Air Force, Dr. Martino became a Senior Research Scientist at the University of Dayton Research Institute (1975–93), where he conducted research for the Army Missile Command, Martin Marietta, AT&T, IT&T, the Hobart Corporation, and other sponsors. He also created and taught graduate-level courses in technological forecasting and technology assessment in the School of Engineering—courses that covered technological forecasting (its application to R&D planning, business, and government) and methods of anticipating the social, economic, and environmental consequences of new technology. He is the author of *Technological Forecasting for Decision Making* (Elsevier Science, 2d ed., 1983) and *Science Funding: Politics and Porkbarrel* (Transaction Pub, 1992).

PATRICK J. MICHAELS is the Virginia State Climatologist, Professor of Environmental Sciences at the University of Virginia, and the CEO of an environmental consulting firm. He holds A.B. and S.M. degrees in biological sciences and plant ecology from the University of Chicago and a Ph.D. in ecological climatology from the University of Wisconsin at Madison. He is a past president of the American Association of State Climatologists and was program chair for the Committee on Applied Climatology of the American Meteorological Society. He is a visiting scientist with the George C. Marshall Institute in Washington, D.C., and a senior fellow of the Cato Institute, also in Washington.

Michaels is a contributing author and reviewer of the United Nations Intergovernmental Panel on Climate Change, and his research papers have been published in the major scientific journals, including *Climate Research, Climatic Change, Geophysical Research Letters, Journal of Climate, Nature,* and *Science.* His writings for the general public have appeared in the *Washington Post, Washington Times, Los Angeles Times, USA Today, Houston Chronicle,* and *Journal of Commerce.* He has appeared on ABC, NPR's "All Things Considered," PBS, Fox News Channel, CNN, MSNBC, CNBC, BBC, and Voice of America. According to *Nature* magazine, Michaels may be the most popular lecturer in the nation on the subject of global warming.

HENRY I. MILLER, M.S., M.D., is a research fellow at the Hoover Institution. His research focuses on public policy toward science and technology, especially pharmaceutical development and the new biotechnology. His work often emphasizes models for regulatory reform. Miller joined the Food and Drug Administration in 1979, where he was the medical reviewer for the first genetically engineered drugs evaluated by the FDA and was instrumental in the rapid licensing of human insulin and human growth hormone. From 1989 to 1994 he was the founding director of the FDA's Office of Biotechnology, and he represented the FDA and the U.S. government on various expert and policy panels. After leaving government service, Miller became the Robert Wesson Fellow in Scientific Philosophy and Public Policy at the Hoover

Institution (1994–96). His monographs about risk assessment and management and regulatory policy and reform include *Policy Controversy in Biotechnology: An Insider's View* (R. G. Landes, 1997), *Biotechnology Regulation: The Unacceptable Costs of Excessive Regulation* (London: Social Affairs Unit, 1997), and *To America's Health: A Proposal to Reform the Food and Drug Administration* (Hoover Institution Press, 2000). In addition, he has published academic papers in prominent medical, scientific, and public affairs journals—*The Lancet, Journal of the American Medical Association, Science, Nature,* and *Nature Biotechnology*—and articles for the general public in magazines and newspapers worldwide, including, the *Weekly Standard, National Review, Wall Street Journal, New York Times,* and *Financial Times* (London). He is a regular commentator on the nationally syndicated John Batchelor–Paul Alexander Program on ABC radio.

ROBERT NILSSON joined the Swedish Environmental Protection Agency in 1974. While the head of the toxicological unit of the Products Control Division, he was instrumental in pushing through regulations on reductions of lead in gasoline, as well as the first general restrictions in the world on the use of cadmium. In 1986, the newly created National Chemicals Inspectorate (KEMI) took over most of the responsibility for chemicals control, and Nilsson was senior toxicologist at KEMI until July 2002. Dr. Nilsson's Ph.D. was earned in biochemistry and radiation biology.

He has worked for OECD in various capacities, for the International Program on Chemical Safety (IPCS) and for WHO, and has advised the Ministries of Environment of the governments of Iran and India. From 1992 through July 2002, with support from U.S. industry and the Commission of the European Union, he conducted research on international environmental activities in his capacity as adjunct professor of molecular toxicology and risk assessment at Stockholm University, and since July 2002 he has continued that research as visiting professor there. His position as member of the executive board for the International Society of Regulatory Toxicology and Pharmacology in the U.S. (1994–99), as well as his role as technical adviser in products liability litigation, sometimes directed against industry interests, underline his continued interest in the "politics of chemical risk."

In July 2002, Dr. Nilsson accepted an appointment as professor in toxicology at the Nofer Institute of Occupational Medicine & WHO Collaborating Centre in Lodz, Poland. As part of his responsibility, he advises the new Polish government about creating and supervising a modern regulatory system for chemicals control.

STEPHEN SAFE is a Distinguished Professor of Veterinary Physiology & Pharmacology at Texas A&M University, where he is the director of the Center for Environmental and Rural Health. Dr. Safe's laboratory research is focused on environmental chemistry, toxicology, biochemistry, and mechanisms of action of polychlorinated biphenyls (PCBs), dibenzo-p-dioxins (PCDDs), dibenzofurans (PCDFs) and related compounds. He received a Phil. D. from Oxford University, and a M.Sc. from Queen's University. Dr. Safe is a Senior Scientist, Institute of Occupational and Environmental Medicine, Texas A&M University, and Adjunct Professor, University of Guelph. He served on the National Academy of Sciences Committee on Hormonally Active Agents in the Environment. A member of chemical, biochemical, and microbiology professional societies, he has received awards for his research and has been an honored lecturer at universities in the United States, Canada, and the United Kingdom. In addition to his research papers, published in premier scientific journals, he has published opinion pieces about risks from environmental chemicals in major newspapers.

S. FRED SINGER's research focuses on global climate change, depletion of stratospheric ozone, acid rain, air pollution, the U.S.

space program, energy resources, and U.S. energy policy. His Ph.D. in physics is from Princeton University.

A pioneer in rocket and satellite technology, Singer devised the basic instrument for measuring stratospheric ozone, was the principal investigator on a satellite experiment retrieved by the space shuttle in 1990, and was the first scientist to predict that population growth would increase atmospheric methane—an important greenhouse gas.

Now president of the Science and Environmental Policy Project, a nonprofit policy research group he founded in 1990, Singer is also Distinguished Research Professor at George Mason University and professor emeritus of environmental science at the University of Virginia. He was the founding Dean of the School of Environmental and Planetary Sciences, University of Miami (1964–67), and director of the Center for Atmospheric and Space Physics, University of Maryland (1953–62). Among his several positions in the U.S. government, he was the first director of the National Weather Satellite Service (1962–64) and Deputy Assistant Administrator for Policy, U.S. Environmental Protection Agency (1970–71).

Singer has received numerous awards for his research, including a Special Commendation from the White House for achievements in artificial earth satellites, a U.S. Department of Commerce Gold Medal Award, and the first Science Medal from the British Interplanetary Society. He has served on state and federal advisory panels, including five years as vice chairman of the National Advisory Committee on Oceans and Atmospheres. He frequently testifies before Congress.

He is the author or editor of more than a dozen books and monographs, including *Is There an Optimum Level of Population?* (McGraw-Hill, 1971), *Free Market Energy* (Universe Books, 1984), *Global Climate Change* (Paragon House, 1989), *Hot Talk, Cold Science: Global Warming's Unfinished Debate* (Independent Institute, 1997), and also has published more than 400 technical papers in scientific, economic, and public policy journals. His editorial essays and articles have appeared in numerous publications, including the *Wall Street Journal, New York Times, New Republic, Newsweek, Journal of Commerce, Washington Times,* and *Washington Post.*

Science, Risks, and Politics

MICHAEL GOUGH

The whole aim of practical politics is to keep the populace alarmed—and hence clamorous to be led to safety—by menacing it with a series of hobgoblins, all of them imaginary.
—H. L. Mencken

Science has changed the world profoundly, bringing great increases in life expectancies[1] and wealth. Along with desirable changes have come some unintended consequences that affect or might affect human health and the environment.

Governments, responding to concerns about such risks, have established "risk assessment and management" organizations to estimate the magnitude of the risks and to control them. The control efforts—almost always accomplished through government regulations—affect the livelihoods of individuals, communities, and industries. It is no surprise that such regulatory efforts lead to conflicts between those who see the risks as proven and

1. J. Oeppen and J. W. Vaupel, "Broken Limits to Life Expectancy." *Science* 296 (2002): 1029–31.

justifying immediate control and those who question the strength of the evidence about risk and see benefits from continuing use of the substance or process.

Ideally, the scientists or analysts who generate estimates of harm that may result from a risk would consider all the relevant facts and alternative interpretations of the data, and remain skeptical about tentative conclusions. Ideally, too, the agency officials and politicians, who have to enact a regulatory program, would consider its costs and benefits, ensure that it will do more good than harm, and remain open to options to stop or change the regulation in situations where the underlying science is tentative.

Those ideals do not exist, have never existed, and probably never will. Interest groups and government agencies succeed in raising a clamor about a purported risk that drowns out other considerations, even, in some cases, in the absence of factual support for the claims. The media, knowing that risks sell papers and draw viewers to news programs, focus on covering the people who assert the importance of the risk. In order to appear fair, a newspaper story about risk might quote a skeptic in the penultimate paragraph, or a two-to-five-minute TV segment might give a skeptic fifteen or twenty seconds at the end. But who will take the skeptic, his facts, and his opinions seriously if the reporters consider them of so little value as to make them appear as afterthoughts.

Politicians, seeing that the public treats a risk as real, often decide to "get out in front of the problem," even though they are aware that they have little or no knowledge of the science that supports the existence or importance of the risk. Scientists, aware of the political interest in risk and the public's awareness of it, will seek research funds, knowing that a result that buoys up the risk, or, at least, a result that does not sink it, is more likely to be published, to receive public attention, and to result in further funding. Or, they may elect to bypass the usual norms of science entirely, call a press conference and try to convince the public about a risk with no scientific peer review.

The authors of the chapters in this volume describe risk assessment and risk management activities that differ from any ideal. They describe scientists masking policy decisions as "scientific," and politicians labeling politically driven decisions as scientific, attempting thereby to place them outside the realm of political discussion, debate, and compromise. But this is an illusion. All policy matters involving human health and the environment are political. The more that political considerations dominate scientific considerations, the greater the potential for policy driven by ideology and less based on strong scientific underpinnings.

Government Involvements in Science

Governments realize the importance and power of science and employ the latest scientific tools and methods to carry out their functions. Science and politics have become inseparable because of funding and regulation policies. Moreover, politicians intervene in the practice of science, sometimes diverting science and the interpretation of scientific findings away from where the evidence leads to directions deemed politically desirable. Three chapters in this volume, by William Happer, Henry I. Miller, and Joseph P. Martino describe some such political interventions.

William Happer, "Harmful Politicization of Science"

Happer, a physicist who was Director of Energy Research at the Department of Energy during George H. W. Bush's presidency, discusses three interventions of politics into science. He describes the starvation and deaths that followed Trofim Lysenko's substitution of patent nonsense for genetics and plant science in the Soviet Union (with the full backing of Joseph Stalin and in accord with Communist scientific thought). He discusses the ultimately failed efforts of cold fusion advocates to corral the U.S. Congress into funding their "invention." He then turns to the politicization of science about environmental risks to human health and risks to the world's climate. He puts environmental risks into perspective with comments that some risks are so serious that everyone agrees that they need attention, while others are less certain because the effects of the risks, if there are any, cannot be measured. He also describes the bias in federal funding toward "research programs that reinforced messages of imminent doom: humanity and planet earth devastated by global warming, pestilence, famine, and flood."

Henry I. Miller, "The Corrosive Effects of Politicized Regulation of Science and Technology"

Miller, a former official of the Food and Drug Administration, describes the confluence of interests that can be arrayed to oppose a particular technology. Bureaucrats, whose power expands with their ability to regulate, and large companies that welcome regulatory hurdles because they have the legal and technical resources to jump them, leaving smaller, less affluent competitors little choice but to merge or to be bought out, can be found in league with activists openly antagonistic to a new technology. He is especially critical of some of the policy decisions about bioengineered products, including food, that arose during the Clinton administration. Miller concludes on a gloomy note, "There is no important constituency for sound science policy. On the contrary, politicization often represents little more than pandering to the [public's] fears, which sometimes verge on superstition."

Joseph P. Martino, "Science and Public Policy"

Martino, an engineer and retired U.S. Air Force colonel, discusses some of the most publicized environmental issues of the last decade or so—spotted owls, lynxes, the reintroduction (or, perhaps, more accurately, the introduction) of wolves into Yellowstone National Park, and attempts to resolve conflicting claims on the water in the Klamath Basin. In all those issues, there is evidence that government officials intentionally selected results, misinterpreted observations, and interfered with experiments in order to advance their goals.

Happer and Miller's chapters to some extent reflect the normal working of politics. New administrations replace the senior officials of federal agencies with appointees who share their political orientations. This is expected and customary, but as Happer and Miller describe, replacements made without consideration of maintaining a solid science base for making technical decisions can lead to mistakes.

Martino's examples should not to be taken to indicate that government scientists are to be mistrusted. There is no more justification for that than wholesale rejection of the results reported by industry scientists because of their funding or dismissing environmental organization scientists because of the pressures their organizations face in raising money. In all cases, skepticism, one of the hallmarks of science, is appropriate.

Science, Risks, Images, and Assertions

In his 1961 book, *The Image*,[2] Daniel J. Boorstin, the former Librarian of Congress, lamented that citizens were losing their skepticism and were too willing to accept what they were told by the media, which he called "news makers." The nomenclature is important. At some time in the past, news makers were the people who made discoveries and decisions, built dams and businesses,

---

2. D. J. Boorstin, *The Image: A Guide to Pseudo-Events in America* (1961; reprint, New York: Vintage Books, 1992).

educated and informed students and others about science; they were the people who did things. Now, they are the people who package stories for the media and the people in the media who decide what news to report. They know that they are competing for the public's attention. They are not so much interested in sifting through information to identify what is right and what is wrong—except in egregious cases, of course—as in attracting and holding an audience.

Government agencies, businesses, and environmental organizations burnish images to reach the public, and agencies' and environmental organizations' images of risk can lead immediately to calls for government action to control the risks. For instance, beginning in the early 1990s, a small group of scientist-activists asserted that tiny amounts of plastics and other industrial chemicals in the environment act as "endocrine disruptors" or "environmental estrogens" that disrupt the normal functioning of hormones and affect almost every aspect of growth and development in humans and animals.

Some media outlets trumpeted the 1996 book *Our Stolen Future*,[3] a compilation of mostly unverified observations and speculations, and a paper published in *Science*[4] that presented startling results purportedly showing that tiny concentrations of some chemicals behaved as endocrine disruptors. Congress rushed legislation that requires billions of dollars to be spent to test chemicals that were regarded as safe except for the alleged estrogenic effects.[5]

Many scientists reported they were unable to repeat the ob-

3. T. Colborn, D. Dumanoski, and J. P. Myers, *Our Stolen Future* (New York: Dutton, 1996).

4. S. F. Arnold et al., "Synergistic Activation of Estrogen Receptor with Combinations of Environmental Chemicals," *Science* 272 (1996): 1489–92 (subsequently retracted).

5. D. Byrd, "Goodbye Pesticides?" *Regulation* 20, no. 4 (1997): 57–62.

servations published in *Our Stolen Future*, and the results in the *Science* paper turned out to be fraudulent.[6] It made no difference to the law that requires chemical testing. Industry is doing the tests and passing the costs on to its customers. When it's all done (if it ever is), money that could have been used to benefit health and the environment will have been spent without great prospect of improving anyone's health. The unintended consequences of the forced misallocation of society's resources are rarely given any attention. But decisions have consequences, and ultimately the costs, whether or not they "buy" anything, are borne by workers or shareholders or society at large.

Three chapters in this volume describe expensive and extensive research efforts devoted to images of risk. Stephen Safe assesses the research that fails to find any health from endocrine disruptors in the environment. Bruce Ames and Lois Swirsky Gold review the collapse of the scientific underpinnings for the assertion that environmental chemicals are a major cause of cancer. Bernard L. Cohen contrasts the absence of data to show that nuclear power plants have caused death and disease with the near-total demise of the nuclear power industry because of assertions about cancer risks from the plants.

Stephen Safe, "Endocrine Disruptors"

The claims that tiny amounts of chemicals with estrogenic (hormonal) activity caused a multitude of health effects have some plausibility. Hormones, present in the body at very low concentrations, affect many biochemical reactions, and it's possible that environmental chemicals that mimic them would affect humans.

---

6. Office of the Secretary, Department of Health and Human Services. "Handling Misconduct: Case Summaries." http://ori.dhhs.gov/html/miscon duct/arnold.asp. The only penalty levied on the guilty scientist was an order that he not apply for federal research funding for five years. It made no difference to the scientist, who decided to go to law school.

Safe, a well-respected biochemist, reviews the extensive scientific literature and finds no convincing data about the putative effects of trace amounts of plastics and other chemicals on human beings. He concludes that too much effort was expended on the research because there is great reluctance on their (our) part to say "enough is enough." With limited funding available, this can seriously impede research that addresses more pressing environmental and human health issues.

Bruce Ames and Lois Swirsky Gold, "Cancer Prevention and the Environmental Chemical Distraction"

Bruce Ames, elected to the National Academy of Sciences in recognition of his research in genetics and genetic control, and his colleague, Lois Swirsky Gold, who has published and continuously updates a compendium of the results of laboratory tests for possibly carcinogenic chemicals, are convinced that those tests have, at most, a questionable bearing on human health. They argue that the high doses of chemicals used in the tests cause toxic effects that are rarely—probably never—seen at the far lower exposures experienced by humans. In the absence of those toxic effects, the chemicals are not a cancer risk. Despite the limited, and perhaps zero, risk from those chemicals, federal regulatory agencies that are interested in preventing cancer have focused their efforts on reducing exposures to them.

So what? Where's the harm in overregulation of chemicals? (1) No, or tiny at best, health gain can be expected from regulations. (2) The focus on "environmental carcinogens" diverts attention from research that is likely to make a difference in health.

To the extent that Ames and Gold are right, and they probably are right to a large extent, the fascination of politicians, regulators, the media, and the public with environment carcinogens will eventually be seen as more than a diversion of resources. It will also be seen as a fascination that retarded improvements in health.

Bernard L. Cohen, "Nuclear Power"

Cohen, a physicist, was a participant in the battle for acceptance of nuclear power that was waged between nuclear scientists and engineers on one side and political activists, aided by a few scientists and endorsed by the gullible media, on the other. The media embraced the activists' claims of great risks and failed to put the (far smaller than the activists claimed) risks from nuclear power into perspective, by, for instance, comparing a person's exposure to natural radiation to his possible exposure to radiation from a nuclear power plant. Nor were comparisons made between the risks of ordinary life—motor and industrial and home accidents that kill thousands—to radiation risks from nuclear power that have killed no one. Cohen speculates that the growing recognition that fossil fuel power plants are a major source of pollution and other problems, including problems arising from foreign sources of supply, will lead to a revival of interest in nuclear power.

The Persistence and Importance of Assertions

Careful research has weakened assertions that environmental chemicals are endocrine disruptors and major causes of cancer. Environmental organizations still tout the risks to raise the public's awareness—they say—and to solicit contributions. Government officials, in charge of programs to investigate the risks, continue to provide funds to scientists who look for evidence to support the assertions and to programs that test chemicals for effects that have little, at best, and more likely, no, relationship to human health. Environmental organizations' publicity and government spending programs can keep assertions alive despite mounting scientific evidence that they are wrong.

Cohen's chapter illuminates a dangerous component of risk assertions. Those who make assertions focus only on risks. They ignore any benefits that come from the substance or process and the possibility that elimination of their targeted risk may increase another risk. In the 1960s and 1970s, during the battle over nuclear power, there was no room in the antinuclear forces' world for any trade-offs. They acted as if shutting down nuclear plants involved no risks, having only the one effect of eliminating the cancer risk that they associated with the plants. In fact, there are few decisions to reduce risks that don't bring other risks, such as, in this case, more emissions of gases that may contribute to global warming.

Science and Risk Assessment

"Risk assessment" is the process for examining links between risks and possible harms—for instance, chemicals in the environment and cancer; increasing concentrations of atmospheric CO_2 and global warming. Risk assessment is often called "science-based" because part of the process—establishing that a chemical causes cancer in laboratory rats or that there is a correlation between CO_2 and atmospheric temperatures—is scientific.

From there on risk assessment is dependent on policy decisions and professional judgments. In the case of the animal studies, a policy decision is necessary about how to extrapolate from the number of cancers seen in rats exposed to high levels of a chemical to estimated numbers of cancers that might occur in people exposed to levels of the same chemical thousands of times lower. We will never be sure of the accuracy of the extrapolation because the expected number of cancers in the human population is too small to be detected.

In the case of global warming, many factors in addition to CO_2

—water vapor and aerosols, fluctuations in the sun's energy output—have been identified as playing a role in surface temperatures.[7] In recognition of the limited knowledge about the effects of those factors as well as uncertainty about the role of CO_2, policy decisions are required to decide which climate models are to be used to predict future temperature changes. Those models, based on uncertain science and policy decisions, may be used to set limits on emission rates and levels for decades into the future, with profound effects upon population, technology, economic growth, and energy systems. It is impossible to know how well the models' predictions will fit with reality until time passes, and, in the meantime, we cannot determine their accuracy, making the predictions unscientific because they cannot be checked by measurements.

Because of the prominence of policy judgments in the interpretations of risk assessments, it is more accurate to say only that risk assessment has some (limited) scientific component. To call it "science-based" is an overstatement because it differs radically from science.

Hypothesis and Science

Karl Popper, generally accepted as the leading twentieth-century philosopher of science,[8] divided science into two basic steps: the formation of a hypothesis (called variously an idea, a hypothesis, or a theory), followed by the testing of the hypothesis. The physicist Paul Davies and the biologist Peter Medawar, both admirers

7. *A Guide to Global Warming* (Washington, D.C.: George C. Marshall Institute, 2000).

8. K. Popper, *The Logic of Scientific Discovery* (New York: Basic Books, 1959). See also D. Miller, ed., *Popper Selections* (Princeton, N.J.: Princeton University Press, 1985). This paperback collection contains some of Popper's essays on science at pp. 133–206.

of Popper, have compared the formation of a hypothesis to a composer imagining the notes of a symphony or an artist mentally combining the colors and shapes that emerge as a painting.[9] Hypotheses can be imagined that require the intervention of God or magic or a specialized skill, but those are not scientific. To be scientific, a hypothesis must describe events in the physical world, and it can be tested in many detailed and specific ways. If the theory passes those tests, our confidence in the theory is reinforced. A theory that is too vague or general, or makes predictions concerning circumstances beyond our ability to test, is of little value.

Predictions of human cancer risks based on results of tests in rats cannot be tested; predictions from climate-change models cannot be tested. In science the capacity to test is the capacity to falsify or confirm a hypothesis.

Assertion and Risk Assessment

Assertions of risk, which in risk assessment are analogous to a hypothesis in science, do not have to withstand tests. Theo Colborn, an author of *Our Stolen Future*, stated, "Just because we don't have the evidence doesn't mean there are no effects."[10] Exactly: we may have overlooked something in our search for evidence. But, in context, Colborn's statement went much further. It was made after several years of scientific research had failed to support her assertions about endocrine disruptors. Her statement brushed the evidence aside. No matter how much information is

9. P. Davies, *The Mind of God: The Scientific Basis for a Rational World* (New York: Simon & Schuster, 1992); P. Medawar, "The Philosophy of Karl Popper," in P. Medawar, *The Threat and the Glory* (Oxford: Oxford University Press, 1991), pp. 91–101.

10. Theo Colborn, quoted in G. Easterbrook, "Science Fiction," *New Republic*, August 30, 1999, pp. 18–22.

piled up against an assertion, there is no reason for its proponents to drop it.

Once an agency or politician accepts an assertion—and acceptance may come easily when a new program can be established or voters' favor curried—the agency or politician can demand evidence to set the assertion aside, no matter how flimsy the evidence for it. The demand cannot be met because it involves proving a negative.

Scientists' Roles in Risk Assessment

The fact that science may play only a limited role in risk assessment makes it that much more important "to get the science right." In addition to their central role in designing studies and collecting the data that go into risk assessments, scientists play a central role in devising models for estimating health risks and climate change and in selecting the models to be used.

Politicians and others interested in the best use of the science that goes into risk assessments should ensure that the scientists who participate in model selection represent the range of opinions about models. They should not leave this task up to the same group of people—scientists or policymakers—who selected the currently used models. New ideas and new perspectives are essential for designing experiments and models and for testing new ideas.

Weighing the Evidence

Scientific studies about a hypothesis, whether supportive of it ("positive") or not supportive ("negative") probably have equal chance of being published because scientists want to be as sure as they can about the hypotheses that they accept as accurate descriptions of the physical world. It is different in risk assessment.[11] Many scientists are convinced that "negative results" about a risk are less likely to be published than "positive results."

Despite that bias, government agencies sometimes confront conflicting data about a risk issue, and someone or some organization is given the responsibility of judging and weighing the data. Ideally, he or she would weigh the evidence in an even-handed fashion. That may be difficult for a regulator considering the effects of saying that a risk no longer requires regulation, or for a research administration that realizes that concluding that enough information has been done requires that no more research funding will be provided.

Consensus Science

When a risk is politically important and the science is uncertain, policymakers who want to appear to be doing something rather than waiting for more certain results can turn to committees of scientists for a review of the available information. The outcome from most such committees is a consensus report.

Consensus panels about risks almost always include people who made the assertion, and they usually steer a careful, centrist path through the scientific information. It is not unusual for them to conclude that the risk is not as big as some asserted, but that it can't be rejected, and that more research is needed. How different from science. Scientists strive to find evidence that supports one conclusion over another. "Splitting the difference" or "finding a consensus" is not science. Robert A. Pielke Jr., of the University

11. M. Gough, "Antagonism—No Synergism—in Pairwise Tests of Carcinogens in Rats," *Regulatory Toxicology and Pharmacology* 35 (2002): 383–92, is an analysis of a study that showed that mixtures of two carcinogens do not cause more cancers than either carcinogen by itself. The study, completed in 1978, was never published by its sponsor, the National Cancer Institute.

of Colorado, wrote, "Consensus science can provide only an illusion of certainty. When consensus is substituted for a diversity of perspectives, it may in fact unnecessarily constrain decision makers' options."[12] In practice, decision makers will never hear some perspectives.

Two chapters in this volume discuss the workings and results of consensus panels. Both provide suggestions about how the panels might work better.

Patrick J. Michaels, "Science or Political Science? An Assessment of the U.S. National Assessment of the Potential Consequences of Climate Variability and Change"

Michaels, the State Climatologist for Virginia, criticizes the work and conclusions of a United States consensus panel, the National Assessment Synthesis Team, which was created to investigate the possible effects of warming on the United States. The team based all its projections on two climate change models that predicted the greatest changes in temperature and rainfall, ignoring other models—compatible with all that is known—that predict smaller changes. Michaels urges that the synthesis team be reconstituted with different members who will take the uncertainty of the models into account.

Michael Gough, "The Political Science of Agent Orange and Dioxin"

By 1990, panels at the EPA, in the Department of Health and Human Services, and the congressional Office of Technology Assessment (OTA), had decided that there was no convincing evidence that Agent Orange had harmed veterans of the war in Vietnam. Members of Congress, who had long before accepted the veterans' claims about harms, directed the Institute of Medi-

12. R. A. Pielke Jr., "Room for Doubt," *Nature* 410 (2001): 151.

cine (IOM) to review the same evidence. The IOM did not review
the data as scientists typically do, but matched it against some
other criteria (never specified), leaving it unclear about what criteria the committee used. Gough also criticizes the composition
of the IOM committee, which was set up to exclude scientists who
had taken a stand of any kind in discussions about Agent Orange,
dioxin, or related substances. That action, he says, eliminated the
most knowledgeable scientists from the panel.

Consensus and Policy

The recommendations of consensus panels should be treated with
caution because they are based on far-from-certain science and
are driven by social dynamics that can substitute the value of
cohesion—"group think"—for independent, critical thinking. Instead they serve as the basis for guiding funding decisions, planning responses to changes that may or may not take place (Michaels's chapter), or providing compensation for diseases that
occur no more commonly in an "exposed" population than in the
population as a whole (Gough's chapter). For the public and the
media, consensus panel recommendations that establish and sustain research programs, response programs, or compensation
programs are a strong message that "there must be something
there."

The Precautionary Principle

Science and risk assessment, with all their flaws, take time, cost
money, and leave some participants unsatisfied. The precautionary principle, which originated among German Greens in the
1970s, is offered as an alternative. It has no definitive definition.
At least twenty can be found in treaties, laws, journal articles and
books, and Cass Sunstein has placed them on a scale from weak

to strong.[13] The "weak" ones, if implemented in the U.S., would result in few changes from the current scheme of risk assessment and managment. Stronger definitions would toss science aside. For instance, one definition says, "action should be taken to correct a problem as soon as there is evidence that harm *may occur*, not after the harm has already occurred" (emphasis added; "may occur" is a low hurdle; any assertion should be able to leap it).

In the United States, the president of Friends of the Earth, testifying before a House of Representatives committee in 2002, said:

> . . . the precautionary principle mandates that when there is a risk of significant health or environmental damage to others or to future generations, and when there is scientific uncertainty as to the nature of that damage or the likelihood of the risk, then decisions should be made so as to prevent such activities from being conducted unless and until scientific evidence shows that the damage will not occur.[14]

Sunstein says that the strong statements mean "that regulation is required whenever there is a possible risk to health, safety, or the environment, even if the supporting evidence is speculative and even if the economic costs of regulation are high."[15] John Graham, administrator of the Office of Information and Regulatory Affairs in the Office of Management and Budget, speaking about the precautionary principle, presented a number of illustrations to show

13. C. R. Sunstein, "Beyond the Precautionary Principle," John M. Olin Law and Economics Working Paper no. 149 (2d series), The Law School, University of Chicago. Available at http://www.law.uchicago.edu/Lawecon/WkngPprs_126-150/149.CRS.Precaution.pdf.

14. B. Blackwelder, testimony before the Senate Appropriations Committee, Subcommittee on Labor, Health, and Human Services, January 24, 2002. Quoted in Sunstein, 2002.

15. Sunstein, p. 7.

that "precaution," by itself, is not a reliable guide for action.[16] (Sunstein argues that it is no guide at all.)

Two chapters in this volume discuss the precautionary principle. For rich countries, application of the principle may result only in some minor irritations and higher prices as products are taken off the market; in poor countries, it can mean death.

Robert Nilsson, "Science and Politics in the Regulation of Chemicals in Sweden"

Sweden is a fervent proponent of the precautionary principle, and Swedish government reviews of risk information place emphasis on studies that suggest a risk, largely exclude consideration of other results, and preclude consideration of benefits. Sweden has imposed restrictions on the use of chemicals that have been approved for use in the European Union (EU), bringing Sweden into conflict with the EU's principles of free trade. Robert Nilsson, until recently a senior scientist in the agency of the Swedish government that regulates exposures to chemicals, sees two possible futures for Sweden's chemical regulations. Sweden's membership in the EU may force it to bring its chemical regulations in line with the rest of Europe's. Alternatively, and chemical regulation plays only a tiny role in deliberations about it, Sweden may leave the EU.

Roger Bate, "How Precaution Kills: The Demise of DDT and the Resurgence of Malaria"

The widespread use of DDT, along with other measures, eliminated malaria from many countries in the world in the 1940s

---

16. J. D. Graham, "The Role of Precaution in Risk Management," speech delivered at the International Society of Regulatory Toxicology and Pharmacology "Precautionary Principle Workshop," Crystal City, Va., June 20, 2002, available at http://www.whitehouse.gov/omb/inforeg/risk_mgmt_speech062002.html.

through the 1960s by controlling the mosquitoes that spread the microbe that causes the disease. After Rachel Carson's *Silent Spring* indicted DDT as the cause of decreasing bird populations in the United States and the publication of some never-replicated tests that showed DDT to be a carcinogen in laboratory animals, the United States and other rich countries reduced, then eliminated, the use of DDT, substituting more expensive insecticides for it. Bate, director of the International Policy Network, traces the sad history as poor countries adopted the environmental policies of the rich world and phased out DDT. Malaria rates rose, and the disease became, once again, a major killer. Bate considers the DDT saga as an example of the likely outcome of increased reliance on the precautionary principle as a guide for international environmental decision making.

Political Throttling of Science

S. Fred Singer is a retired university professor and the president of a nonprofit policy research organization. In the final chapter in this volume, he describes an attempt by a politically affiliated scientist to silence him, by an attack on his honesty. The attack failed, but a court case was necessary to stop it. The chapter also includes a description of a subsequent attempt by Vice President Al Gore to belittle Singer's reputation because of his accepting funds from industry. A TV newsperson stopped that attempt.

S. Fred Singer, "The Revelle-Gore Story:
Attempted Political Suppression of Science"

In 1991, three scientists, S. Fred Singer, Chauncey Starr, and Roger Revelle, published a paper about global warming in a small-circulation journal, *Cosmos*. In the paper, they concluded that there was no need to take immediate action to counter global warming. Later, after Dr. Revelle had died, Singer was contacted about preparing a paper for a collection of essays on climate change, and he asked the editor of the collection to republish the *Cosmos* paper. The editor agreed.

At about the same time, a journalist quoted then-Senator Al Gore as having credited Dr. Revelle with introducing him to the idea of climate change and contrasted Dr. Revelle's statement in the *Cosmos* paper with Mr. Gore's calls for immediate action to counter global warming. Subsequently, a scientist involved in the preparation of the collection of essays demanded that Singer remove Revelle's name from the paper before it was republished. Singer refused. That scientist, in close contact with Senator Gore's staff, began a campaign saying that Singer had coerced Revelle, described as having been sick and enfeebled, to attach his name to a paper that he had not written. A suit was brought on Singer's behalf that was settled when the accusing scientist retracted his accusations and apologized for making them. The retraction specifically acknowledged that there was no evidence that Dr. Revelle had been coerced.

Later, Vice President Gore made a more direct assault on Singer. He called Ted Koppel, the TV news anchor, and asked him to investigate Singer's sources of funding. The attempt blew up in Gore's face. On his February 24, 1994, program, Koppel asked, "Is this a case of industry supporting scientists who happen to hold sympathetic views, or scientists adapting their views to accommodate industry?" And he chastised Gore.

There is some irony in the fact that former Vice President Gore, one of the most scientifically literate men to sit in the White House in this century, resorted to political means to achieve what should ultimately be resolved on a purely scientific basis.

"The Acid of Truth"

In his response to Vice President Gore, Ted Koppel characterized science in no uncertain terms: "The measure of good science is neither the politics of the scientist nor the people with whom the scientist associates. It is the immersion of hypotheses into the acid of truth. That's the hard way to do it, but it's the only way that works." Koppel's ringing defense of scientists and the importance of looking at their work and not at their funding was the most significant stop to Vice President Gore's attempts to discredit Dr. Singer and other scientists with whom he disagreed. It is remarkable, however, that in a country that prides itself on a scientific base a TV newsman was the vocal defender of science.

Congress and members of the administration, of any administration, can demonstrate their commitment to sound science by deflecting attacks based on funding or association, whether the attacks are directed at industry scientists, government scientists, or environmental organization scientists. Yet they rarely do. To find errors in a scientist's data or interpretations is a legitimate task for a scientist or a nonscientist, but besmirching his reputation instead of examining his work is not.

To ask for consideration of science on its merits is a bit like a plea based on Mom and apple pie. It's actually worse because it's relatively easy to dismiss a scientist on the basis of "What do you expect? Look where she gets her money." It's more difficult to examine her research and find out if it's good or bad. In fact, that's usually well beyond the ability of a nonscientist, but it's not beyond his or her ability to ask that the examination be made.

Recommendations

From the contents of the chapters in this book, it is apparent that better policy decisions and better use of society's resources will come from an examination of all available science carried out in ways to encourage critical thinking by scientists and policymakers. The three recommendations that follow are directed at Congress and the Executive Branch. They are equally applicable to other citizens interested in improving the usefulness of science in risk management decisions.

1. Demand Transparency

Congress recognized the importance of review of the science that goes into agency decisions when it included the "data quality section" (sometimes called "data quality act") in the FY 1999 Omnibus Appropriations Act (P.L. 105–277). Commencing October 1, 2000, federal agencies are required to provide all information produced under a federal award to interested parties. Such data will be of value to those who want to understand and to support or challenge the scientific bases for an agency decision.

As agencies receive requests, Congress and the Office of Information and Regulatory Affairs (OIRA) in the Office of Management and Budget should monitor the adequacy of agency responses. As information about agency responses is acquired, OIRA, which administers the "data quality act," can alter guidelines for its implementation as needed.

Congress and the Executive Branch can also use the Supreme Court's decisions about the admission of expert testimony in courts as a starting point for establishing standards for consideration of experts and their opinions. In the 1993 "Daubert Case,"[17] the U.S. Supreme Court set down some guidelines for courts to use to decide whether an expert and his or her testimony is ad-

---

17. *Daubert v. Merrell Dow Pharmaceuticals, Inc.*, 509 U.S. 579 (1993). Subsequently in "the Kumho Tire case" (*Khumo Tire Co. v. Charmichael,* 526 U.S. 137 (1999)), the Supreme Court extended the rules laid down in Daubert for admission of scientific evidence to testimony based on "technical" and "other specialized knowledge" such as that of mechanics or economists. The Kumho case ended the practice of some lawyers of putting experts on the stand to testify that the witness wasn't subject to Daubert because the testimony wasn't, strictly, scientific.

missible in Federal Courts.[18] Federal advisory committees could establish requirements that have to be met—say, publication of results in a peer-reviewed journal or access to the underlying data that go into a calculation—before the data or opinions will be heard.

2. Establish Advisory Panels and Get Rid of Consensus Committees

Almost every decision in our society comes from resolving disagreements: labor/management; prosecutors/defense attorneys; even sports events. Why should the resolution of scientific controversies that are important enough to warrant governmental attention be among the few settled by consensus?

Democracy can suffer from decisions based on "scientific consensus," which usually means that, though the science is not clear, some group of people has chosen a path through the controversies to a resolution of fewest regrets or maximum funding for research. Those decisions, cloaked in the authority of science, are too often removed from the checks and balances of politics. Politicians who like the consensus can deflect criticism by saying, "It's a scientific decision, well beyond my understanding and out of my hands." Those who dislike it may find it difficult and inappropriate to question or to argue about "the science." Thus politicians who benefit from a consensus decision are able to evade responsibility for their actions; it takes authority away from those who disagree; it politicizes science.

Currently, Congress and the Executive Branch depend on committees of the National Academy of Sciences for advice. They

18. D. Goodstein, "How Science Works," *Reference Manual on Scientific Evidence*, 2d ed. (Washington, D.C.: Federal Judicial Center, 2000) pp. 67–82. Available at http://air.fjc.gov/public/pdf.nsf/lookup/sciman00.pdf/$file/sciman00.pdf.

could improve the quality of advice by insisting that the committees include knowledgeable partisans about the issue under review and that the committees place a high priority on vigorous debate rather than focus on consensus. Reports should, of course, draw attention to issues on which there is genuine consensus, but they should also include minority and divergent views on issues for which there is a range of credible scientific views. "Group think" is not a good route to resolving complex science based policy issues.

3. Continue U.S. Policies About
Science, Risk, and the Environment

Making decisions about risks to health and the environment is difficult for Congress, for regulatory agency administrators, for officials of industry, and for the public that awaits the decisions. Questions about science, economics, trade-offs, and uncertainty seldom have clear-cut answers. Many countries, many international treaties, and many environmental organizations have offered the precautionary principle as a shibboleth, a near-magic principle, to guide decisions about risks.

The many definitions of the precautionary principle do no more than provide comfort to those who think that the science and economics and politics that go into risk decisions can be put aside in favor of a magic bullet. There is no magic bullet. The precautionary principle(s) is (are) the product of philosophers considering the fate of the earth, and it is supposed to provide direction for decision making, including the use of science. With that in mind, it is worthwhile to recall the statement of the physicist Richard Feynman, "Philosophers say a great deal about what is absolutely necessary for science, and it is always, so far as one can see, rather naive, and probably wrong."

The U.S. Congress has established science-based regulatory

agencies and has written specific laws to deal with risks to health and the environment. The agencies and various government-appointed committees have accumulated the world's knowledge about risks and established procedures for considering the nuances of the information. As is apparent to readers of this book, improvements can be made.

Improvement will not come from policies based on the precautionary principle or any similar principle, which ignores the specifics of different risks and the benefits that accompany the substance or process that is being examined. Good policy cannot be derived by skipping over the fact that we live in a world of trade-offs and that actions have consequences. A regulatory and policy system that produces greater value for society must have a foundation of credibility. Far better to emphasize science in the risk assessment process and to examine the process and evaluate how well it works than to chase after lofty aspirations embodied in a principle without definition.

ONE

Harmful Politicization of Science

WILLIAM HAPPER

Politicization is inevitable when governments provide funding for science. The public expects to get something back from the science they support—for example, better health, national security, jobs. This normal politicization does no harm and may even be good for science and society. But politicization taken to the extreme can be very harmful. In extreme politicization, governments or powerful advocacy groups use science and scientists who share or benefit from the politicization to drive science out of technical decisions and to promote a nonscientific agenda.

My discussion of politicization of science begins with what must be its most extreme manifestation, when the Soviet Union used denial of income, imprisonment, and execution to impose its political will on the science of biology. The same desires for wealth, recognition, and power that propelled the politicization of Soviet biology exist in our democracy, but tyranny is absent. In its place, those who seek to politicize science here attempt to divert federal research funds to their ends and to stifle dissenting opinions, using the power of the press, congressional hearings, and appeals to patriotism.

The proponents of cold fusion in the United States used all those means in their quest for money and fame and standing. In the end, they failed because their claims were shown to be based on corrupt or misinterpreted experiments. While the debate was going on, at least one politician testified that scientists who expressed skepticism about cold fusion were unpatriotically inhibiting pursuit of the most important scientific breakthrough since the invention of fire. Worse, those who stood in the way of cold fusion were delaying development of a scientific breakthrough that would reverse many of the world's environmental problems because it would provide pollution-free energy.

Protection and improvement of the environment are now the siren song of politicians, businessmen, and scientists who claim that their conclusions about global climate change and their proposals to stave off catastrophic change are the only thing standing between mankind and a bleak, blasted planet in the future. They have, to some degree, succeeded in strangling the flow of research money to scientists who question their conclusions and prescriptions.

In my own case, I lost a federal position because of citing scientific research findings that undermined a politician's rhetoric. I did not suffer for my actions as did the Soviet biologists, but my dismissal surely serves as a warning to other government scientists and, perhaps more importantly, to nongovernment scientists who act as advisers to the government, that politics can trump science even in purely technical topics.

The politicization of science is impossible without the participation of some scientists in it. Politicians in both tyrannies and democracies are susceptible to scientists who say that they can show the way to manage nature without all the complicated baggage of ordinary science. How attractive the bright, adventurous, and brave individuals are who cast off the burdensome limitations of facts and theory that constrain the scientists who disagree with them. But politicians and citizens alike should question scientists who are unwilling to subject their observations and theories to independent tests, and their ideas and conclusions to discussion among technically qualified peers. Unhappily for society, such scientists, with sufficient political backing, can subvert the funding process so that information critical to their claims cannot be developed. At the present time, it is very difficult to obtain funding, either from U.S. governmental sources or from private foundations, for research that does not presuppose impending environmental doom. Suggestions that moderate global warming may actually be a good thing for humanity are treated with ridicule and hostility.

Lysenko's Destruction of Biology in the Soviet Union

Some of the worst consequences of politicized science have come from the seemingly noble aim of improving human well-being. Those who promise to circumvent the limitations that scientific laws place on human existence can always count on adulation, power, and wealth. A particularly egregious and well-documented example of this was Trofim Lysenko's destruction of biology in the Soviet Union. From the time he burst into public view in 1928 until the downfall of Khrushchev in 1964, Lysenko replaced real biology in the Soviet Union with falsehoods, prisons, and executions. Many details about Lysenko's career can be found in the excellent books by Valery N. Soyfer, *Power and Science* (in Russian), and *Lysenko and the Tragedy of Soviet Science* (in English).[1] A "people's academic," Trofim Lysenko promised to revolutionize the laws of agriculture, just as his Communist masters were trying to revolutionize human society.

The Soviet Union forcibly collectivized agriculture in 1928 and forced peasants to surrender their land, livestock, and machinery and to join collective farms. All grain was confiscated from the peasants, even grain needed for planting the following year's crops. Massive famines followed in 1929 and the early 1930s. Several million peasants starved to death in the Ukraine, and the Red Army was used to collect the grain harvest, such as it was, because whole villages had perished from hunger.

Hard-working and successful small farmers remained productive and were an affront to Soviet collectivism. Referring to these enterprising farmers as *kulaks* (clenched fist in Russian), Stalin orchestrated the "liquidation of kulaks as a class." Thousands were executed, and millions were deported to Siberia or Central Asia.

To try to cope with the disastrous effects of collectivization, the Communist Party ordered the rapid development of more productive varieties of wheat and other important crops. It imposed impossible demands on agricultural research institutions to improve (within one year) crop yields, resistance to diseases and pests, ease of harvest, food value, and so on.

The plant breeders and geneticists of the Soviet Union were some of the best in the world. Moreover, they had some of the finest genetic pools of wheat to start with; indeed, wheat varieties of Russian ancestry were the sources of the most productive wheat strains grown in the United States and Canada.

With the best of planning and luck, the time scale for intro-

---

1. V. N. Soyfer, *Vlast' i Nauka* (Power and Science) (Tenafly, N.J.: Hermitage Press, 1988); V. N. Soyfer, *Lysenko and the Tragedy of Soviet Science* (New Brunswick, N.J.: Rutgers University Press, 1994).

ducing effective new varieties is much longer than one year. Several years are needed to evaluate hybrids or to select varieties with desirable properties. More years are needed to produce sufficient seed for massive plantings. Lenin himself, responding to a complaint by the Russian author Gorky about the arrest of intellectuals, replied, "In fact, they are not the brain of the nation, but shit."[2] So it was not surprising that both the popular and the scientific press labeled those hapless Russian agronomists who pointed out the impossibility of producing effective new plant varieties in one year as "enemies of the Soviet people."

No wonder the Communists paid attention when young Trofim Lysenko declared that the genetics of Mendel's peas and Morgan's fruit flies was incorrect and simply a capitalist plot to exploit the peasants and working class. Lysenko believed that environmental factors determined the performance of plants and that acquired characteristics could be inherited. Having unmasked the evil Western myth of gene-based inheritance, Lysenko promised almost instant improvements in agricultural production.

Lysenko's origins—a peasant background, and little education—helped him avoid the hatred of the Soviet authorities for the intelligentsia. He first became famous in 1928 by claiming that a series of simple steps, within reach of any farmer, produced markedly improved yields of wheat. All that was necessary was "vernalization"—soaking winter-wheat seed in the fall, burying it in sacks under the snow, and planting it in the spring like ordinary spring wheat. This was all a fraud, supported by corrupted experiments and falsified statistics.

Stalin himself joined the fray, praising Lysenko and his people's scientists, and dismissing as old-fashioned and counterrevolutionary those who believed in genes. Many opportunistic biologists hopped on the Lysenko bandwagon, and he and his

2. Soyfer, *Vlast' i Nauka*, p. 6.

supporters founded Scientific Institutes of Vernalization, while his disciples took over existing institutions. Some brave Soviet biologists opposed Lysenko and many paid for this with their jobs or even their lives. N. I. Vavilov, a plant breeder of international renown, died in prison. Others were simply shot.

Honest scientists from other disciplines were alarmed about what was happening, but for many years they did little to interfere. By the outbreak of World War II, Lysenko and his henchmen were in full control of biology in the Soviet Academy of Sciences.

During the war, Lysenko's younger brother Pavel, a scientific worker in Kharkov, defected to the Germans when they overran the city. The younger Lysenko so impressed the German occupation forces that they named him mayor of occupied Kharkov. After the defeat of the Germans, Pavel managed to escape to the West and he made unflattering comments about the Soviet Union in Voice of America broadcasts. This made Trofim "a family member of an enemy of the people," a criminal offense in the Soviet Union. At about this same time, many in the top levels of the Soviet government were beginning to realize that Lysenko was a fraud who had done much damage to the Soviet Union. Lysenko's hold on Soviet biology weakened as articles in both the popular and scientific press began to assert that chromosomes and genes really did have something to do with inheritance and were important factors in practical agricultural science.

But Lysenko was not so easily defeated. By great good luck he was saved by Stalin himself. Someone had sent Stalin samples of branched wheat from his home republic of Georgia. Up to seven ears would grow on each stalk of this wheat, and Stalin was convinced that widespread planting of branched wheat would be the solution to the periodic crop failures and famines that still plagued the Soviet Union. Stalin invited Lysenko to visit him in his office, gave Lysenko a handful of seeds of the branched wheat, and ordered him to improve the wheat and make enough seed for the entire country. This Lysenko cheerfully promised to do, and as part of the bargain, he gained permission to deal once and for all with his remaining scientific enemies.

With Stalin's support Lysenko carefully orchestrated a trap for his opponents during the meeting of the All-Union Academy of Agricultural Sciences in August 1948. Lysenko's agents encouraged the few remaining honest geneticists to speak up in favor of genes and chromosomes. On the last day of the conference Lysenko stunned the conference by announcing that Stalin himself had decreed that henceforth there would be only one approved biology in the Soviet union, that of Lysenko. From then on, taking genes and chromosomes seriously was tantamount to treason.

In the aftermath of the 1948 conference, most of the remaining honest geneticists in the Soviet Union were fired from their jobs and replaced by Lysenko's protégés. The famous branched wheat that gained Stalin's support for Lysenko turned out to give much poorer yields than ordinary, unbranched wheat, but with Stalin's support, this was no problem for Lysenko. After Stalin's death, it was not long before Lysenko hypnotized his successor, Nikita Khrushchev, who provided the same top-level political support to which Lysenko had become accustomed.

In spite of Lysenko's complete triumph over his scientific enemies in 1948, it was increasingly clear to objective observers in the Soviet Union and abroad that Lysenko's bizarre agricultural practices, together with the disincentives of Soviet economic policies, were ruining Soviet food production. Nevertheless, Lysenko continued to enjoy the full support of the leadership of the Communist Party, and no biologists who disagreed with him remained in any position to challenge or question him. The only effective scientific opposition came from outside biology.

The physicists Peter Kapitza, who later won a Nobel Prize for his work on low-temperature physics, Igor Tamm, and Andrei

Sakharov were some of the most fearless defenders of honest genetics. Lysenko hated them all, but Tamm and Sakharov were credited with the invention of the Soviet hydrogen bomb, and Lysenko did not have sufficient political power to have them jailed or shot, as he had done with his opponents in the field of biology. In 1964, Tamm and Sakharov led a successful campaign to thwart Lysenko's attempt to pack the Soviet Academy of Sciences with his cronies. This so infuriated Khrushchev that he decided to dissolve the Academy of Sciences. Luckily for Soviet science, Khrushchev was so confident of success that he took a vacation before completing his dismantlement of the Academy. On October 14, 1964, Anastas I. Mikoyan and an impressive contingent of Red Army generals showed up at Khrushchev's vacation spot and announced that he, Khrushchev, had just retired and would be drawing his pension from now on. So the "Little October Revolution," as the Russians like to call this episode, saved Soviet science from Lysenko.

The Lysenko episode shows that an entire scientific discipline can be destroyed if the attractions of false science are great enough and if its proponents are ruthless enough. The great Russian poetess Anna Axmatova, who lost her husband and nearly lost her son, a distinguished historian, to Stalin's executioners, in a few lines of verse summarizes the tragedies Lysenko and other opportunists brought to Russia:

TO THE DEFENDERS OF STALIN

Those are the ones who shouted,
"release Barrabas to us for our holiday,"
those who commanded Socrates to drink the hemlock
in the dim confines of the dungeon.
We should pour out the same drink for them,
in their innocent, slandering mouths,

these amiable lovers of tortures,
these experts in the production of orphans.[3]

The Lysenko affair is one of the most thoroughly documented and horrifying examples of the politicization of science, but no country or age is immune. In totalitarian societies politicized science often leads to tragedy; in democratic societies politicized science often ends in wasted time and effort and sometimes in farce.

To illustrate the different histories of politicized science in totalitarian societies and democracies, I will compare Lysenko's biology in the Soviet Union with the history of "cold fusion" in the United States. Most of my discussion of cold fusion has been taken from the excellent book by John Huizenga, *Cold Fusion: The Scientific Fiasco of the Century.*[4]

Cold Fusion

What can be more annoying than the difficulty of getting controlled fusion energy on earth? If we could only figure out how to do it, we could provide the world's energy needs indefinitely with the practically inexhaustible supplies of deuterium and lithium available in the oceans. We know how to get large amounts of energy from fusing deuterium and tritium nuclei in a thermonuclear weapon. But after nearly fifty years of hard work and large expenditures of research funds, the world has yet to harness fusion energy to generate electrical power. Magnetic fusion devices are large, costly, and still far from practical; imploding small sam-

---

3. A. Axmatova, *Stikhov Moikh Belaya Staya* (The White Flock of My Verses) (Moscow: Exmo Press, 2000).
4. John R. Huizenga, *Cold Fusion: The Scientific Fiasco of the Century* (Rochester, N.Y.: University of Rochester Press, 1992).

ples of deuterium and tritium gas with large lasers also still has a long way to go before it can be a practical energy source.[5]

In light of the great effort and limited results, Professor B. Stanley Pons and his colleague, Dr. Martin Fleischman, surprised the whole world on March 23, 1989. Pons, chairman of the Chemistry Department at the University of Utah, and Fleischman, a distinguished electrochemist from England, announced that they had observed the generation of substantial heat from deuterium nuclei fusing in the palladium electrodes of electrochemical cells under the benign conditions of temperature and pressure found in an ordinary room. Television and newspapers trumpeted "controlled fusion in a fruit jar," in glowing terms all over the world.

Pons and Fleischman had not submitted a scientific paper about their discovery at the time of their press conference, so it was very hard for other scientists to judge the claims, but as details began to leak out, there was skepticism in the nuclear physics community, even as many other scientists and the public at large were greatly enthusiastic.

There were many parallels to Lysenko's vernalization announcements in 1928. The simplicity and importance of the cold fusion process intoxicated the press. Eager scientific imitators hurried to join the bandwagon. And there was soon high-level political attention. President George Bush asked for advice from Glen Seaborg, the great nuclear chemist who discovered plutonium. Seaborg gave a sober briefing to President Bush, and he stressed the inconsistency of the claimed results with fifty years of painstaking work in nuclear physics.

Whatever his opinion of Seaborg's analysis, President Bush realized that cold fusion, if true, would be a revolution of great importance to the United States and to the world. Unlike Stalin, who immediately embraced Lysenko, Bush directed that a panel

5. H. Furth, "Fusion," *Scientific American*, September 1996.

of scientific experts be established to investigate the claims. The nuclear chemist John Huizenga and the physicist Norman Ramsey chaired the panel, and I was a member of it.

The potential for commercialization of cold fusion was an important consideration from the very start of the cold fusion episode, and patent considerations may have influenced the timing of the first press conference. Many people—Pons and Fleischman, the University of Utah, and various imitators—hoped to get fabulously wealthy from this wonderful new energy source. Much as Lysenko had managed to get a hearing at the highest levels of the Soviet Union, Pons and Fleischman were granted a hearing by the Committee on Science, Space, and Technology of the U.S. Congress on April 26, 1989, barely a month after their cold fusion press conference.[6] Opening the hearing, the committee chairman, Congressman Robert A. Roe of New Jersey, said, "The potential implications of a scientific breakthrough that can produce cold fusion are, at the least, spectacular." Many other committee members, both Democrats and Republicans, made similar enthusiastic comments.

Dr. Chase N. Peterson, the president of the University of Utah, made a point very similar to some made by Lysenko about why radically new discoveries were prone to happen far from the deadening restraints of establishment science:

> A capacity to see an old problem from new perspectives was required. Chemists, electrochemists, looked at a problem traditionally reserved to physicists. In fact therein lies some of the humor and bite of the scientific controversy that is raging. I would like to think that it may not be by chance that it happened in Utah, at a university which has encouraged unorthodox thinking while being viewed by the world as a

6. "Recent Developments in Fusion Energy Research," 101st Cong., 1st sess., April 26, 1989; no. 46.

conservative, even socially orthodox place. There in fact may
be something valuable in isolation from more traditional
centers. America has prospered and innovated at the frontier
and the University of Utah is still a frontier that attracts faculty who highly value their intellectual freedom.[7]

One of the most interesting witnesses was Ira C. Magaziner,
who later gained fame as the architect of President William Clinton's ill-fated health care plan. At the time of the congressional
hearings on cold fusion, Mr. Magaziner was president of the management consulting firm TELESIS, USA, Inc. In introducing his
consultant Magaziner to the committee, Peterson described him
as "one of the world's renowned business consultants on issues
of world competition." After a rousing sales pitch to convince
Congress to send $25 million immediately to the University of
Utah, Magaziner summarized with an appeal to patriotism:

> So now I hope you can understand why I came here today,
> even though I am not from Utah and have no interest in
> palladium. I have an interest in America's future. I see this
> as an opportunity for America both to develop this science
> into future American prosperity and also to develop a model
> for how America can regain preeminence in commercializ-
> ing other new sciences in the coming decade.
>
> I have come here today to ask you to prevent another TV
> or VCR or computerized machine tool or solar cell or super-
> conductor story. I have come to ask you to lead so that we
> will not be the first of our nation's ten generations to leave
> its children a country less prosperous than the one it inher-
> ited. I have come here to ask you, for the sake of my children
> and all of America's next generation to have America do it
> right this time.[8]

In spite of Magaziner's testimony and a well-orchestrated

---

7. Ibid.
8. Huizenga, *Cold Fusion*, p. 51.

campaign to begin a crash program in cold fusion, sober skeptics convinced the U.S. Congress to resist appropriating massive new funds. The furor died down and the enthusiasm for supporting the research ebbed as weeks and months went by and many laboratories reported that they could not reproduce the results of Pons and Fleischman and other embarrassed laboratories withdrew hasty but mistaken confirmations of their results.

A few loyalists still maintain that a sinister conspiracy by big government and industry killed cold fusion, but cold fusion was thoroughly discredited in society at large. Unlike the Lysenko affair, there was no all-powerful political establishment that could declare cold fusion to be politically correct or incorrect and its opponents enemies of the people.

Before ending the discussion of cold fusion, let me cite Representative Wayne Owens, representing Utah's Second District, who also testified at congressional hearing:

> Some say solid-state fusion may be man's greatest discovery since fire. Others say, as I do, that it may also be the innovation to protect and perpetuate the Earth's dying life support system, more important than the possible salvation of the dying industrial superiority of America. Man cannot stand another century like the last. In those 100 years, we have consumed more of the nonrenewable richness of the Earth than was used during all of man's previous history. We polluted and poisoned our environment with its use, and it literally threatens our continued existence. The revolutionary discovery, solid state fusion, arrives simultaneously with our entry into the age of true environmental alarm. So, bursting with pride, Utah's Congressional Delegation brings to the committee the prospect of a second economic chance and a second environmental opportunity. This morning we tell you not only of the discovery which may revolutionize the world's energy system, but more importantly, it may be the answer to the preservation of our home, Planet Earth. Within

the next two weeks, the United Utah Congressional Delegation will present you with an innovative legislative plan, one which will precipitate a whole new concept for national partnership for action. It will combine private and public investment and the opportunity for America to develop, engineer and champion the most far-reaching innovation of our time.[9]

Samuel Johnson once commented that "patriotism is the last refuge of a scoundrel." In their enthusiastic testimony, the supporters of cold fusion made ample use of patriotism, but as Representative Owens's statements show, "preservation of our home, Planet Earth" was also a favored theme. What might Samuel Johnson have said about extreme environmentalism, which is my final example of politicized science?

Extreme Environmentalism

Most Americans want to protect the environment and think of themselves as moderate environmentalists. As a country, we have made much progress in protecting and restoring the environment. Our rivers and air are cleaner than they have been for over a hundred years. Increasingly large areas of land are being set aside as wilderness. Our forests are growing back. But even as we clean up and protect the environment, "environmentalism" has attracted some whose motives—fame, power, wealth—are hard to distinguish from those of Lysenko or the cold fusion enthusiasts.

Unlike Lysenko's vernalized wheat, or cold fusion in a fruit jar, environmental issues are harder to dismiss as patent nonsense. Anyone can see that dumping raw sewage into a river degrades the downstream water quality. But how is one to respond to much subtler claims—that magnetic fields from electrical power lines cause childhood leukemia, that freon will destroy the

9. "Recent Developments in Fusion Energy Research."

ozone layer and ultimately life on earth, that pestilence, famine, rising sea levels, or worse will come from increasing atmospheric carbon dioxide and global warming? These are only some of exaggerated environmental fears promoted by one group or another.

Changes in environmental conditions are not easy to detect, as demonstrated by the massive outlays of research money to develop and maintain devices to measure them. Even with the best instruments, the great natural variability in what can be measured can mask the smaller changes that are of interest to those studying possible human-caused effects. In light of these difficulties, the average citizen must hope that scientific specialists give correct advice on important policy issues. But scientists make mistakes. If they don't make mistakes, they are not trying hard enough. Mistakes get corrected in the normal course of science as attempts are made to repeat the experiments, and conclusions are corrected or reinterpreted if appropriate.

Even without political malice, such as Lysenko's, which crippled Soviet biology, correction of a scientific mistake can take many years. A good example is the nineteenth-century dispute about the age of the earth and the sun. On one side were physicists, and on the other, geologists and evolutionists. The Scottish physicist William Thomson, later to become Lord Kelvin, had first articulated the second law of thermodynamics, which says that the entropy of the universe cannot decrease. So it was natural for him to use thermodynamic considerations for age estimates. From measurements in mine shafts, he knew that the temperature of the earth increased by 2 or 3 degrees C per 100 meters of increasing depth. So heat had to be flowing to the surface of the earth from the hot interior, since heat naturally flows from warmer to cooler regions, or the second law of thermodynamics would be violated. Assuming that the earth had cooled by conduction of heat, and that there were no sources of heat inside the earth, Kelvin was able to estimate that the earth must have been molten no more than 98 million years ago.

Kelvin also used thermodynamics arguments to estimate the age of the sun. Supposedly, the sun was formed from accumulating "meteors," and Kelvin therefore called his theory of the sun's energy "the meteoric theory." As the meteors that formed the sun gradually collapsed to smaller and smaller volumes under the influence of their gravitational attraction for each other, they became hotter and hotter and this provided the heat for the sunlight. Kelvin's theory, published in 1900, reflected forty years of study:

> That some form of the meteoric theory is certainly the true and complete explanation of solar heat can scarcely be doubted, when the following reasons are considered: (1) No other natural explanation, except by chemical action, can be conceived. (2) The chemical theory is quite insufficient, because the most energetic chemical action we know, taking place between substances amounting to the whole sun's mass, would only generate about 3,000 years' heat. (3) There is no difficulty in accounting for 20,000,000 years' heat by the meteoric theory.[10]

While 20 million years seems like a long time, Charles Darwin, supported by geologists, had estimated that some 300 million years were required to account for geological processes, like the erosional formation of the "Weald," a large valley across the south of England.[11] Even longer times seemed to be needed to explain other geological observations. And the theory of evolution also required times much longer than Kelvin's estimates.

In the end, Kelvin, the great mathematical physicist and president of the Royal Society, was wrong, and Darwin and the geol-

10. Sir William Thomson, Lord Kelvin, "The Age of the Sun's Heat," in *Essays in Astronomy*, ed. Edward Singleton Holden (New York: D. Appleton and Co., 1900), p. 51.

11. Ibid.

ogists were right. The earth is around 4.5 billion years old. Unlike Darwin and his geologist friends, who based their estimates of the earth's age on observed erosion rates and other empirical evidence, Kelvin relied on models, for which the mathematics was impeccable, but some of the fundamental physics was incomplete. Commenting on Darwin's age estimates, Kelvin says:

> What, then are we to think of such geological estimates as 300,000,000 years for the "denudation of the Weald"? Whether is it more probable that the physical conditions of the sun's matter differ 1,000 times more than dynamics compel us to suppose they differ from those of matter in our laboratories; or that a stormy sea, with possibly Channel tides of extreme violence, should encroach on a chalk cliff 1,000 times more rapidly than Mr. Darwin's estimate of one inch per century.[12]

Contrary to Kelvin's confidence that matter in the sun behaved like matter in his laboratory, the matter in the sun is subject to nuclear interactions, which do not occur at the low temperatures and pressures of the earth. Neither Kelvin nor anyone else knew anything about the atomic nucleus. The first inklings of nuclear physics had shown up only four years before Kelvin's rather pompous dismissal of the geological evidence for the antiquity of the earth. In 1896 Becquerel discovered that uranium and a few other elements are radioactive. Although not recognized until Rutherford's brilliant discovery of the atomic nucleus in 1909, radioactivity was due to nuclear interactions with energies not just 1,000 times larger than any Kelvin had ever observed in his laboratory but 1,000,000 times larger. This was completely new physics that had not been included in Kelvin's models of the age of the sun or the age of the earth, and it was responsible for the spectacularly wrong estimates he made of both ages.

12. Ibid., p. 49.

Kelvin did not realize that heat is continuously generated inside the earth by the radioactive decay of uranium and other naturally radioactive elements. Nor did he realize that enormous amounts of heat are being continuously produced in the core of the sun by the fusion of light elements like hydrogen nuclei, ultimately yielding helium nuclei. There is enough hydrogen in the sun to keep it shining at about the same level as now for billions of years. This is "hot fusion," and unlike cold fusion, it really works and we owe our lives to it.

Lord Kelvin's understanding of the earth's age was limited by his ignorance of nuclear interactions. The current debates about global climate change are complicated by our not understanding the physics of the sun or of the earth's atmosphere and oceans well enough to dismiss them as major causes of climate change on the earth. Dramatic climate changes like the medieval warm period at the time of the Viking settlements of Iceland and Greenland from about A.D. 900 to 1250, and the subsequent "little ice age," from about 1250 to 1700, which led to extinction of the Greenland settlements, were certainly not caused by manmade changes in the concentration of carbon dioxide in the atmosphere. Subtle changes of the sun's output and perhaps other poorly understood factors must have been much more important in causing those large climate changes than changing levels of atmospheric carbon dioxide.

Global warming pressure groups would have the world believe that catastrophic changes in the earth's climate will occur without drastic limitations of carbon dioxide emissions—this in spite of the fact that the carbon dioxide levels in the earth's atmosphere have been much higher than today's for much of geological history. For example, as documented by the work of Berner,[13] atmospheric carbon dioxide concentrations were some five

13. R. Berner, "The Rise of Plants and Their Effect on Weathering and Atmospheric CO_2," *Science* 276 (1997): 544–46.

times higher than those now from about 300 million years to 30 million years ago, a geological period of flourishing life on earth. For most of the time since the first fossils of advanced forms of life appeared in the Cambrian era, some 600 million years ago, the earth's climate has been somewhat warmer than at present, and the poles have had little or no ice cover. The exceptions were two ice ages, similar to the present one, the Gondwanian, about 280 million years ago, and the Ordovician, about 430 million years ago. Both ice ages coincided with unusually low levels of carbon dioxide in the atmosphere, much as we have experienced at present. It is hard to understand hysteria over manmade increases in carbon dioxide levels that will not even bring atmospheric carbon dioxide levels up to their norm for most of geological history, and which will probably help to prevent the next advance of ice sheets. So we should be very careful about taking actions that will certainly cause great economic harm.

False biology prevailed for forty years in the Soviet Union because Lysenko gained dictatorial control. His type of control —dependent upon prison, exile, and bullet—is not possible in democratic societies, but the control of research funding enables those in political favor to restrict research that might undermine political opinions and positions. For instance, when I was the Director of Energy Research of the Department of Energy in the early 1990s I was amazed that the great bulk of federal funds for environmental studies from the DOE, NASA, EPA, and other federal agencies flowed into research programs that reinforced a message of imminent doom: humanity and planet earth devastated by global warming, pestilence, famine, and flood. I was particularly disturbed by the ridiculous claims by then-Senator Al Gore that recent NASA studies had shown that there was an "ozone hole over Kennebunkport." I remember reacting angrily to a briefing by Mr. Gore's political ally, Bob Watson of NASA, when he used the same words, an "ozone hole over Kennebunkport," to brief high-level members of the Bush administration in the West Wing of the White House.

After the election of Bill Clinton and Al Gore in the fall of 1992, I was soon the only "holdover" from the previous Bush administration in the Department of Energy. There I worked with the new Secretary of Energy, Hazel O'Leary, to defend basic science in the Department of Energy. Although most political appointees are replaced after the White House changes hands in a presidential election, it is not unusual for those occupying scientific posts to remain for some time in a new administration. However, after a few months, Secretary O'Leary called me in to say that I was unacceptable to Al Gore and his environmental advisers, and that I would have to be replaced. She was apologetic and gracious during this discussion, and she did not elaborate on the exact reasons for Gore's instructions.

The modern Greek poet Constantine Cavafy wrote a poem, "Things Ended," which is worth remembering as we contemplate our supposedly dying planet:

> Possessed by fear and suspicion,
> mind agitated, eyes alarmed,
> we desperately invent ways out,
> plan how to avoid the inevitable
> danger that threatens us so terribly.
> Yet we're mistaken, that's not the danger ahead:
> the information was false
> (or we didn't hear it, or didn't get it right).
> Another disaster, one we never imagined,
> suddenly, violently, descends upon us,
> and finding us unprepared—there's no time left—
> sweeps us away.[14]

---

14. C. P. Cavafy, *Collected Poems*, edited by George Savidis (Princeton, N.J.: Princeton University Press, 1992).

Summary

Politicized science is an inevitable part of the human condition, but society must strive to control it. Although history shows that politicized science does much more damage in totalitarian societies than in democracies, even democracies are sometimes stampeded into doing very foolish and damaging things.

The Kyoto Treaty, based on assertions that mankind's generation of carbon dioxide will cause global warming, is an example of such a foolish and damaging thing. The effects of the Kyoto Treaty, if the treaty is enacted, are likely to be more like those of Prohibition, than Lysenko's biology. The demonizations of rum and carbon dioxide have much in common. In 1920, the U.S. Congress passed the Eighteenth Amendment to the Constitution of the United States. This amendment, which prohibited the manufacture, sale, or transport of alcoholic beverages, was intended to rid the country of the accidents, disease, and violence associated with those beverages. It didn't. It began a disastrous era that helped organized crime to flourish as never before and nourished contempt for the law that has not entirely dissipated today. In 1933, the Twenty-first Amendment repealed the Eighteenth Amendment, the only time in history that an amendment to the U.S. Constitution has been repealed. Demonization of anything is hard to combat, since it is so easy to join the supposed high ground of virtue, while scorning those who go through the painstaking effort of looking at the facts for themselves. This was why it was so hard to stop the bandwagon of prohibition or Lysenko's biology.

The same human motives that cause other problems in our lives also drive extreme politicized science. As the examples here show, a common motive is the love of power and domination. This was clearly one of the most important motives for Lysenko. There is no surer way to build a powerful bureaucratic empire in a democracy than to promote a supposed peril and then staff up a huge organization to combat it.

The intoxication of fame and glory is an important motive, especially for the scientists themselves. What bliss to be a sainted savior of the planet, to be the provider of agricultural abundance as communism dumps capitalism into the dustbin of history, or to be a new Prometheus, bringing the fire of cold fusion to desperate humanity!

Greed is often a motive. The University of Utah was transfixed by the untold dollars they thought would flow to the inventors of cold fusion. The Enron Corporation, a politically correct darling of many environmental advocacy groups, was a stalwart supporter of the Kyoto Treaty to limit carbon dioxide emissions. Enron envisaged huge profits from the trading of emission rights. Moreover, Enron's holdings of natural gas, the fossil fuel that emits the least carbon dioxide per BTU of combustion energy, would also greatly increase in value as the constraints of the Kyoto Treaty began to hurt the coal industry.

One can go down the list of deadly sins of almost any religion, and most can be found in politicized science. This should come as no surprise, since scientists are as fallible as anyone else in their personal lives. We recall that the first biblical mention of science (from "knowing" in Latin) occurs in the story of Eve's temptation by the Serpent, "*Eritis sicut Deus,* scientes *bonum et malum;* Thou shalt be as God, knowing good and evil." Science has always been associated with good and evil, and it will always be a struggle to be sure that the good prevails.

TWO

The Corrosive Effects of Politicized Regulation of Science and Technology

HENRY I. MILLER

There is politicization, and there is politicization. The Random House dictionary defines "political" in a number of ways, including: "pertaining to, or connected with a political party; and exercising or seeking power in the governmental or public affairs of a state, municipality, etc." So when we talk of the politicization of public policy concerned with the oversight of science and technology, we can mean a number of things, not all of them necessarily bad. Not necessarily, but commonly. The term is usually used to imply politicians' undue or inappropriate influence over governmental activities or processes in order to achieve some sort of partisan gain.

When political fortunes change and a new party comes into power in the Executive Branch, one expects a change in overall philosophy of government—and the same is true of the Congress, which exerts oversight over the activities and actions of executive departments and agencies. Such changes are part and parcel of the political process. However, the imposition of heavy-handed, improper coercion and influence on governmental, science-based activities during the Clinton administrations were outside the usually recognized rules of the game.

Science Gored

As congressman, senator, and vice president, Al Gore was one of the most ruthless and determined politicians of his generation. As vice president, he exercised unprecedented interference in public policy related to technology. What could be the motivation for what were, in fact, antitechnology actions by this man who extolled the importance of technology, and whose spin doctors presented him as something of a science and policy wonk? Vice President Gore's attitudes, ascertained from his extensive writings over many years, provide a clue.

While a congressman and self-styled expert on biotechnology issues, Al Gore praised Jeremy Rifkin's shoddy antibiotechnology diatribe, *Algeny*, as "an important book" and an "insightful critique of the changing way in which mankind views nature."[1] In a 1991 article in the *Harvard Journal of Law and Technology*, then-Senator Gore displayed an astounding lack of appreciation of the historically positive linkage between science and economic development. He disdainfully described investors' eager reception of Genentech's 1980 stock offering as the first sellout of the "tree of knowledge to Wall Street,"[2] ignoring that much of the modern economy is built on physics, chemistry, and geology, and that

1. A. Gore, Jacket quotes for J. Rifkin, *Algeny* (New York: Penguin Books, 1983).
2. A. Gore, "Planning a New Biotechnology Policy," *Harvard Journal of Law and Technology* 5 (1991): 19–30.

biotechnology was a $100 billion industry long before the gene-splicing industry emerged, regularly making impressive contributions to the betterment of human health and the environment, using microorganisms to produce antibiotics, enzymes, vaccines, beverages and other products, and genetics to breed more nutritious crops requiring less cultivated land.

In the same article, Gore coined a "principle that applies to regulating new and strange technologies such as biotechnology": "If *you* don't [regulate], you know somebody else will" (emphasis in original).

Gore was not entirely pessimistic about biotechnology's possible contributions to better processes and products, but, in an original but bizarre twist, he worried about biotechnology's possible success:

> The most lasting impact of biotechnology on the food supply may come not from something going wrong, but from all going right. My biggest fear is not that by accident we will set loose some genetically defective Andromeda strain. Given our past record in dealing with agriculture, we're far more likely to accidentally drown ourselves in a sea of excess grain.

It is doubtful that that apprehension is shared by developing countries, confronted by the prediction that over the next century the world's population is expected to more than double, from 5.5 billion to about 11.3 billion people, with more than 80 percent of the additions expected to reside in their regions.

Gore's attitudes toward biotechnology are consistent with his views of science generally, which he presents in *Earth in the Balance*.[3] Throughout the book, he employs the damning comparison that those who believe in technological advances are as sinister, and polluters are as evil, as the perpetrators of the World

3. A. Gore, *Earth in the Balance* (New York: Plume, 1992).

War II Holocaust. He decries the separation of science and religion. He accuses Americans of being dysfunctional because we've
developed "an apparent obsession with inauthentic substitutes
for direct experience with real life," such as "Astroturf, air con-
ditioning and fluorescent lights . . . Walkman and Watchman,
entertainment cocoons, frozen food for the microwave oven," and
so on. Should we assume, then, that Mr. Gore has returned to an
air-conditioning-, microwave-, TV-, VCR-, and DVD-free existence in Tennessee?

The Gore Appointments

As the Clinton administrations' science and technology czar, Gore
chose many high-level appointees to regulatory agencies—and,
thereby, politicized agency policies and decisions. And what a
collection of yes-men and antiscience, antitechnology ideologues
they were:

- *Presidential science adviser Jack Gibbons,* one of the less distinguished people to occupy that important post;

- *Environmental Protection Agency Administrator and Gore ac-
  olyte Carol Browner,* whose agency was condemned repeatedly by the scientific community and admonished by the
  courts for flawed policies and decisions;

- *Food and Drug Administration Commissioner Jane Henney,*
  rewarded with that position after politicizing the agency's critical oversight of food and drugs while she was its deputy head;

- *Jerrold Mande,* an untalented nonentity whom FDA officials
  regarded as Vice President Gore's "political commissar" at the
  agency;

- *State Department Under Secretary Tim Wirth,* who worked
  tirelessly to circumvent Congress's explicit refusal to ratify

radical, wrong-headed treaties signed by the Clinton administration;

- *Agriculture Under Secretary Ellen Haas,* former director of an antitechnology advocacy group, who reconstructed science thusly, "You can have 'your' science or 'my' science or 'somebody else's' science. By nature, there is going to be a difference."[4]

Public Policy Gored

Gregory Simon, Vice President Al Gore's senior domestic policy adviser, represented a low point of the Clinton administration appointments that politicized science. A lawyer without scientific training or experience (and, therefore, a typical Gore choice for directing science policy), Simon had been a nemesis of the new biotechnology even before his tenure in the White House. While a staffer on the House Science, Space, and Technology Committee, Simon had authored the Biotechnology Omnibus Act of 1990, HR 5232, which was science-averse, would have created potent regulatory *dis*incentives to the use of the most precise and predictable genetic technology, and had no pretense of protecting consumers from genuine risks. The bill, had it become law, could have initiated the devastation of the biotech industry several years before the Clinton administration's health care reform and regulatory policies actually began it in the mid-1990s.

After becoming the vice president's aide, Simon in his public utterances revealed no diminution of his troglodytism. Simon said that the actual degree of biotech's risks is irrelevant, that the new biotechnology must be subjected to a high degree of governmental

---

4. E. Haas, "Diet Risk Communication: A Consumer Advocate Perspective," in G. E. Gaull and R. A. Goldberg, eds., *The Emerging Global Food System* (New York: Wiley & Sons, 1993), pp. 133–46, esp. p. 134.

control and regulation in order to calm a "hysterical" public. He went on to opine that, for regulatory purposes, biotech products simply cannot be compared to traditional products and that "consumers will have to change their concept of how food is made" before they will accept the technology.[5] His statements cannot be reconciled with consumers' actual attitudes and behaviors or with scientific consensus about the safety of the new technology.

Eliminating Opponents

The intolerant nature of their practices was as troubling as the substance of the Clinton-Gore policies. Gore, Simon, et al. brooked no dissension or challenge to their views and acted to purge those whom they considered to be their "enemies." In order to slant— that is, to "politicize"—federal science and technology policy and to rid the civil service of dissenting views, Gore and Simon interfered in federal personnel matters to an unusual degree.

For example, Simon threatened a high-ranking official at the Department of Energy with retaliation if she hired David Kingsbury, the former assistant director of the National Science Foundation. (Simon and Kingsbury had clashed on biotechnology policy in earlier years, and, as a congressional staffer, Simon had hounded Kingsbury from government with unsubstantiated charges of conflict of interest.) Simon also improperly ordered FDA to remove a senior civil servant from his position at FDA. Agency officials admitted that this was retribution for the "transgression" of having implemented Reagan-Bush policies effectively.

William Happer, in his chapter in this volume, describes his

5. B. Davis, Harvard University, personal communication; R. Hoyle, "Comments from the White House's Greg Simon," *Bio/Technology* 11 (1993): 1504–5.

dismissal from a senior scientist position at the Department of Energy because his interpretation of the scientific evidence about ozone depletion and global warming conflicted with those of the vice president's advisers. Similar incidents occurred at the departments of State, Energy, and Interior, and at EPA, where a number of prominent civil servants were moved to less visible positions and a number of others were replaced—for their own "protection"—with more "acceptable" officials during interactions with the White House.

Green Accounting

In 1994, the Commerce Department's Bureau of Economic Analysis introduced its so-called economic-environmental accounting framework to calculate the country's "Green GDP."[6] Just as a conventional accounting ledger includes an entry for depreciation of plant and equipment, the bureau's system attempted to record the "degradation of natural assets." In this theory of accounting, U.S. government grants for solar energy research could be considered *income*, while funding on nuclear energy could be counted as *expenditures* and grants from the World Bank to radical environmental groups could be counted among the bank's *income*, while the value of electricity from a new dam financed by the organization could be counted among the bank's *expenditures*.

Gore tried to move his ideas into international relations by a policy that would punish countries that didn't go along. At Gore's direction, the State Department produced *Environmental Diplomacy*, a slick but bizarre document with forewords by the vice president and Secretary of State Madeleine Albright. It includes statements such as "[the world bank should factor] environmental

6. "Al Gore and the Environment." http:/www.whitehouse/gov/wh/eop/ovp/html/Enviro_GDP.html, May 1, 1996.

implications into its lending decisions," with which few would disagree, but, on balance, it reads like a Greenpeace manifesto or, not coincidentally, like Gore's *Earth in the Balance*, echoing the claim that "[c]lassical economics defines productivity narrowly and encourages us to equate gains in productivity with economic progress. But the Holy Grail of progress is so alluring that economists tend to overlook the bad side effects that often accompany improvements."

The statement ignores the repeated efforts of economists to incorporate and evaluate externalities in their assessments, but Gore's proposed remedy for the "fault" he had identified was to redefine the relevant measures of economic activity. As adopted by the State Department, the new accounting system had a clear purpose: to enable governments to obscure the costs of environmental protection by calling them "benefits" and to force businesses to list wealth-creating activity as societal "costs." The effects of this doublespeak, if widely implemented, would be profound: companies around the world would see their regulatory expenses skyrocket and their markets shrink. Consumers would pay inflated prices for fewer products and higher taxes to support bloated bureaucracies.

Environmental Diplomacy stated that the State Department would focus its regional and bilateral environmental diplomacy on several key areas, one of which was "land use."[7] The State Department would add decisions about foreign countries' "local and national leaders weigh[ing] the competing goals of protecting a forest against providing additional croplands" in deciding on U.S. foreign policy. Such purely domestic actions by sovereign nations acting in what they consider to be their best interests "have social, environmental, and economic implications, which in turn affect our foreign policy." Mr. Gore and Ms. Albright in-

7. *Environmental Diplomacy* (Washington, D.C.: U.S. Department of State, 1997).

tended that U.S. policy toward foreign countries should turn on those countries' domestic economic decisions—whether, for example, the French government chose to harvest an old-growth forest in Burgundy or Mexico City decided to build additional highways instead of a subway system.

If this U.S. policy seems extreme, so are its philosophical underpinnings, as laid out in *Earth in the Balance.* The apocalyptic central thesis of Mr. Gore's book is that we need to take "bold and unequivocal action . . . [to] make the rescue of the environment the central organizing principle for civilization." The events of September 11, 2001, and the ensuing efforts against international terrorism illustrate how unspeakably myopic and self-absorbed was this view of the "civilization's" appropriate priorities.

Gore's Policies and Science
at Federal Agencies

Citizens, business people, members of consumer and environmental groups, and officials of state and local governments who have business with the federal government seldom interact directly with the White House or the State Department. Instead, their routine contacts are with federal agencies, such as the Food and Drug Administration (FDA) or the Environmental Protection Agency (EPA). Gore-influenced appointments to those agencies tilted FDA and EPA to his antitechnology, antibusiness positions, with potentially long-lasting consequences for the health of the nation's citizens and the nation's applications of science and technology to its problems.

Dr. Kessler's FDA

There is wide agreement that reform of the FDA has long been necessary. Bringing a single new drug to market in the United

States now takes twelve to fifteen years and costs the manufac-turer on average more than $800 million, by far the highest price tag in the world. Profits only sometimes offset these costs, and a Duke University study reveals a sobering corollary—fewer than three out of every ten drug products generate revenues that cover their development costs.[8]

This trend is at least partly the result of the FDA's capricious decisions about clinical trials necessary to establish the safety and efficacy of new drugs and its continual raising of the bar for ap-proval. The average number of clinical trials performed on an average drug increased from 30 in the early 1980s to 68 during 1994–95; the average number of patients in clinical trials for each drug more than tripled; the average time required for clinical trials of a new drug increased from 85 to 92 months between the first and second halves of the 1990s. In all, between five and eight years are necessary for basic research, preclinical (animal) stud-ies, clinical trials, and review time before a drug receives mar-keting approval from the FDA (if approval is granted).

During the 1990s, the FDA changed rules and policies that added further costs and time to the development of new drugs, but provided little or no additional protection of public health. The agency's policies mean that drug companies increasingly can af-ford to develop only products that are potential financial block-busters, while drugs for life-saving but narrower uses are ne-glected. Already-huge drug companies find it necessary to merge in order to achieve even greater economies of scale.

When he became FDA commissioner in 1991, David Kessler promised dramatic changes, that—to use a term he repeated in many lectures—he "would teach the elephant to dance." And Kessler did—to a tune called by flacks and politicians. Right out

8. H. G. Grabowski and J. M. Vernon, "Returns to R&D on New Drug Introductions in the 1980s," *J. Health Economics* 13 (1994): 383–406.

of the gate, Kessler chose a high-profile but ludicrous case that was calculated to get him on the evening news in a virile demonstration of being tough on industry. Defective heart valves, a contaminated vaccine, a drug causing sudden death? No, Citrus Hill orange juice. Kessler commanded federal marshals to confiscate 15,000 gallons of juice. Was it spoiled, contaminated, unfit for human consumption? Nope. It was labeled "fresh" when it was actually made from concentrated orange juice. Federal guidelines say it is inaccurate to call orange juice "fresh" if it's made from concentrate.

On CBS' *60 Minutes*, Kessler expressed his indignation, "[the juice] was made from concentrate. My grandmother could have told you, I mean, it wasn't fresh. It wasn't very hard [to tell the difference]."

Wouldn't consumers have been justified in asking Dr. Kessler: "If we can so easily tell by taste that the juice came from concentrate and is inferior, why not simply let *us* decide whether we like the product well enough to buy it again? Why aren't you more concerned about our taxpayer dollars footing the bill for FDA's regulatory compliance staff and lawyers, and for the federal marshals who corralled the outlaw juice? And doesn't FDA have anything more important to worry about?"

One suspects that Kessler's *grand-mère* might have been more pragmatic. In private and public, Kessler admonished his staff to "get tough," publicly he said that FDA is an "enforcement agency" and that, by God, industry will know it. (I know from personal experiences that Kessler took a different line when meeting privately with industry. He explained that the bluster about enforcement was just for show, to keep FDA's left-wing critics off his back. He assured them that he was very sympathetic to industry. Kessler's statements reflect the overtones expressed by Gore when he said that it was important that people who agreed with him regulate because otherwise someone else would. Someone else, of course, wouldn't do it right.)

Pressures to alter FDA's practices and methods had been building for years, and they continued in the early years of the Clinton administration, reaching fruition in the sweeping Drugs and Biological Products Reform Act of 1996, HR 3199. The bill went down to ignominious defeat. The demise of this attempt to reform the nation's premier regulatory agency offers an interesting case study in political dishonesty and mendacity.

The bill would have permitted the FDA to dispense with the requirement that manufacturers turn over voluminous raw data from clinical trials. Manufacturers instead would have delivered condensed, tabulated, or summarized data—just as they do now in submissions to the FDA's foreign counterparts—and the agency would have retained authority to obtain additional material when needed.

The legislation would also have established a more liberal approval standard for drugs intended to treat any "serious or life-threatening" condition. Like the then-current standard for review and approval of AIDS drugs, the new criterion would have allowed easier patient access to a drug when there is "a reasonable likelihood that the drug will be effective in a significant number of patients and that the risk from the drug is no greater than the risk from the condition." That common-sense, humane principle would have extended to patients with diseases like stroke, multiple sclerosis, Alzheimer's disease, emphysema, crippling arthritis, and heart failure the benefits reserved for those with AIDS.

The bill would also have ameliorated to a large extent the FDA's censorship of scientific and medical information concerning off-label uses by permitting the legitimate dissemination of information about non–FDA approved uses of drugs to health professionals and the public via textbooks and articles from peer-reviewed journals.[9] It would also have permitted retrospective evidence from clinical research to be used for approval of additional, off-label uses of drugs already on the market. Normally, FDA requires expensive and time-consuming new studies for such uses even when some data from the original tests (collected in studies to address other medical conditions) are perfectly adequate. Such reforms would have cut down both on the time and the costs involved in securing FDA approval for additional uses of drugs.

The legislation's most significant reform—along the lines of proposals made by William C. Wardell and me in the Progress and Freedom Foundation's study, *Advancing Medical Innovation* —would have introduced nongovernmental alternatives to some FDA oversight.[10] Under its provisions, pharmaceutical manufacturers could have opted for product review by FDA-accredited nongovernmental organizations—private- or public-sector (e.g., academic) entities. Each of these institutions would have been subject to periodic FDA audits, and strict requirements backed by civil and criminal sanctions would have assured the confidentiality of data and the absence of conflicts of interest. Alternatively, the manufacturer could still have opted for review by the FDA, and in all cases the agency would have retained the responsibility for final sign-off of marketing approvals.

Of course, permitting both governmental and private-sector alternatives while maintaining FDA's sign-off on its competitors' recommendations is rather like giving the Coca-Cola Company

9. Drugs that are developed, approved, and marketed for a particular disease or diseases are sometimes found to be effective for other diseases, for diseases that don't appear on the "label" that describes the benefits of the drug. About half of all prescriptions are written for such "off-label" uses.

10. W. C. Wardell and H. I. Miller, "Therapeutic Drugs and Biologics," in R. A. Epstein et al., *Advancing Medical Innovation* (Washington, D.C.: Progress and Freedom Foundation, 1989), pp. 79–102.

the right to sign off on Pepsi taste tests. In spite of such shortcomings, had it been enacted the bill would have been a significant step toward loosening the FDA's monopoly grip on drug testing and evaluation and making drug regulation more efficient.

Politics sealed the fate of HR 3199. The FDA and its supporters in the Clinton administration saw the legislation as a threat to the federal government's regulatory hegemony, and they pulled out all the stops to defeat it. Phil Lee, the Assistant Secretary of Health and Human Services, dismissed the bill and anything resembling it as nothing more than veto-bait. FDA Commissioner David Kessler registered the FDA's opposition to the House bill in a nine-page statement, "The Impact of the House FDA Reform Proposals," that was remarkable for revealing the lengths to which an agency head will go to protect the status quo.[11]

Kessler asserted, "FDA would be forced to approve new drugs using summaries of safety data prepared by drug companies." Untrue. The bill would have allowed FDA experts to depend on condensed, tabulated, or summarized data (when considered adequate) rather than reviewing the voluminous raw data from clinical trials, often running to hundreds of thousands of pages. In all cases, agency reviewers would have had access to additional materials as well, and could have obtained them by a simple request from an FDA supervisory official.

To make his case, Kessler cited the example of a drug called Dilevalol, which he said was approved in Japan, Portugal, and England on the basis of data summaries. Americans, he said, were spared morbidity and mortality because "the FDA medical reviewer noted in the raw data evidence that some patients had severe liver injury." Another untruth. The record shows it was

11. Food and Drug Administration. "The Impact of the House FDA Reform Proposals [background paper]" (Washington, D.C.: FDA, 1996), 9 pp.

the *company*, Schering-Plough, that identified the toxicity and ultimately withdrew the application for U.S. approval.[12]

Kessler claimed that the legislation would weaken the effectiveness standard for drugs and that the FDA would be forced to approve a new use for a drug on the bases of "anecdotal evidence of effectiveness" and "common use by physicians (with no objective evidence)." The price, he concluded, would be "the unnecessary pain and suffering patients would undergo until they were given an effective treatment." These are more distortions of the truth. The reality is that, as surveys and analyses have shown repeatedly, the FDA's policies have made life progressively more dangerous for patients and difficult for physicians.[13]

Congress abandoned HR 3199 in face of the Clinton administration's vehement opposition and the threat of a presidential veto. This was a significant loss, given the consensus within the scientific and public policy community that real reform was badly needed. Neither before nor since has Congress tackled FDA reform so aggressively, although the agency's policies and performance have begged for it. The legislation that eventually passed in the next congressional session was meager and disappointing.

It is ironic that "get tough" Kessler left the FDA under a cloud, resigning three weeks after public accusations that he had falsified travel vouchers, double-billed travel expenses, and the like. Eventually, he made partial restitution to the government.

Dr. Henney's FDA

As the FDA's Deputy Commissioner from 1992 to 1994, Jane Henney had demonstrated a willingness to play politics with products

12. A. R. Giaquinto, Schering-Plough Research Institute, letter to House Commerce Committee, May 14, 1996.

13. See, e.g., Anon., "A National Survey of Oncologists Regarding the Food and Drug Administration" (Washington, D.C.: Competitive Enterprise Institute, 1995), 4 pp.

under review by America's most omnipresent regulatory agency, which is charged with assuring the safety of food, drugs, and medical devices, with a value of more than $1 trillion annually. While she occupied the number-two job at the FDA, Henney's decisions gave the appearance of being motivated by politics and self-interest.

As the co-chairman of the Public Health Service Task Force on Breast Implants in 1992, she collaborated prominently in the disastrous government decisions that needlessly left millions of women fearful and confused and that destroyed the silicone implant industry. As an FDA official, Henney was willing to delay the approval of products such as bovine somatotropin, a protein that enhances milk production in cows, because genetically engineered products were thought to be politically incorrect by Vice President Gore and his staff. She expedited others, such as a female condom with a high failure rate, after being instructed to do so by Health and Human Services Secretary Donna Shalala, who lauded it as a "feminist" product. President Clinton rewarded Henney for such actions by appointing her as FDA Commissioner.

EPA: Neither the Best Nor the Brightest

Since its creation in 1972, the EPA has been subject to nearly continual criticism for ignoring or misusing science in its regulatory actions. It has been criticized too for skirting the regulatory process and imposing large costs on industry without ever having "to show its work" about any scientific justification. One of the best-known examples was initiated in the late 1980s, well before Clinton and Gore reached the White House, when the Natural Resources Defense Council (NRDC) launched a media campaign against Alar, an agricultural chemical that permits apples to ripen uniformly and increases yield. In response to NRDC's promoted public outcry about Alar, the EPA pressured apple growers to abandon using it. Because of "inescapable and direct correlation" between exposure to UDMH" (the primary degradation of product of Alar) and "the development of life threatening tumors," Assistant Administrator John Moore "urged" farmers who were using Alar to stop. He also said that EPA would soon propose banning Alar. Coming from Dr. Moore, a senior federal regulator, his statement was akin to an armed mugger "urging" the victim to relinquish his wallet. Separately, EPA admitted that no data supported a finding of carcinogenicity.[14]

During the Alar episode, one of Moore's senior subordinates, lawyer Steven Schatzow, attempted to intimidate the members of an advisory panel because their opinion differed from his own:

> Apparently, the EPA officials had expected the SAP [Scientific Advisory Panel] to rubber-stamp its decision [that Alar or UDMH was a carcinogen]. When it did not, Uniroyal [the manufacturer of Alar] officials were jubilant. But after the meeting, Steven Schatzow, then director of EPA's Office of Pesticide Programs, herded SAP members into his office. The angry Schatzow demanded, "How can you do this to us?" After a heated exchange with the scientists, he concluded, "Look, I can't tell you what to do, but you might like to think about this one again." The scientists were stunned by such flagrant interference, and all refused to back down.[15]

Often EPA has ignored scientific evidence and bona fide public health considerations in favor of unsubstantiated fears expressed by influential special-interest groups. As long ago as 1992, an expert panel commissioned by then-EPA Administrator William Reilly reported: "(i) The science advice function—that is, the pro-

14. P. Shabecoff, "Hazard reported in apple chemical: E.P.A. cites a risk of cancer but will not bar use yet," *New York Times*, February 2, 1989, p. 23.
15. M. Fumento, *Science Under Siege* (New York: Morrow, 1993), pp. 19–44. See also R. J. Bidinotto, "The Great Apple Scare," *Reader's Digest*, October, 1990, pp. 55–56.

cess of ensuring that policy decisions are informed by a clear understanding of the relevant science—is not well defined or coherently organized within EPA. (ii) In many cases, appropriate science advice and information are not considered early or often enough in the decision making process."[16] And while "(iii) EPA should be a source of unbiased scientific information . . . EPA has not always ensured that contrasting, reputable scientific views are well-explored and well-documented."[17] Most damning of all, the panel concluded that "EPA science is perceived by many people, both inside and outside the Agency, to be adjusted to fit policy. Such "adjustments" could be made consciously or unconsciously by the scientist or the decision maker.[18]

The panel was charitable. The EPA was by far the most scientifically challenged agency that I encountered in almost two decades of public service, a period during which I interacted frequently with many government departments and agencies.

The EPA's capacity to propose and apply flawed scientific assumptions or paradigms to regulatory policy is intimately related to the manner in which the agency handles its advisory process, and scientists on advisory panels who offer independent perspectives anger EPA officials. For example, University of California microbiologist Dennis Focht, an academic member of the EPA's Biotechnology Science Advisory Committee, wrote a letter to the committee's chairman that said a policy decision to regulate on the basis of genetic technique rather than on an assessment of risk was based on nonscientific considerations. In response, EPA Assistant Administrator Linda Fisher, a lawyer, sent this distin-

16. Anon., *Safeguarding the Future: Credible Science, Credible Decisions, The Report of the Expert Panel on the Role of Science at EPA* (EPA document no. 600/9-91/050) (Washington, D.C.: U.S. Environmental Protection Agency, March 1992).
17. Ibid.
18. Ibid.

guished scientist a written rebuke that chided him on his inability to "provide the Agency with [an] unbiased assessment of the scientific issues at hand," and, in effect, invited him to resign from the committee.[19]

In accord with the federal government's unwritten rule that no bad deed goes unrewarded, the current Bush administration has reappointed Fisher to EPA and promoted her to Deputy Administrator. Not unexpectedly, the combination of an agency head —the scientifically unschooled EPA Administrator Christie Whitman—with an aggressive, unscientific, unprincipled deputy has been anathema to the creation of sound public policy (and a source of continuing embarrassment for the Bush administration).

Focht, an eminent and principled academic scientist, had acted as would be expected of an extramural adviser genuinely committed to providing rigorous, objective, and apolitical advice to federal regulators and officials at agencies like the National Institutes of Health (NIH) and FDA. NIH and FDA usually ask their advisers to provide narrow scientific expertise in reviewing and ranking grant applications, expressing opinions about research areas for additional or reduced funding, or evaluating the results of clinical trials. A different and perverse situation frequently prevails at the EPA. Instead of narrow scientific questions, the biotechnology-related committees are often asked for opinions on policy issues, and asked in such a way as to invite rubber-stamping of a course of action that directly benefits EPA.

The EPA consistently chooses policy directions that serve bureaucratic ends (such as larger budgets and regulatory empires), while disadvantaging academic and most industrial research. This places extramural advisers in a position that is, at the least,

19. L. J. Fisher, EPA assistant administrator, letter to Dennis Focht, University of California, August 21, 1992.

uncomfortable, and at worst, frankly conflicted. It is noteworthy that at the time that the EPA was proposing and its advisory committees were recommending scientifically indefensible and regressive policies, some chairmen and members of EPA's Biotechnology Science Advisory Committee were receiving substantial agency funding.

Some of EPA's programmatic and policy deficiencies can be ascribed to career civil servants with their own agendas, who manipulate EPA-inexperienced political appointees (most often lawyers). A pertinent example is Dr. Elizabeth Milewski, an EPA mid-level manager who has had primary responsibility for biotech policies in the Office of Pesticides and Toxic Substances. At a 1991 interagency meeting that I attended, she announced that the EPA could not accept a certain scientifically based policy because "our constituency won't stand for it."

Most civil servants apprehend their "constituency" to be the American taxpayers and consumers who offer the government their trust and treasure, but Milewski and others have something quite different in mind. Their "constituency" is a small but vocal and highly organized minority composed of politically potent, antibiotechnology activists at such groups as Environmental Defense, National Wildlife Federation, Union of Concerned Scientists, and Greenpeace who think of government regulation as something with which to bludgeon technologies, products, industries, or companies they dislike. In other words, not without justification, they see themselves allied with government in a war against capitalism and "globalization."

Government That Was Neither
Leaner Nor Less Mean

I have heard it said that Bill and Hillary Clinton are the enemy of normal people. But the epitome of that description is Al Gore, whose cynical and erroneous view of science and its role in public policy places him among an infinitesimal minority and serves as a reminder that ignorance is not a simple lack of knowledge but an active aversion to knowledge—the refusal to know—issuing from hubris or laziness of mind. More disturbing still, because of its practical implications, is his philosophy of government, particularly with respect to the federal oversight of new technology and environmental protection. Gore's views are (to borrow a phrase from George Will) paradigmatic of paternalistic liberalism, of government that is bullying because it is arrogant, and arrogant because it does not know what it does not know. President Clinton repeatedly promised "leaner but not meaner government," but what we got was quite the opposite.

No Reason for Optimism

There appears little likelihood that science policy will become less politicized or more rational and centered on science. Unhappily, there are several reasons for this pessimism.

There is no important constituency for sound science policy. On the contrary, politicization often represents little more than pandering to the fears, which sometimes verge on superstition, of a scientifically illiterate and statistics-phobic public. Federal regulator-bureaucrats excel at the Emperor's New Clothes school of formulation of self-serving policy. They have learned to confer legitimacy on almost any policy, no matter how flawed or antithetical to the public interest, by moving from step to bureaucratic step according to the specified rules, with everyone pretending that the evolution and substance of the policy are plausible. There is a saying in Washington that something that has been said three times becomes a fact, and adherence to the requirements of federal rule-making—publishing appropriate notices in the *Federal Register*, holding public meetings, responding to public comments, publishing final rules, and so on—is the apotheosis of that idea.

In the end, regulatory policy is often crafted under the influence of a kind of "happy conspiracy" among activists, government regulators, and even some segments of industry. Clemson University economist Bruce Yandle has proposed the "bootleggers and Baptists" model of policymaking. Yandle points out that in the American South, Sunday closing laws make it illegal to sell alcohol on Sunday. These laws are maintained by a coalition of Baptists and bootleggers. The Baptists (and other religious denominations) provide the public outcry against liquor on Sunday, while the bootleggers (who actually sell liquor on Sunday) quietly persuade legislatures and town councils to maintain the closing laws.[20]

An application of this theory about public choice is apparent in the formulation of policy toward the regulation of science and technology. The Baptists are the environmental and other anti-technology groups, and the bootleggers are the companies that are seeking excessive regulation that will create market-entry barriers to competitors. Then, when the competition has been eradicated, they'll lobby for a loosening of the strict regulation that was needed in the first place only in order to "permit the public to gain confidence in the technology."

The government's self-interest in the process is best served not by doing as little as possible as efficiently as possible, but by taking on greater responsibilities, demanding bigger budgets, and expanding bureaucratic empires. Too often, any correlation between government policymakers' self-interest and the public interest is purely coincidental.

20. B. Yandle, "Bootleggers, Baptists, and Global Warming," in T. L. Anderson and H. I. Miller, eds., *The Greening of U.S. Foreign Policy* (Stanford: Hoover Institution Press, 2000).

During my quarter century in or studying government, I have seen nothing to disprove historian Barbara Tuchman's observation, "Mankind . . . makes a poorer performance of government than of almost any other human activity."[21]

21. B. Tuchman, *The March of Folly: From Troy to Vietnam* (New York: Knopf, 1984), p. 4.

THREE

Science
and
Public
Policy

JOSEPH P. MARTINO

Government is coercion. George Washington said: "Government is not reason. Government is not persuasion. It is force." When science becomes involved in government, science will be involved in politics and coercion. When government carries out scientific studies, tests, and experiments and interprets the results without consideration of other studies, tests, and experiments and results, the "science" should be viewed with even more skepticism than industry or activist group science.

Politicized Science

Government agencies should, and often insist they do, base their decisions on sound science. In some, science is either warped to support a decision made on other grounds, or completely absent.

In this chapter, I describe cases in which government scientists fell short of any usual expectation for unbiased, open-minded, and fairly reported investigations and results.

Spotted Owls

How valid was the "science" used to justify an end to logging in spotted owl habitat? The answer to that question is to be found in knowledge of whether or not further logging would further endanger a species that was already endangered. Or was it?

The three populations of spotted owls in the United States—the Northern Spotted Owl, the California Spotted Owl, and the Mexican Spotted Owl—interbreed readily, and DNA analysis shows that they are genetically almost identical.[1] In 1986 the Audubon Society estimated that 1,500 pairs was the minimum breeding population needed to avoid extinction, and the U.S. Fish and Wildlife Service (USFWS) estimated that there were "somewhere between 3,000 and 4,000 spotted owl pairs" in the United States;[2] the number was uncertain because spotted owls in much of California and the Southwest had never been counted. At the same time, it was apparent that the number of Northern Spotted Owls was declining because of reduction in habitat as timber was clearcut.

In 1989 the USFWS proposed to list the Spotted Owl as "Threatened," under the Endangered Species Act (ESA). In July 1989, Congress appropriated $13 million to study the spotted owl. One important "finding" of the studies was that there were more spotted owls in "old growth" forests than there were in very young

1. Greg Easterbrook, "The Spotted Owl Scam," http://www.olypen. com/solidarity/spotted.htm.
2. Ibid.

forests (REF). However, "intermediate growth" forests were not studied.

Two years later, in 1991, federal judge William Dwyer, citing research that showed the number of spotted owls was approaching the minimum number required to maintain a breeding population, banned most logging in Oregon and Washington to assure that at least 3,000 pairs would survive. The key to the ban was the "finding" that the Northern Spotted Owl required "old growth" timber in order to nest and survive.

"Old growth" timber is the most valuable kind of timber for logging, and the ban shut down logging in the Northwest, put thousands of loggers out of work, and killed towns that depended on the logging industry. It added nearly $5,000 to the price of an average new home.

Lost in the rhetoric was the fact that the spotted owl does not require old growth timber. The Mexican Spotted Owl lives in the scrub desert of the Southwest, a habitat much different from the humid old-growth forests of the Northwest. Gregg Easterbrook notes: "The California Department of Fish and Game has found spotted owls living and reproducing in several types of non-ancient woodlands, including oak savannas—low-tree habitats unlike any in the Cascade Range of Washington and Oregon."[3] Large numbers of the California Spotted Owl have been found on private lands, including "industrial" forests maintained by logging companies. Genetically nearly identical birds are found in widely differing habitats. This means the "old growth" finding is simply bad science.

Spotted owl survival turns out to depend not on specific type of habitat, but on availability of habitat, and availability of prey.

Spotted owls in Washington and Oregon prey mainly on fly-

3. Ibid.

ing squirrels, whose Cascades population is relatively low. In California, spotteds prey mainly on the dusky-footed wood rat. California's managed woodlands [industrial forests] have sunlight on the forest floor, because foresters space and trim trees to maximize yield. The warm climate further encourages plant growth. The result is forests with lots of wood rats.[4]

In 1998 Federal Claims Court judge Lawrence S. Margolis ruled that the Forest Service did not have a "rational basis" for halting timber sales to the Wetsel-Oviatt Lumber Company, and that the Forest Service action was "arbitrary, capricious, and without rational basis." Moreover, he ruled that the Forest Service officials knew their findings were faulty when they canceled a sale to the timber company. He ruled: "The Forest Service therefore breached its contractual obligation to fairly and honestly consider Wetsel's bid on the sale."

The Forest Service denied logging in this case based on aerial photography of the area, which showed some old trees supposedly suitable for spotted owl nests. However, they made no attempt to verify their findings through a ground inspection. A private contractor and another government agency reviewed the Forest Service's analysis. Both found it unreliable.

There may be as many as 10,000 pairs of spotted owls in the U.S.[5] The cry to stop logging to preserve the spotted owl is based purely on politicized science. The emphasis on preserving old-growth forests has nothing to do with science or spotted owls. There may be justification for maintaining "old growth" forests as valuable in themselves. However, the spotted owl is not a reason for "protecting" old-growth forests. The spotted owl story is an example of politicized science used to achieve a political objective.

4. Ibid.
5. Ibid.

Lynx Hair

In 1998, the U.S. Fish and Wildlife Service proposed listing the Canada lynx, which ranges across the "northern tier" of states from Washington State to Maine, as an endangered species. To determine the number of lynx, the Rocky Mountain Research Station of the U.S. Department of Agriculture Forest Service developed a sampling kit to be used to collect lynx hairs at more than 10,000 "scratching posts" in a dozen states.

Everything in the survey was standardized as much as possible. The kit for each scratching post included hair snares, visual attractants, bait, and glass vials, plastic bags, and other paraphernalia for returning the samples. The field protocol specified baiting the lure with a standard amount of bait. Two weeks later, any hair found on the bait was to be enclosed in the glass bottles, the bait was to be placed in the plastic bag, and everything returned to the Station.

Once returned to the Station, the hair was sent to the University of Montana, where a laboratory analyzed the DNA in the hair to identify the species. A "positive control," a sample of Canada lynx hair, was run in each test to verify that the test could detect the species, and water was run in each test as a "negative control." At the completion of each test, the extracted DNA samples were frozen, and hair samples were stored to permit checking any specific sample if questions arose.[6]

In 1999 and again in 2000, seven officials of the U.S. Forest Service, the U.S. Fish and Wildlife Service, and the Washington Department of Fish and Wildlife sent Canada lynx hair samples to the laboratory with statements that the samples had been re-

---

6. The description of the survey is taken from the testimony of Kevin S. McKelvey, U.S.D.A. Rocky Mountain Research Station, to the House Committee on Resources, March 6, 2002.

trieved in the Gifford Pinchot and Wenatchee National Forests in Washington State. In reality, the hair had been taken from a pen holding captive lynx and from a stuffed animal, as became known the day after one of the officials who had sent in the samples retired.

On that day, the official reported the submission of the samples to his former superior. When questioned about why the hair from the captive and stuffed lynx had been submitted, the then-retired official and the others who had made the submissions said they wanted to test the laboratory to be certain it could detect lynx hair. They did so with no authorization, and because such "testing of the laboratory" was not included in the survey design, they had no way to inform the laboratory of the unauthorized submissions. The laboratory, not knowing the origin of the samples, counted the hair from the captive and stuffed animals as indicating that lynx were present at scratching posts in the forests in Washington State.

In a letter to *Nature*, Dr. L. Scott Mills, director of the laboratory that analyzed the samples, stated that the protocol used for the lynx survey had been validated with appropriate controls in two labs. His testing protocol had been peer reviewed and published. He said, "For a field worker to arbitrarily decide 'to test the lab' by labeling a hair from elsewhere as if it were a field-collected sample corrupts the integrity of the data and does not constitute a blind control."[7]

There was no need to "test the lab," and it was impossible for the persons submitting the bogus hair specimens to know the results of their "tests" anyway. In a report to the House Resources Committee, the General Accounting Office (GAO) stated:

7. L. S. Mills, "False Samples Are Not the Same as Blind Controls," *Nature* 415 (2002): 471.

In 2000, one of the participants, a biologist with the Forest Service, notified the field coordinator for the National Survey that a control sample had been submitted in connection with the survey for the Gifford Pinchot National Forest. However, he did not identify which sample was the control. As a result, the laboratory and the Forest Service decided not to analyze the hair samples submitted as part of the 2000 survey for the region that included the Gifford Pinchot and the Wenatchee National Forests until the Forest Service completed an investigation and identified all of the unauthorized submissions.[8]

Land-use advocates characterized the incident as an attempt by "biologists with a green tilt" to close off National Forests. Environmental activists accepted the officials' statements that they only intended to "test the lab." Officials of the agencies involved have publicly recognized that the lynx hair incident reflects badly on their agencies and are attempting damage control.

Interior Department Inspector General Earl Devaney reported that he found no criminal intent in the employees' actions, and the Justice Department declined to prosecute them. However, he said the USFWS' failure to administer "meaningful punishment" showed the service's "bias against hold[ing] employees accountable for their behavior."[9]

The USFWS employees involved in the false submissions were taken off the lynx survey, "counseled," and given bonuses. Considering the potential impact of a false finding of lynx presence in the Pinchot and Wenatchee Forests, this seems like a slight tap on the wrist. Indeed, the Inspector General said: "Awarding the involved employees with monies and specifically praising

8. R. Malfi, "Canada Lynx Survey: Unauthorized Hair Samples Submitted for Analysis (GAO-02-496T)" (Washington, D.C.: Government Accounting Office, March 6, 2002).

9. R. Gehrke, "No Criminal Intent Found in Lynx Study," Seattle-Times.com, March 2, 2002.

their work on the lynx study so soon after the incident is not only an incredible display of bad judgment, but also highlights the FWS's excessively liberal award policy and practice."[10]

Only the perpetrators know whether the incident was intentional fraud. In any case, it reinforced the suspicions of those who charge the government with using politicized science to justify ideologically motivated decisions.

"Reintroducing" Wolves in Yellowstone

Historically, wolves ranged from Canada well down into the United States, and from the West Coast to the East Coast. There are numerous accounts of wolf attacks on humans and livestock. One of the earliest on record was reported by the naturalist John James Audubon, and occurred about the year 1830.[11] Attacks continued up through the 1990s, and one attack, in 1996, was the basis for an article in *Reader's Digest*.[12] Healthy as well as rabid wolves, which some blame for all the attacks, have been identified at autopsy when attacking wolves have been killed and examined.

It was with good reason that wolves were hunted to extinction in most of the United States. Wolves are incompatible with livestock, pets, and human beings. It is only because of "green ideology" that they are being reintroduced.

The government systematically misled the public about the numbers of wolves that would be involved in the reintroduction into Yellowstone Park. The organization Defenders of Wildlife cited thirty-five to forty-five wolves as being the target numbers.

10. Anon., "Here a Lynx: There a Lynx," www.cfif.org/5_8_2001/ Free_lines/current/lynx.htm.
11. J. J. Audubon and J. Bachman, *The Quadrupeds of North America*, 3 vols. (New York, 1851–54); reference in http://www.natureswolves.com/ humans/aws_wolfattacks.htm.
12. Kathy Cook, "Night of the Wolf," *Reader's Digest*, July 1997, pp. 114–19.

The National Park Service's initial estimates of between thirty and forty wolves grew to plans calling for ten packs of ten wolves each.

Later, the USFWS upped the ante. Breeding packs are assumed to average ten wolves each, but each pack is assumed to have only one breeding pair. The "recovery plan" calls for ten packs of ten wolves in each of three "recovery areas," for a total of 300 wolves.

Where did this number come from? In 1987, the USFWS stated: "The goal of 10 breeding pairs in each of three recovery areas was established after extensive literature review and consultation with a number of U.S. and Canadian biologists/wolf researchers."[13] Contrary to that published estimate, USFWS responded to a Freedom of Information Act request for the data with a letter that stated the service

> "[had] not contracted or undertaken any studies which deal with minimum viable populations of the Northern Rocky Mountain Wolf," and added "there are no records in the files of our Denver Regional Office or the Cheyenne Fish and Wildlife Enhancement Office referencing any specific materials [which were] used in determining recovery numbers for the Northern Rocky Mountain Wolf."[14]

In short, the current numbers have no scientific basis, and, apparently, the original numbers were set low to minimize public resistance.

A further bit of junk science involves an alleged "balance of nature," in which wolves prevent their prey (elk, deer, caribou, etc.) from overgrazing the land, and moreover strengthen the prey

---

13. "Northern Rocky Mountain Wolf Recovery Plan (Denver: U.S. Fish and Wildlife Service, 1987).

14. C. E. Kay, "Wolf Recovery, Political Ecology, and Endangered Species," www.natureswolves.com/usfws/recovery.htm.

herd by removing the old, the sick, and the unfit. In fact, wolves attack the calves and the yearlings, not the aged and the sick.

> During the 1950s and 1960s, when wolf control was widespread and effective, game herds grew and the north country [Canada and Alaska] became known as a hunter's paradise. Government wolf control ended by 1970, and predator populations began to expand . . . In Wood Buffalo National Park, for instance, there were approximately 12,000 bison when wolf control was terminated; today there are fewer than 3,500, and the population is still dropping. Wolf predation of calves has been identified as the primary factor responsible for the decline.[15]

If only wolves and buffalo were involved, the number of wolves should decline along with the population of buffalo until an equilibrium is reached. In practice, as C. E. Kay also points out, wolves can drive a vulnerable prey population almost to extinction without effect on their own numbers, if they have an alternative though less vulnerable prey population available:

> In Northern British Columbia, wolves caused a substantial decline in the most vulnerable ungulate species and then switched to the next most vulnerable ungulate until it also declined. The wolves cascaded down the list of available ungulate species from the most vulnerable to the least vulnerable until all ungulate populations had been substantially reduced.[16]

The USFWS attempted to develop computer models to prove that wolf recovery would not be detrimental to prey populations. Dr. Robert Taylor, a noted computer modeler and predation expert, testified to the Wolf Recovery Committee at Helena, Mon-

---

15. "Here a Lynx: There a Lynx."
16. Kay, www.natureswolves.com/usfws/recovery.htm.

tana, regarding two of these models.[17] Of one, he said: ". . . this is a wholly unacceptable effort. It relies on datasets of questionable utility . . . it employs obsolete simulation approaches, and it reflects inadequate attention to uncertainty in assumptions and parameters."[18] Of the other model, Taylor testified:

> The model is conceived in such simplistic terms that it cannot, at best, be expected to provide much more than a gross approximation to what will happen [if wolves are reintroduced because] it misrepresents the predatory impact of wolves and their internal population dynamics. . . . The sensitivity analysis is inadequate, considering that many of the parameter values are mere guesses. . . . The net effect of these problems is that none of the conclusions [on probable wolf-ungulate interactions] can be justified at this time.[19]

Taylor later obtained the computer codes for this model, made a single, yet reasonable, change to one of the model's assumptions of wolf-ungulate prey interactions, and found that the model's output was drastically different from what has been published by the agencies.[20]

In addition, the computer models assumed only 100 to 200 wolves in each of three recovery areas. The reality is that ESA mandates will require 1,500 to 2,000 wolves. Moreover, the models do not take into account additive predation by bears or mountain lions, also undergoing expansion as protected species.

The word "reintroduction" assumes that wolves were once common in Yellowstone, but that assumption appears to be without a factual basis. Kay examined journals left by early explorers,

17. At the time Dr. Taylor was a faculty member of the Fish and Wildlife Department at Utah State University. He is now a wildlife consultant and professional computer programmer.
18. Kay, www.natureswolves.com/usfws/recovery.htm.
19. Ibid.
20. Ibid.

and found that, "Between 1835 and 1876, 20 different expeditions spent a total of 785 days traveling through the Yellowstone Eco-system on foot or horseback," without "seeing or killing even a single wolf." No evidence "remotely suggest[s] that large numbers of wolves were common in Yellowstone during the 1835–1876 period."[21]

From 1914 to 1926, Park Service employees, eradicating wolves from Yellowstone, killed 136 wolves in Yellowstone. This included only 56 adults over an eleven-year period.[22] Kay concluded that even pre-Columbian ungulate populations were held to low levels by intense hunting, thereby keeping wolf populations low.

If, as pointed out earlier, wolves and humans in the same territory are incompatible, it is to be expected that the alleged "reintroduction" of wolves into settled areas has caused problems. Indeed, it has. Wolves are killing livestock, including cattle and horses, and pets, including large "working dogs" used in cattle herding.[23]

Poorly done science or, perhaps, politically motivated science, bolstered the push to "reintroduce" wolves to their former range, including areas like Yellowstone where they probably never existed in great numbers before. Unfortunately, that was not the end of the poor science.

Chairman Dan Fuchs of the Montana House of Representatives reports that USFWS has known since 1997 that elk-calf ratios were being drastically reduced in areas of high wolf concentration. However, when Montana Fish and Wildlife Protection per-

21. Ibid.
22. Ibid.
23. Some reports, including some grisly photos, can be found at http://www.natureswolves.com.

sonnel attempted to release this evidence to the public, the USFWS barred them from doing so.

A study begun in 1997 showed that calf ratios were dropping precipitously—zero to 10 elk calves per 100 cows—in areas of high wolf concentration inside Yellowstone while the ratio outside high wolf concentration areas remained at 46 calves per 100. However, USFWS officials hid wolf predation in the annual reports because they published averages for the entire northern herd, combining the 0 to 10 calf ratios in high wolf areas with the 46 calf ratios from elsewhere, bringing the average to near the 30-calf ratio needed to sustain herd viability.[24]

In 1997 and 1998, the low calf ratio was confined to areas of high wolf concentration. In more recent years, as dense wolf populations have reached critical mass across the entire northern Yellowstone Range, the area of low calf ratio also expanded to encompass the entire herd.

The introduction of wolves in areas where they had been eliminated or never existed is a case of ideology overpowering not only science but common sense.

Klamath Basin Water Supply

In 2001 the Bureau of Reclamation shut off irrigation water from the Klamath Basin, which originates in the Cascade and Siskiyou Ranges of southwest Oregon, to save an allegedly endangered species, the suckerfish. While the shut-off was widely described as a case of "people versus fish," there were people on both sides of the issue: people using water for irrigation and people dependent on fish.

Rogue Valley pear farms draw off some Klamath Basin water

---

24. Personal communication from Mr. Joe Balyeat, Montana House of Representatives.

before it reaches Klamath Lake, and an adequate flow of water below the lake must be maintained to allow migration of coho salmon, which is essential for two American Indian tribes' way of life. In 1864, a treaty created a reservation for Klamath Indian bands living in the Klamath area and recognized the Indians' legal rights to water. The water rights were reaffirmed in the 1954 Termination and Relocation Act, in the subsequent Restoration Act of 1973, and a federal case (*U.S. v. Adair*). In addition, the Yurok Indians, who depend on coho salmon for their way of life, have a reservation on both sides of Klamath River, downstream from Klamath Lake.

In 1905 the Bureau of Reclamation started the Klamath Basin project. Lake Klamath, largest of the lakes in the basin, is thirty-five miles long but averages only seven feet deep, which results in the water in the lake becoming warm in the summer. In the 1930s and 1940s, the Klamath Basin land was awarded to home-steaders, with the promise of ample water. Many of the home-steaders were veterans of World War I or World War II.[25]

Several varieties of suckerfish apparently migrated into Upper Klamath Lake at some time during the Klamath Basin project. As of 1970, the official count of Lost River suckerfish was "unknown," and the shortnose suckerfish was "very rare." By 1976, estimates rose to 94,000 Lost River suckerfish and 252,000 shortnose suck-erfish. Since then, suckerfish kills have taken place during years of high water levels—1995, 1996, and 1997—and by 1997, the suckerfish populations were estimated to have declined about 50 percent to 46,000 Lost River suckerfish and 146,000 shortnose suckerfish. There were no suckerfish kills in 1992 and 1994, when water levels in the lake were low. In only three years since 1991

---

25. A copy of a *Life* magazine article about the land lottery for veterans can be found at http://www.klamathcrisis.org/Photos/life-cover.htm.

was the water level in Upper Klamath Lake higher than it was in 2001.

The lake and river and the fish within them are essential for the 500 to 1,000 bald eagles that normally reside in the Lower Klamath Wildlife Refuge, downstream from the irrigation canals, during winter months. The same refuge is a stopping place for some two million ducks, geese, cranes, and other waterfowl that pass through on migrations and depend on water and fish for survival.

The government overpromised the water in the basin. It guaranteed homesteading farmers irrigation water "in perpetuity," and the treaties with Indian tribes guaranteed water to maintain the coho salmon.

On April 7, 2001, the Bureau of Reclamation shut off water for irrigation in the Klamath Basin. The water was needed for salmon and suckerfish, and the Endangered Species Act took priority over Indian treaties and irrigation guarantees. Some 1,500 family-owned farms could not grow crops without the irrigation water. Farmers and agriculture-dependent businesses in the Klamath Basin lost about $200 million.

Given the situation as of April 2001, did the government use sound science to allocate the limited available water as effectively as possible? It did not. Were the suckerfish endangered? Possibly those in the Klamath Basin were. However, they exist elsewhere. No evidence was given that the species was endangered anywhere else. Moreover, it appears that the suckerfish in the Klamath Basin were "exotic" invaders, no more native to the area than the Zebra Mussels in Lake Erie. Hence the very basis for declaring them "endangered" was questionable at best.

The matter of whether the coho salmon were endangered also represents "junk science." In September 2001, a Federal district court in Eugene, Oregon (*Alsea Valley Alliance v. Donald L. Evans*), ruled that the government had improperly counted only the number of wild coho salmon in determining whether they were "endangered," ignoring thousands of genetically identical salmon raised in hatcheries. The court ruled that coho salmon must be taken off the Endangered Species list. (This ruling has been appealed.)

On February 4, 2002, a National Academy of Sciences report (NAS "Scientific Evaluation") stated that the Council found no research showing that higher water levels in the lake benefited suckerfish or that reduced flows of Klamath water harmed coho salmon.[26] On the contrary, suckerfish kills were associated with high lake levels, and the lake was already higher than in all but three of the previous ten years. The report also stated that salmon would be hurt by releasing extra waters during drought years because the warmer water would "equal or exceed the lethal temperatures" for coho salmon in summer months. What little science was available to the USFWS should have led to a different decision from the one made by the service.

Now that everyone realizes there isn't enough water to meet Indian treaty and irrigation guarantees, corrective action is being taken. In April 2002, the USFWS and the Bureau of Reclamation released a draft Ten-Year Plan, and with the attention focused on mistakes of the past, science may be better used than it was in the decision to shut off the irrigation water.

Tip of the Iceberg?

The problem is not these few cases where science was misused for political or ideological ends. The real problem is that there

26. National Academy of Sciences, *Scientific Evaluation of Biological Opinions on Endangered and Threatened Fishes in the Klamath River Basin: Interim Report* (Washington, D.C.: National Academy Press, February 2002). Available at: http://www.nap.edu/books/0309083249/html.

may be many more such cases that have not been discovered. There is no way of knowing.

As Representative James Hansen of Utah said of the lynx hair issue: "This lynx debacle calls into question everything the Fish and Wildlife Service has done for the past eight years. . . . It makes me wonder if past studies have been marred by sloppy or faulty research."[27] He went on to add: "We came very close to impacting the economy of an entire region because of a handful of dishonest people. The use of sound science and peer review could have prevented this whole problem."

Government agencies claim to make decisions on the basis of "the best science available." These examples show that science may be carefully sifted and selected to support an extreme view, that estimates can be skewed to mislead, and that no science may be used. Even if the examples I mention are the only ones in which government agencies and their employees have played fast and loose with science, they are sufficient to remind citizens that they should not suspend skepticism when considering government's claims based on science.

27. Comments of James Hansen at www.house.gov/pombo/wc/articles2002/january3_02.htm.

FOUR

Endocrine Disruptors

STEPHEN SAFE

My initial involvement with endocrine disruptors and the endocrine disruption hypothesis began, unknowingly, in the early 1970s when I was a research officer at the National Research Council of Canada in the Atlantic Regional Laboratory in Halifax, Nova Scotia. Following the identification of polychlorinated biphenyls (PCBs) as highly stable environmental contaminants, my friend and colleague, Otto Hutzinger, persuaded me to collaborate with him on some of the first studies of those chemicals. To investigate concerns that PCBs would not undergo degradation in the environment through chemical/photochemical or metabolic pathways, our initial studies focused on the synthesis of PCB standards that were then used to demonstrate that PCBs undergo photochemical degradation and are metabolized by rats, fish, and birds.[1] We also carried out similar studies with several different classes of halogenated aromatic pollutants including the infamous and highly toxic 2,3,7,8-tetrachlorodibenzo-*p*-dioxin (TCDD, dioxin) and related compounds.

During the 1980s, my research focused on the structure-activity relationships for TCDD and related compounds, and this led to the development of the toxic equivalency factor approach for risk assessment of "dioxin-like" compounds (including PCBs).[2] Our studies on the mechanism of action of TCDD were greatly influenced by a paper by Kociba and coworkers who reported the results of their two-year ("lifetime") dioxin feeding studies in male and female Sprague-Dawley rats. In this study, male rats did not develop TCDD-induced tumors, whereas in female rats there was a significant increase in liver tumors.[3] Buried within their extensive analysis of each tissue for tumors or precancerous lesions were some intriguing results on uterine and mammary tumors, both of which spontaneously develop in older female rats *that have normal estrogen levels.* Decreases in both tumors were apparent in rats maintained on the TCDD diet, consistent with the idea that TCDD inhibited estrogen-dependent tumor formation and development.

Thus, TCDD exhibited antitumorigenic activity by disrupting

1. S. Safe and O. Hutzinger, "Polychlorinated Biphenyls: Photolysis of 2,4,6,2′,6′ Hexachlorobiphenyl," *Nature* 232 (1971): 641–42; O. Hutzinger et al., "Polychlorinated Biphenyls: Metabolic Behavior of Pure Isomers in Pigeons, Rats, and Brook Trout," *Science* 178 (1972): 312–14; O. Hutzinger et al., "Identification of Metabolic Dechlorination of Highly Chlorinated Biphenyl in Rabbits," *Nature* 252 (1974): 698–99.

2. S. Safe, "Polychlorinated Biphenyls (PCBs), Dibenzo-*p*-dioxins (PCDDs), Dibenzofurans (PCDFs) and Related Compounds: Environmental and Mechanistic Considerations Which Support the Development of Toxic Equivalency Factors (TEFs)," *C. R. C. Crit. Rev. Toxicol.* 21 (1990): 51–88.

3. R. J. Kociba et al., "Results of a 2-Year Chronic Toxicity and Oncogenicity Study of 2,3,7,8- Tetrachlorodibenzo-*p*-dioxin (TCDD) in Rats," *Toxicol. Appl. Pharmacol.* 46 (1978): 279–303.

or blocking the formation and growth of age- and estrogen-dependent mammary (and uterine) tumors in rats, and this observation was subsequently confirmed in other laboratory animal studies. Moreover, women accidentally exposed to TCDD in Seveso, Italy, had reduced incidence of breast and endometrial cancers compared to usual rates of these tumors.[4]

TCDD acts through the Ah receptor, a cellular component that binds to the TCDD molecule, and my laboratory has been investigating the unique Ah receptor-mediated antiestrogenic/anticarcinogenic actions of TCDD and developing new nontoxic analogs of TCDD for treating breast cancer.[5] Some of these compounds are in preclinical studies, and we are also investigating their use for treatment of prostate cancer.

My involvement in the endocrine disruptor controversy began in response to an article reporting that PCB and DDE levels were higher in breast cancer patients than in women who did not have the disease, "comparisons" or "controls." It was suggested that the estrogenic activity of organochlorine compounds such as PCBs and DDE may increase the risk for breast cancer.[6] I expressed several concerns regarding this hypothesis, including the fact that the human diet contains contaminants such as TCDD and PCBs, which exhibit antiestrogenic activity, as well as dietary phytochemicals, compounds found in plants that exhibit both es-

4. P. A. Bertazzi et al., "Health Effects of Dioxin Exposure: A 20-year Mortality Study," *Am. J. Epidemiol.* 153 (2001): 1031–44.

5. S. Safe et al., "Selective Ah Receptor Modulators (SAhRMs): Progress Towards Development of a New Class of Inhibitors of Breast Cancer Growth," *J. Women's Cancer* 3 (2001): 37–45; A. McDougal et al., "Tamoxifen-induced Antitumorigenic/Antiestrogenic Action Synergized by a Selective Ah Receptor Modulator," *Cancer Res.* 61 (2001): 3901–7.

6. F. Falck et al., "Pesticides and Polychlorinated Biphenyl Residues in Human Breast Lipids and Their Relation to Breast Cancer," *Arch. Environ. Health* 47 (1992): 143–46.

trogenic and antiestrogenic activity and have been linked to disease prevention.[7]

The Endocrine Disruptor Hypothesis

In the early 1990s, authors of several publications heightened concerns about the potential adverse human health effects associated with background environmental exposures to chemicals that disrupt endocrine signaling pathways.[8] The adverse effects of TCDD and related compounds on wildlife and laboratory animals had already been established,[9] and it was hypothesized that other endocrine-active compounds such as estrogenic chemicals that bind directly to the estrogen receptor (ER) (direct-acting estrogens) may pose environmental and human health problems. Colborn and coworkers also pointed out numerous environmental contaminant-induced wildlife problems, especially those associated with reproduction and development, and suggested that these could be sentinels for ongoing human health problems.[10]

7. S. Safe, "Dietary and Environmental Estrogens and Antiestrogens and Their Possible Role in Human Disease," *Environ. Sci. Pollut. Res.* 1 (1994): 29–33.

8. K. B. Thomas and T. Colborn, "Organochlorine Endocrine Disruptors in Human Tissue," in *Chemically Induced Alterations in Sexual Development: The Wildlife/Human Connection,* T. Colborn and C. Clement., eds. (Princeton, N.J.: Princeton Scientific Publishing, 1992), pp. 365–94; T. Colborn, F. S. Vom Saal, and A. M. Soto, "Developmental Effects of Endocrine-Disrupting Chemicals in Wildlife and Humans," *Environ. Health Perspect.* 101 (1993): 378–84; D. J. Hunter and K. T. Kelsey, "Pesticide Residues and Breast Cancer: The Harvest of a Silent Spring," *J. Natl. Cancer Inst.* 85 (1993): 598–99; K. El-Bayoumy, "Environmental Carcinogens That May be Involved in Human Breast Cancer Etiology," *Chem. Res. Toxicol.* 5 (1993): 585–90; R. M. Sharpe and N. F. Skakkebaek, "Are Oestrogens Involved in Falling Sperm Counts and Disorders of the Male Reproductive Tract?" *Lancet* 341 (1993): 1392–95.

9. L. S. Birnbaum, "Developmental Effects of Dioxin," *Environ. Health Perspect.* 103 (1995): 89–94.

10. Colborn et al., "Developmental Effects."

They were particularly concerned about possible effects of *in utero* or early postnatal exposures on the development of the male and female reproductive tracts, which are highly sensitive to steroid hormone levels.

In one of the first studies of data collected about sperm quality over time, Carlsen and coworkers analyzed 61 sperm-count studies from several countries published between 1938 and 1991 and showed that there was "a significant decrease in mean sperm count from 113×10^6/ml in 1940 to 66×10^6/ml in 1990 (p $<$ 0.0001)" and concluded that "there has been a genuine decline in semen quality over the past 50 years."[11] Sharpe and Skakkebaek later hypothesized "that the increasing incidence of reproductive abnormalities in the human male may be related to increased oestrogen exposure *in utero*."[12] At about the same time, Mary Wolff and her coworkers[13] reported that either PCBs or 1,1-dichloro-2,2-bis(*p*-chlorophenyl)ethylene (DDE, a long-lived degradation product of DDT) levels were elevated in breast cancer patients as compared to levels in controls, and it was subsequently hypothesized that synthetic estrogenic compounds (xenoestrogens) in combination with genetic factors may be preventable causes of breast cancer.[14]

The observed wildlife responses coupled with indications of a worldwide decrease in sperm counts and reports of higher PCB/DDE levels in breast cancer patients (vs. controls) immediately captured the attention not only of scientists and government reg-

11. E. Carlsen et al., "Evidence for the Decreasing Quality of Semen during the Past 50 Years," *Br. Med. J.* 305 (1992): 609–12.

12. Sharpe and Skakkebaek, "Oestrogens."

13. Falck et al., "Pesticides"; M. S. Wolff et al., "Blood Levels of Organochlorine Residues and Risk of Breast Cancer," *J. Natl. Cancer Inst.* 85 (1993): 648–52.

14. D. L. Davis et al., "Medical Hypothesis: Xenoestrogens as Preventable Causes of Breast Cancer," *Environ. Health Perspect.* 101 (1993): 372–77.

ulators but also of the media and public. Numerous reports on television and in newspapers and magazines highlighted decreased sperm counts, smaller penises (in alligators living in a pond near a Superfund site), and chemical-induced breast cancer. Perhaps the classic statement belongs to Dr. Louis Guillette of alligator-penis fame, who informed a congressional panel that "every man in this room is half the man his grandfather was."

In her article entitled "Hormone Hell" in *Discover Magazine* (in September 1996), Catherine Dold wrote: "Industrial chemicals —from plastics to pesticides—paved the road to modern life. Now it appears that these same chemicals, by mimicking natural hormones, can wreak havoc in developing animals. And the road we once thought led to material heaven is heading somewhere else entirely."

Lawrence Wright in his *New Yorker* article (January 15, 1996) entitled "Silent Sperm" extensively discusses the falling sperm count issue and the studies by Skakkebaek, Sharpe, and their colleagues. Mr. Wright also mentions an interview with Dr. Harry Fisch who "claims that his work refutes the whole notion of a decline in the world's sperm count." Unfortunately, Dr. Fisch's paper could not be released prior to its publication and therefore the impact of his work was not fully appreciated.

My comments on the sperm count issue and the role of estrogens were among the few statements in this (and many other) articles that disputed the hypothesis:

> "The estrogen link is total bunk," Stephen Safe, a professor of toxicology at Texas A&M University told me. . . . Safe admitted that he didn't have a clue to what could be causing lower sperm counts and other male reproductive problems. "Lord only knows," he said. "It may be a very regional thing. But just because Denmark has a problem and a few alligators in a swamp below a Superfund site develop small penises doesn't mean our sperm counts are going down or our re-

productive success has declined. I just don't think we should extrapolate."

Other early articles in *Newsweek* (March 21, 1994, "The Estrogen Complex"), *Time* (March 18, 1996, "What's Wrong with Our Sperm?"), *Science News* (January 8, 1994, "The Gender Benders," and January 22, 1994, "That Feminine Touch"), and a British television special entitled "Assault on the Male" forecast a gloomy future for mankind!

Not surprisingly, environmental and health research and regulatory agencies in most developed countries have issued lengthy reports on endocrine disruptors, and review articles on every aspect of this hypothesized problem have appeared in scientific journals. In addition, increased funding for research on endocrine disruptors has resulted in new data as well as the generation of several controversies regarding interpretation of laboratory animal and cell culture data from different laboratories. Those results and controversies continue to attract media attention. In contrast, results from human studies have been less controversial and somewhat reassuring; however, reporting of these data has been minimal. Who cares if we are more than half the men our grandfathers were! Unfortunately, many in the news media fail to report good news on environmental issues, which is a disservice to their readers/viewers.

Endocrine Disruptors and Male Reproductive Capacity

The initial report suggesting a worldwide decrease in sperm counts coupled with a hypothesis that this may be part of larger syndrome (i.e., decreased male reproductive capacity)[15] spurred research efforts around the world. In addition to sperm counts,

---

15. Sharpe and Skakkebaek, "Oestrogens"; Carlsen et al., "Evidence."

scientists have investigated other potential indicators of diseases/
problems associated with the male reproductive tract including
testicular cancer, prostate cancer, fertility, male/female birth ratios, hypospadias (displaced urethral opening), and cryptorchidism (undescended testicles) in infants.

All but one of these studies addressed only changes over time
and did not attempt to measure exposures to chemicals. The one
study that attempted to correlate levels of exposure to endocrine
disruptor chemicals with an adverse response examined testicular cancer. As summarized in this section, it should be clear that
facts do not support the frightening "assault on the male" scenarios presented in the media and by some scientists.

Sperm Counts

The issue of time-dependent decreases or increases in sperm
counts had been frequently raised prior to the report by Carlsen
and coworkers on their meta-analysis of 61 selected sperm count
studies.[16] Their work was highly provocative, and the results of
their meta-analysis study have been hotly debated by academic
and nonacademic scientists, and the difficulties in obtaining consistent sperm count/quality data have also been documented.

Since 1993, there has been a host of new studies on sperm
counts and quality from men at various clinics (Table 1).[17] Results

16. Carlsen et al., "Evidence."

17. D. A. Adamopoulos et al., "Seminal Volume and Total Sperm Number
Trends in Men Attending Subfertility Clinics in the Greater Athens Area
During the Period 1977–1993," *Hum. Reprod.* 11 (1996): 1936–41; I. S. Tum-
mon and D. Mortimer, "Decreasing Quality of Semen," *Br. Med. J.* 305 (1992):
1228–29; J. Auger et al., "Decline in Semen Quality Among Fertile Men in
Paris During the Past 20 Years," *N. Engl. J. Med.* 332 (1995): 281–85; S. Irvine
et al., "Evidence of Deteriorating Semen Quality in the United Kingdom:
Birth Cohort Study in 577 Men in Scotland Over 11 Years," *Br. Med. J.* 312
(1996): 467–71; K. Van Waeleghem et al., "Deterioration of Sperm Quality in
Young Healthy Belgian Men," *Hum. Reprod.* 11 (1996): 325–29; J. Gyllenborg

Table 1. Sperm Counts/Quality Studies: 1993–Present

Cohort	Location	Years of Data Collection	Sperm Counts (10^6/ml)
A. DECREASED SPERM COUNTS/QUALITY			
Fertility clinic (20)	Greece (Athens)	1977–1993	51–39
Husbands (infertile women) (21)	UK (London)	1978–1989	101–76
Sperm donors (22)	France (Paris)	1973–1992	89–60
Sperm donors (23)	Scotland	birth cohort	98–78
Infertile men (24)	Belgium	birth cohort (1950–1970)	—
B. NO CHANGE OR SLIGHTLY INCREASED SPERM COUNTS/QUALITY			
Volunteer donors (25)	Denmark (Copenhagen)	1977–1995	53–72.7
Infertile couples (26)	Venezuela (Merida)	1981–1995	—
Volunteer donors (27)	Australia (Sydney)	1980–1995	69
Husbands (infertile women) (28)	Denmark (Odense)	birth cohort[a] (1950–1970)	183.7
Husbands (infertile women) (29)	Slovenia	1983–1996	81
Fertility clinics (30)	Spain (Barcelona)		44
Vasectomy clinics (31)	New York	1970–1994	131.5
	California	1970–1994	72.7
	Minnesota	1979–1994	100.8
Sperm donors (32)	France (Toulouse)	1977–1992	68.4
Sperm donors (33)	Washington (State)	1972–1993	52
Sperm donors (34)	Japan (Sapporo)	1975–1998	70.9–79.6
C. VARIABLE RESULTS–DEPENDING ON SELECTION OF TIME PERIOD			
Infertile men (35)	Denmark	1950–1971 (decrease)	
		1922–1971 (no change)	
Fertility clinics (36)	Canada	1984–1996 (decrease)	variable
		1975–1996 (no change)	

Note: a. This approach presents sperm counts based on a defined range of birth dates (e.g., 1950–1970) for individuals in a study.

from some clinics indicated decreased sperm quality; however, most studies indicate that there has not been a significant decline in sperm quality during the last fifteen to twenty-five years.

The work by Fisch and coworkers on sperm quality of men from vasectomy clinics in New York, California, and Minnesota revealed no change in sperm counts, sperm volume, or sperm motility in the period 1970 through 1994.[18] They did, however, show surprisingly large differences in sperm counts between the three locations. Sperm counts in New York, California, and Minnesota were 131.5, 72.7, and 100.8 × 10⁶/ml, respectively, and still

---

et al., "Secular and Seasonal Changes in Semen Quality Among Young Danish Men: A Statistical Analysis of Semen Samples from 1927 Donor Candidates during 1977–1995," *Int. J. Androl.* 22 (1999): 28–36; I. Tortolero et al., "Semen Analysis in Men from Merida, Venezuela, Over a 15-Year Period," *Arch. Androl.* 42 (1999): 29–34; D. J. Handelsman, "Sperm Output of Healthy Men in Australia: Magnitude of Bias Due to Self-selected Volunteers" *Human Reprod.* 12 (1997): 101–5; P. E. Rasmussen, K. Erb, and L. G. Westergaard, "No Evidence for Decreasing Semen Quality in Four Birth Cohorts of 1,055 Danish Men Born Between 1950 and 1970," *Fertil. Steril.* 68 (1997): 1059–69; B. Zorn et al., "Semen Quality Changes Among 2343 Healthy Slovenian Men Included in an IVF-ET Programme from 1983 to 1996," *Int. J. Androl.* 22 (1999): 178–83; P. Andolz, M. A. Bielsa, and J. Vila, "Evolution of Semen Quality in North-Eastern Spain: A Study in 22,759 Infertile Men Over a 36-Year Period," *Hum. Reprod.* 14 (1999): 731–35; H. Fisch et al., "Semen Analyses in 1,283 Men from the United States Over a 25-Year Period: No Decline in Quality. *Fertil. Steril.* 65 (1996): 1009–14; L. Bujan et al., "Time Series Analysis of Sperm Concentration in Fertile Men in Toulouse, France Between 1977 and 1992," *Br. Med. J.* 312 (1996): 471–72; C. A. Paulsen, N. G. Berman, and C. Wang, "Data from Men in Greater Seattle Area Reveal No Downward Trend in Semen Quality: Further Evidence that Deterioration of Semen Quality Is Not Geographically Uniform," *Fertil. Steril.* 65: (1996): 1015–20; N. Itoh et al., "Have Sperm Counts Deteriorated Over the Past 20 Years in Healthy, Young Japanese Men? Results from the Sapporo Area," *J. Androl.* 22 (2001): 40–44; Y. Zheng et al., "Is Semen Quality Related to the Year of Birth Among Danish Infertility Clients?" *Int. J. Epidemiol.* 26 (1997): 1289–97; E. V. Younglai, J. A. Collins, and W. G. Foster, "Canadian Semen Quality: An Analysis of Sperm Density Among Eleven Academic Fertility Centers," *Fertil. Steril.* 70 (1998): 76–80.

18. Fisch et al., "Semen analyses."

lower sperm counts, 52×10^6/ml, were reported from the state of Washington,[19] indicating large demographic differences in sperm counts within the United States. Such variability has also been observed in other countries.[20] The effects of geographic differences on sperm counts were particularly striking in Canada, where the values from eleven different centers ranged from 51–121 $\times 10^6$/ml in 1984 and 48–137 $\times 10^6$/ml in 1996.[21]

These results suggest that persistent organic pollutants (POPs), such as PCBs, DDE, and other organochlorine pesticides, are unlikely to be causative agents for decreases in sperm counts (geographic or temporal) because human levels of these environmental contaminants tend to be similar within most countries except for a few specific groups (e.g., people whose diets include lots of fish). Since sperm counts in males are highly variable and are influenced by many different factors, this parameter may not be a useful indicator for determining potential adverse exposures to environmental endocrine disruptors. Nevertheless, results of more recent studies in Japan indicate that sperm counts are not decreasing in many areas.[22] Future studies that investigate differences in sperm counts within various countries and regions may provide new insights on sperm-count variability.

Fertility

Temporal changes in fertility may be a more reliable indicator than sperm counts regarding possible alterations in male reproductive capacity, and the World Health Organization has devel-

19. Paulsen et al., "Data."
20. Younglai et al., "Canadian Semen Quality"; J. Auger and P. Jouannet, "Evidence for Regional Differences of Semen Quality Among Fertile French Men," *Hum. Reprod.* 12 (1997): 740–45.
21. Younglai et al., "Canadian Semen Quality."
22. Itoh et al., "Sperm Counts."

oped protocols for determining human fertility changes.[23] At least two studies have investigated the effects of *in utero* exposure to pharmacologic (high) doses of estrogen (with or without progestins) or the potent synthetic estrogenic drug diethylstilbestrol (DES) on the fertility of male offspring.

In the 1950s and early 1960s, estrogens and DES were prescribed for women experiencing problems during pregnancy, and a study in Chicago in the early 1960s investigated the effects of DES on pregnancy outcomes by comparing outcomes in women who received DES to outcomes in a control group of women who received a placebo. After data became available that demonstrated harmful effects of DES, Wilcox and coworkers contacted the sons of women in this study to evaluate the long-term effects of DES exposure on their fertility.[24] Based on their analyses, Wilcox and coworkers concluded that "High doses of DES did not lead to impairment of fertility or sexual function in adult men who had been exposed to the drug *in utero*."

Lamuela-Raventos and coworkers studied a group of men and women in Finland (1954–63) exposed *in utero* to pharmacologic doses of estrogens alone or estrogens/progestins (combined) and concluded that these "drugs as used in the study population did not have much impact on the fertility of offspring."[25] These data, coupled with studies showing no decrease in fertility in Sweden and Britain,[26] indicate that there is not a global decrease in male fertility.

23. T. M. Stewart et al., "Feasibility of Surveillance of Changes in Human Fertility and Semen Quality" *Hum. Reprod.* 16 (2001): 177–87.

24. A. J. Wilcox et al., "Fertility in Men Exposed Prenatally to Diethylstilbestrol," *N. Engl. J. Med.* 332 (1995): 1411–16.

25. R. M. Lamuela-Raventos et al., "Direct HPLC Analysis of *Cis*- and *Trans*-resveratrol and Piceid Isomers in Spanish Red *Vitis vinifera* Wines," *J. Agric. Food Chem.* 43 (1995): 281–83.

26. O. Akre et al., "Human Fertility Does Not Decline: Evidence from

Sex Ratios at Birth

Davis and coworkers examined birth sex ratios in several industrial countries and reported that the "usual" 1.06:1.0 male to female ratio had declined.[27] Their conclusions stated, "We propose that reduced male proportion at birth be viewed as a sentinel health event that may be linked to environmental factors," and as a potentially useful measurement for determining the role and identities of endocrine active chemicals that could affect birth sex ratios. Interestingly, some recent studies indicate that the male birth fraction is dependent on multiple factors including race, parental age, and birth weight. A study in Finland investigated sex ratios in that country over a period of 250 years (1751–1997), and concluded that decreased sex ratios have not been observed since 1920.[28] Moreover, after examination of multiple parameters including chemical usage and human levels of organochlorine contaminants, they concluded that "we were not able to confirm that chemicalization (in the sense of exposure to agricultural or industrial chemicals) is a significant source of changes in sex ratio."[29]

Sex ratios were determined in families who were accidentally exposed to high levels of dioxin (in Zone A) as a result of an industrial accident that occurred in Seveso, Italy, in 1976.[30] From

---

Sweden," *Fertil. Steril.* 71 (1999): 1066–69; M. Joffe, "Time Trends in Biological Fertility in Britain," *Lancet* 355 (2000): 1961–65.

27. D. L. Davis, M. B. Gottlieb, and J. R. Stampnitzky, "Reduced Ratio of Male to Female Births in Several Industrial Countries: A Sentinel Health Indicator," *JAMA* 279 (1998): 1018–23.

28. T. Vartiainen, L. Kartovaara, and J. Tuomisto, "Environmental Chemicals and Changes in Sex Ratio: Analysis Over 250 Years in Finland," *Environ. Health Perspect.* 107 (1999): 813–15.

29. Ibid.

30. P. Mocarelli et al., "Change in Sex Ratio with Exposure to Dioxin," *Lancet* 348 (1996): 409.

April 1977 to December 1984 there was a decrease in the male/ female sex ratio (26/48); in contrast, from 1985 to 1994, this ratio increased to normal values (60/64). These results suggest that high-level exposure to TCDD may affect birth sex ratios; however, no changes in sex ratios have been observed as a result of parental occupational exposure to relatively high doses of TCDD,[31] and no other data corroborate the Seveso findings.

Hypospadias and Cryptorchidism

It has been hypothesized that hypospadia and cryptorchidism in newborns may also be contributors to a global decrease in male reproductive capacity. Paulozzi has summarized studies of inter-national trends in the rates for those conditions, which were highly variable among different countries.[32] For example, in 1990, hypospadias for the following countries varied from 38 to 7 per 10,000 births, with the United States > Australia > Sweden > Norway > New Zealand > Netherlands > Finland > Japan, and there were also differences within countries. Inter-country vari-ability was also observed for cryptorchidism. There are, however, no correlations in the rates of the two birth defects in various countries.

Paulozzi indicated that the increases in hypospadias "leveled off in many systems after 1985," whereas for cryptorchidism "since 1985, rates declined in most systems" ("systems" refers to health systems in countries/regions that collect these data). Pau-lozzi suggested that "it is unlikely that further inspection of inter-

31. T. M. Schnorr et al., "Spontaneous Abortion, Sex Ratio, and Paternal Occupational Exposure to 2,3,7,8-Tetrachlorodibenzo-*p*-dioxin," *Environ. Health Perspect.* 109 (2001): 1127–32.

32. L. J. Paulozzi, "International Trends in Rates of Hypospadias and Cryptorchidism," *Environ. Health Persp.* 107 (1999): 297–302.

national trends alone will shed additional light on the question of endocrine disruption as a cause of birth defects."

Testicular Cancer

The incidence of testicular cancer has been increasing in most countries, and since the risks are highest among younger men, it is possible that initiation of this tumor could be related to *in utero/* early postnatal exposure to some unknown factors including estrogens.[33] There are large differences in the incidence rates of testicular cancer in various countries, and such variability in rates is a common observation in studies of many male reproductive tract problems. For example, between 1985 and 1989, the incidence rates for testicular cancer in highly susceptible thirty-to-thirty-four-year-olds was 2.7, 3.3, 3.4, 5.6, 5.9, 11.1, 18.2, 22.2, and 24.5 per 10^5 in Lithuania, Latvia, Estonia, Finland, Poland, Sweden, Norway, East Germany, and Denmark, respectively.[34] Differences among these northern European countries was >9-fold, and among the Scandinavian countries, there was a >4-fold difference between Denmark (high) and Finland (low).

Sharpe suggested that DDE (which inhibits male sex hormones—androgens—and is an "antiandrogen") may play a role in the hypothesized increases in diseases or problems in the male reproductive tract.[35] However, breast-milk levels of DDE (a commonly used measure for DDE exposures) are comparable in all four Scandinavian countries and therefore do not correlate with

33. R. H. Depue, M. C. Pike, and B. E. Henderson, "Estrogen Exposure During Gestation and Risk of Testicular Cancer," *J. Natl. Cancer Inst.* 71 (1983): 1151–55.

34. R. Bergstrom et al., "Increase in Testicular Cancer Incidence in Six European Countries: A Birth Cohort Phenomenon," *J. Natl. Cancer Inst.* 88 (1996): 727–33.

35. R. M. Sharpe, "Reproductive Biology. Another DDT Connection," *Nature* 375 (1995): 538–39.

different incidence rates for testicular cancer in these countries.[36] This investigation of a possible linkage of an environmental chemical and a specific disease of the male reproductive tract found no support for an association of DDE with the development of testicular cancer.

Summary

The hypothesis that environmental endocrine disruptors may contribute to diseases of the male reproductive tract has spurred considerable research on this area, with a particular emphasis on changes that have occurred over time. There are no apparent global changes in sperm counts and fertility, rates of hypospadias and cryptorchidism, and birth sex ratios. Testicular cancer is increasing in most countries, but it is not correlated with other indicators of male reproductive capacity. Moreover, testicular cancer is increasing while DDE and other POPs are decreasing, suggesting that exposure to these compounds is not linked to testicular cancer.

For many of these responses, there are large differences in incidence rates between and within various countries, and possible etiologic factors that can account for these differences are unknown. Persistent organic pollutants that bioaccumulate are not highly variable within most countries/regions and therefore cannot be responsible for the observed demographic-dependent differences in incidence rates. Research designed to study the reason for region-specific differences in diseases/problems in the male reproductive tract will require new hypotheses and paradigms that include genetic susceptibility, diet, lifestyle factors, and

36. A. Ekbom, A. Wicklund-Glynn, and H. O. Adami, "DDT and Testicular Cancer," *Nature* 347 (1996): 553–54.

other environmental exposures (including chemical contaminants).

Role of PCBs/DDE in Breast Cancer

The reports of Falck and coworkers[37] and Wolff and coworkers[38] that levels of PCBs or DDE were higher in breast cancer patients compared to controls in two cohorts from Connecticut and New York raised concerns that such persistent xenoestrogens (estrogens that originate outside the body, and are often used to denote synthetic estrogens) may play a role in development of breast cancer. Other authors and I[39] criticized the xenoestrogen-breast cancer hypothesis because PCBs/DDE are not mammary carcinogens in high-dose human exposures or in animal tests and some PCBs exhibit antiestrogenic activity in female rats.[40] Subsequent studies on cohorts of breast cancer patients and controls in several

37. Falck et al., "Pesticides."

38. Wolff et al., "Blood Levels."

39. S. Safe, "Environmental and Dietary Estrogens and Human Health —Is There a Problem?" *Environ. Health Perspect.* 103 (1995): 346–51; U. G. Ahlborg et al., "Organochlorine Compounds in Relation to Breast Cancer, Endometrial Cancer, and Endometriosis: An Assessment of the Biological and Epidemiological Evidence," *Crit. Rev. Toxicol.* 25 (1995): 463–531.

40. Ahlborg et al., "Organochlorine Compounds"; K. C. Silinskas and A. B. Okey, "Protection by 1,1,1-trichloro-2,2-bis(p-chlorophenyl)ethane(DDT) Against Mammary Tumors and Leukemia During Prolonged Feeding of 7,12-dimethylbenz(a)anthracene to Female Rats," *J. Natl. Cancer Inst.* 55 (1975): 653–57; J. D. Scribner and N. K. Mottet, "DDT Acceleration of Mammary Gland Tumors Induced in the Male Sprague-Dawley Rat by 2-acetamidophenanthrene," *Carcinogenesis* 2 (1981): 235–39; S. Safe, "Modulation of Gene Expression and Endocrine Response Pathways by 2,3,7,8-tetrachlorodibenzo-*p*-dioxin and Related Compounds," *Pharmacol. Therap.* 67 (1995): 247–81; T. Zacharewski, and S. Safe, "Antiestrogenic Activity of TCDD and Related Compounds," in K. S. Korach, ed., *Reproductive and Developmental Toxicology* (New York: Marcel Dekker, 1998), pp. 431–48.

countries have demonstrated that total PCBs and DDE levels were not elevated in patient groups.[41]

41. N. Krieger et al., "Breast Cancer and Serum Organochlorines: A Prospective Study Among White, Black, and Asian Women" *J. Natl. Cancer Inst.* 86 (1994): 589–99; L. López-Carrillo et al., "Dichlorodiphenyltrichloroethane Serum Levels and Breast Cancer Risk: A Case-control Study from Mexico," *Cancer Res.* 57 (1997): 3728–32; P. Van't Veer et al., "DDT (Dicophane) and Postmenopausal Breast Cancer in Europe: Case Control Study," *Br. Med. J.* 315 (1997): 81–85; D. J. Hunter et al., "Plasma Organochlorine Levels and the Risk of Breast Cancer," *New Engl. J. Med.* 337 (1997): 1253–58; A. Schecter et al., "Blood Levels of DDT and Breast Cancer Risk Among Women Living in the North of Vietnam," *Arch. Environ. Contam. Toxicol.* 33 (1997): 453–56; K. B. Moysich et al., "Environmental Organochlorine Exposure and Postmenopausal Breast Cancer Risk," *Cancer Epidemiol. Biomarkers. Prev.* 7 (1998): 181–88; A. P. Hoyer et al., "Organochlorine Exposure and Risk of Breast Cancer," *Lancet* 352 (1998): 1816–20; S. Guttes et al., "Chlororganic Pesticides and Polychlorinated Biphenyls in Breast Tissue of Women with Benign and Malignant Breast Disease," *Arch. Environ. Contam. Toxicol.* 35 (1998): 140–47; G. Liljegren et al., "Case-control Study on Breast Cancer and Adipose Tissue Concentrations of Congener Specific Polychlorinated Biphenyls, DDE and Hexachlorobenzene," *Eur. J. Cancer Prev.* 7 (1998): 135–40; K. J. Helzlsouer et al., "Serum Concentrations of Organochlorine Compounds and the Subsequent Development of Breast Cancer," *Cancer Epidemiol. Biomarkers. Prev.* 8 (1999): 525–32; J. F. Dorgan, "Serum Organochlorine Pesticides and PCBs and Breast Cancer Risk: Results from a Prospective Analysis," *Cancer Causes and Control* 10 (1999): 1–11; G. A. S. Mendonca et al., "Organochlorines and Breast Cancer: a Case-control Study in Brazil," *Int. J. Cancer* 83 (1999): 596–600; E. M. Ward et al., "Serum Organochlorine Levels and Breast Cancer: A Nested Case-control Study of Norwegian Women," *Cancer Epidemiol. Biomarkers. Prev.* 9 (2000): 1357–67; D. Bagga et al., "Organochlorine Pesticide Content of Breast Adipose Tissue from Women with Breast Cancer and Control Subjects," *J. Natl. Cancer Inst.* 92 (2000): 750–53; I. Romieu et al., "Breast Cancer, Lactation History, and Serum Organochlorines," *Am. J. Epidemiol.* 152 (2000): 363–70; R. Millikan et al., "Dichlorodiphenyldichloroethene, Polychlorinated Biphenyls, and Breast Cancer Among African-American and White Women in North Carolina," *Cancer Epidemiol. Biomarkers. Prev.* 9 (2000): 1233–40; S. D. Stellman et al., "Breast Cancer Risk in Relation to Adipose Concentrations of Organochlorine Pesticides and Polychlorinated Biphenyls in Long Island, New York," *Cancer Epidemiol. Biomarkers. Prev.* 9 (2000): 1241–49; T. Zheng et al., "Risk of Female Breast Cancer Associated with Serum Polychlorinated Biphenyls and 1,1-dichloro-2,2'-bis(*p*-chlorophenyl)ethylene," *Cancer Epidemiol. Bio-

Some investigators have used high-resolution analytical techniques to show that one or more individual PCB congeners or other organochlorine pesticides (e.g., dieldrin) were elevated in breast cancer patients, but these increases have not been observed in other studies. For example, Hoyer and coworkers reported that dieldrin levels were higher in a cohort of Danish breast cancer patients and were inversely correlated with breast cancer survival.[42] In contrast, serum levels of dieldrin were not elevated in Norwegian breast cancer patients[43] or in patients from Missouri.[44] Similar inconsistencies between studies have been observed for PCBs where PCB congeners (but not mixtures) were higher in patients vs. controls.

Studies from several countries have vindicated early skepticism about the postulated causal role of PCBs and DDE in the development of breast cancer. Dr. Mary Wolff, a coauthor of the two initial studies showing higher levels of PCBs and/or DDE in breast cancer patients, was also involved in several of the later

---

markers. Prev. 9 (2000): 167–74; T. Zheng et al., "Breast Cancer Risk Associated with Congeners of Polychlorinated Biphenyls," *Amer. J. Epidemiol.* 152 (2000): 50–58; A. P. Hoyer et al., "Organochlorine Exposure and Breast Cancer Survival," *J. Clin. Epidemiol.* 53 (2000): 323–30; T. R. Holford et al., "Joint Effects of Nine Polychlorinated Biphenyl (PCB) Congeners on Breast Cancer Risk," *Int. J. Epidemiol.* 29 (2000): 975–82; M. S. Wolff et al., "Organochlorine Exposures and Breast Cancer Risk in New York City Women," *Environ. Res.* 84 (2000): 151–61; F. Laden et al., ",1-Dichloro-2,2-bis(*p*-chlorophenyl)ethylene and Polychlorinated Biphenyls and Breast Cancer: Combined Analysis of Five U.S. Studies," *J. Natl. Cancer Inst.* 93 (2001): 768–76; F. Laden et al., "Plasma Organochlorine Levels and the Risk of Breast Cancer: An Extended Follow-up in the Nurses' Health Study," *Int. J. Cancer* 91 (2001): 568–74; K. J. Aronson et al., "Breast Adipose Tissue Concentrations of Polychlorinated Biphenyls and Other Organochlorines and Breast Cancer Risk," *Cancer Epidemiol. Biomarkers. Prev.* 9 (2000): 55–63.

42. Hoyer et al., "Organochlorine Exposure and Risk"; Hoyer et al., "Oganochlorine Exposure and Survival."

43. Ward et al., "Serum Organochlorine."

44. Dorgan et al., "Serum Organochlorine."

studies and one of these reports concluded, "combined evidence does not support an association of breast cancer risk with plasma/serum concentrations of PCBs or DDE."[45]

Endocrine Disruptors—
Personal Reminiscences

My participation in the debate on environmental endocrine disruptors and their potential adverse impacts on human health has been a learning experience. During the 1970s and early 1980s, my research on PCBs and related compounds and the TEF concept contributed to the development of regulatory measures that have resulted in reduced emissions and environmental levels of these compounds. This research was primarily supported by federal funding agencies (the Environmental Protection Agency and the National Institute of Environmental Health Sciences).

Although I am still concerned about environmental impacts of organochlorine pollutants and some endocrine disruptors, I have remained skeptical of the hypothesis that these chemicals are currently having global impact on human health. My skepticism is reinforced by the recently published scientific data that have been referenced in this chapter. My views are also due, in part, to the concepts put forward by Bruce Ames and Lois Gold, who pointed out that the human diet contains multiple toxins and carcinogens that occur naturally in food or are formed during cooking.[46] Moreover, levels and often the potencies of "natural" carcinogens in the diet are far higher than those of carcinogenic industrial contaminants. A similar argument also holds true for endocrine disruptors where dietary intakes of phytoestrogens,

45. Laden et al., "1,1-Dichloro-2,2-bis(p-chlorophenyl)ethylene."
46. B. N. Ames and L. S. Gold, "Environmental Pollution, Pesticides, and the Prevention of Cancer: Misconceptions," *FASEB J.* 11 (1997): 1041–52, and see also Ames and Gold chapter, this volume.

and other endocrine-active substances including Ah receptor-active compounds, far outweigh the intakes of endocrine-active manmade environmental contaminants.

Unlike many other scientific controversies, the endocrine disruptor issue has engendered partisan and inflammatory debate on both sides of the issue. My views and statements contributed to this problem, particularly in two articles written as editorials in the *Wall Street Journal* (August 20, 1997) and the *New England Journal of Medicine.*[47] Both articles commented on recently published data that clearly did not support the endocrine disruptor hypothesis, and it was (and is) my view that scientists and the public should be made aware of these results and their significance.

I drew attention to the extensive worldwide coverage in 1996–97 of a report in *Science* indicating that combinations of weakly active estrogenic pesticides interacted synergistically and that this observation strongly supported the endocrine disruptor hypothesis. Scientists in my laboratory, among many others, had not observed these interactions, and about a year later, the authors of the *Science* paper withdrew it, stating that they had been unable to reproduce their own results. In contrast to zealously reporting the original finding, the media paid scant attention to scientific data showing "no synergism," and I believed (and believe) that it was important to point this out.

The *Wall Street Journal* article resulted in a less than complimentary letter from a member of the National Research Council (NRC) panel on endocrine disruptors to NRC staff indicating that "Safe has undermined the work of the panel" and has "contaminated the pending report." Needless to say, there were demands for my removal from the panel, and the letter asserted that my

47. S. Safe, "Xenoestrogens and Breast Cancer," *N. Engl. J. Med.* 337 (1997): 1303–4.

article was part of a conspiracy linked to "specific interest groups that Safe represents."

At that time (1994–96), I had research support for a project on estrogenic compounds funded by the Chemical Manufacturers Association (CMA); my only official contact with the association was Ann Mason, Director of Scientific and Regulatory Affairs (Chlorine Chemistry Council, CMA), who asked for a yearly report. My opinions on the endocrine disruptor hypothesis have been based on analysis of scientific publications and have been consistent prior to, during, and after the research (not personal) support from the CMA.

The editorial in the *New England Journal of Medicine* (*NEJM*) commented on an article that showed that plasma DDE levels in breast cancer patients from several states in this country were not significantly different from levels in control patients.[48] Similar results have been reported in other studies,[49] and my final comments pointed out that "it is incumbent on scientists, the media, legislators, and regulators to distinguish between scientific evidence and hypothesis, and not to allow a 'paparazzi science' approach to these problems." The editors received several negative reactions to my article and these included complaints that I had not disclosed my financial interests.

At the time, based on the then-current *NEJM* guidelines, which asked for current support, I had not declared my previous grant support from the CMA. In retrospect, I agree that full disclosure, even of potential conflicts, is the best course and I should have been more perceptive of this issue.

The subject of endocrine disruptors and fear of chemicals (chemophobia) has been addressed in several recent books on both sides of this contentious issue. *Our Stolen Future; Hormone*

48. Hunter et al., "Plasma Organochlorine."
49. See note 41.

Deception; Hormonal Chaos; and *The Feminization of Nature—Our Future at Risk* chronicle the perceived, predicted, and observed problems associated with endocrine disruptors.[50] Skepticism regarding the human impact of environmental contaminants has been discussed in several books including *The Skeptical Environmentalist* and *Naturally Dangerous: Surprising Facts About Food, Health and the Environment,*[51] and John Stossel (ABC television) remains a consistent skeptic with his features on junk science.

The concern regarding human exposure to relatively low environmental levels of estrogenic contaminants and other endocrine disruptors must take into account higher exposures to phytoestrogens and other naturally occurring endocrine-active compounds in the diet. Although there is evidence linking some wildlife problems to chemical exposures (e.g., organochlorines) that act through endocrine pathways, there have also been surprising observations. Studies in Britain initially raised concern regarding feminization of fish in British rivers, and this was initially linked to estrogenic alkylphenols (industrial products) that contribute to this response in the vicinity of sewage outflows. However, the problems in many of the British rivers where feminization of male fish was observed were not associated with synthetic alkylphenols. Instead, the problem has now been linked

50. See T. Colborn, D. Dumanoski, and J. P. Myers, *Our Stolen Future: Are We Threatening Our Fertility, Intelligence and Survival? A Scientific Detective Story* (New York: Penguin Books, 1996); L. D. Berkson, *Hormone Deception* (Chicago: Contemporary, 2000); S. Krimsky, *Hormonal Chaos: The Scientific and Social Origins of the Environmental Endocrine Hypothesis* (Baltimore: John Hopkins University Press, 2000); and D. Cadbury, *The Feminization of Nature: Our Future at Risk* (London: Penguin Books, 1998).

51. Glassner, B. *The Culture of Fear* (New York: Basic Books, 1999); National Research Council: Committee on Hormonally Active Agents in the Environment, *Hormonally Active Agents in the Environment* (London: Penguin Books, 1999).

to natural estrogens (17β-estradiol/estrone) from human and animal waste and possibly ethynylestradiol, used in birth control pills.[52]

My skeptical comments on the endocrine disruptor hypothesis have been extensively criticized from both a scientific and personal point of view. In the book *Hormonal Chaos*, Dr. Krimsky states: "Safe's role in disputing different components of the hypothesis has also raised eyebrows among some of his colleagues who consider his industrial funding sources a matter of dishonor in these sensitive areas of science." Tony Tweedale (whom I have never met), writing for an environmental group, referred to me as "one loud and inane mouth" and "He'll relatively soon get his come-uppance on these ridiculous arguments of his. . . . I only hope we ensure he gets it good and hard."

Mindless personal attacks by individuals whom you do not know are disappointing, particularly in light of results of continuing studies that have not identified linkages between exposure to endocrine disruptors and human disease. I have always acknowledged the adverse impact of environmental endocrine-active compounds on fish and wildlife populations in some areas, but have questioned their impact on human health. Scientific studies published in the past six to eight years have addressed many of the critical issues associated with endocrine disruptors and human health, and extensive references to these papers have been intentionally included in this chapter. Results of the more recent studies indicate that initial concerns regarding hypothesized endocrine disruptor-induced human problems may not be justified.

52. E. J. Routledge et al., "Identification of Estrogenic Chemicals in STW Effluent. 2. *In vivo* Responses in Trout and Roach," *Environ. Sci. Technol.* 32 (1998): 1559–65; C. Desbrow et al., "Identification of Estrogenic Chemicals in STW Effluent. 1. Chemical Fractionation and In Vitro Biological Screening," *Environ. Sci. Technol.* 32 (1998): 1549–58.

Gregg Easterbrook in an editorial entitled "Science Fiction" in the *New Republic* (August 30, 1999) critically examines the endocrine disruptor issue and concedes that there may be "dangerous endocrine disruptors." However, he concludes his editorial with a statement that is highly relevant: "It's strange to think how quickly speculative, lightly researched claims, advanced by advocates with a fund-raising interest can go straight to the top of the national policy agenda, while so many undeniably genuine problems languish." I do not entirely agree that the endocrine disruptor hypothesis was lightly researched or did not deserve serious scientific study and evaluation by regulatory agencies. The concern with this issue and others is that scientists/regulators develop vested interests in specific problems, and there is great reluctance on their (our) part to say "enough is enough." With limited funding available, this can seriously impede research that addresses more pressing environmental and human health issues.

FIVE

Cancer Prevention and the Environmental Chemical Distraction

BRUCE AMES
LOIS SWIRSKY GOLD

Entering a new millennium seems a good time to challenge some old ideas about cancer cause and prevention, which in our view

This paper has been adapted in part from L. S. Gold, T. H. Slone, N. M. Manley, and B. N. Ames, *Misconceptions About the Causes of Cancer* (Vancouver, Canada: Fraser Institute, 2003), and B. N. Ames and L. S. Gold, "Paracelsus to Parascience: The Environmental Cancer Distraction," *Mutation Res.* 447 (2000): 3–13. The reader is referred to these publications for further details and references. This work was supported by a grant from the Office of Biological and Environmental Research (BER), U.S. Department of Energy, grant no. DE-AC03-76SF00098 to L.S.G. at Lawrence Berkeley National Laboratory; by a grant from the National Foundation for Cancer Research to B.N.A.; by the National Institute of Environmental Health Sciences Center Grant ESO1896 at the University of California, Berkeley; and by a grant for research in disease prevention through the Dean's Office of the College of Letters and Science, University of California, Berkeley, to L.S.G. and B.N.A.

are implausible, have little supportive evidence, and might best be left behind. In this chapter, we summarize data and conclusions from fifteen years of work, raising five issues that involve toxicology, nutrition, public health, and government regulatory policy:

1. *There is no cancer epidemic other than that due to smoking.*

2. *The dose makes the poison.* Half of all chemicals tested, whether natural or synthetic, cause cancer in high-dose rodent cancer tests. Evidence suggests that this high rate is due primarily to effects that are unique to high doses. The results of these high-dose tests have been used to regulate low-dose human exposures, but are not likely to be relevant.

3. *Even Rachel Carson was made of chemicals: natural vs. synthetic chemicals.* Human exposure to naturally occurring rodent carcinogens is ubiquitous and dwarfs the exposure of the general public to synthetic rodent carcinogens.

4. *Errors of omission.* The major causes of cancer (other than smoking) do not involve exposures to exogenous chemicals that cause cancer in high-dose tests; rather, the major causes are dietary imbalances, hormonal factors, infection and inflammation, and genetic factors. Insufficiency of many vitamins and minerals, which is preventable by supplementation, causes DNA damage by a mechanism similar to radiation.

5. *Damage by distraction: regulating low hypothetical risks.* Regulatory policy places unwarranted emphasis on reducing low-level exposures to synthetic chemicals. Putting large amounts of money into small hypothetical risks can damage public health by diverting resources and distracting the public from major risks.

The Dose Makes the Poison

The main rule in toxicology is that "the dose makes the poison." At some level, every chemical becomes toxic, but there are safe levels below that.

In contrast to that rule, a scientific consensus evolved in the 1970s that we should treat carcinogens differently, that we should assume that even low doses might cause cancer, even though we lacked the methods for measuring carcinogenic effects at low levels. In large part, this assumption was based on the idea that mutagens—chemicals that cause changes in DNA—are carcinogens and that the risk of mutations was directly related to the number of mutagens introduced into a cell. It was also assumed that (1) only a small proportion of chemicals would have carcinogenic potential, (2) testing at a high dose would not produce a carcinogenic effect unique to the high dose, and (3) carcinogens were likely to be synthetic industrial chemicals. As we enter the new century, it is time to take account of information indicating that all three assumptions are wrong.

Laws and regulations directed at synthetic chemicals got a big push from the widely publicized "cancer epidemic," which supposedly stemmed from exposures to those chemicals. In fact, there is not now and there never was a cancer epidemic, and cancer mortality, excluding lung cancer mortality, has declined 19 percent since 1950.[1] Lung cancer mortality began dropping about 1990 as a result of reduced smoking rates, and that trend is likely to continue. Regardless of the absence of evidence for a cancer epidemic, the "epidemic" has left a long-lasting legacy—a regulatory focus on synthetic chemicals.

---

1. L. A. G. Ries et al., *SEER Cancer Statistics Review, 1973–1997* (Bethesda, Md.: National Cancer Institute, 2000).

Table 1. Proportion of Tested Chemicals Classified as Carcinogenic

Chemicals tested in both rats and mice[a]	
Chemicals in the CPDB	350/590 (59 percent)
Naturally occurring chemicals in the CPDB	79/139 (57 percent)
Synthetic chemicals in the CPDB	271/451 (60 percent)
Chemicals tested in rats and/or mice	
Chemicals in the CPDB	702/1348 (52 percent)
Natural pesticides in the CPDB	38/72 (53 percent)
Mold toxins in the CPDB	14/23 (61 percent)
Chemicals in roasted coffee in the CPDB	21/30 (70 percent)
Commercial pesticides	79/194 (41 percent)
Innes negative chemicals retested[b]	17/34 (50 percent)
Physician's Desk Reference (PDR):	
drugs with reported cancer tests[c]	117/241 (49 percent)
FDA DATABASE OF DRUG SUBMISSIONS[d]	125/282 (44 percent)

Notes: a. L. S. Gold and E. Zeiger, eds., *Handbook of Carcinogenic Potency and Genotoxicity Databases* (Boca Raton, Fla.: CRC Press, 1997), http://potency.berkeley.edu/crcbook.html (Gold and Zeiger, *Handbook of Carincogenic Potency*).

    b. J. R. M. Innes et al., "1969 Tested 120 Chemicals for Carcinogenicity," *Journal of the National Cancer Institute* 42 (1969): 1110–14. They reported that only eleven of the chemicals were carcinogens, and that observation was important to the idea that only a small proportion, say 10 percent, of all chemicals were carcinogens. To date, fully half the negative chemicals from the Innes study, when retested, have been shown to be carcinogenic.

    c. T. S. Davies and A. Monro, "Marketed Human Pharmaceuticals Reported to be Tumorigenic in Rodents," *J. Am. Coll. Toxicol.* 14 (1995): 90–107.

    d. J. Contrera, A. Jacobs, and J. DeGeorge, "Carcinogenicity Testing and the Evaluation of Regulatory Requirements for Pharmaceuticals," *Regul. Toxicol. Pharmacol.* 25 (1997): 130–45.

Source: Carcinogenic Potency Database (http://potency.berkeley.edu)

About 50 percent of chemicals, both natural and synthetic, that have been tested in standard, high-dose, animal cancer tests are rodent carcinogens (Table 1).[2] What explains the high per-

    2. L. S. Gold et al., *Misconceptions About the Causes of Cancer,* L. S. Gold and E. Zeiger, eds., *Handbook of Carcinogenic Potency and Genotoxicity Databases* (Boca Raton, Fla.: CRC Press, 1997); L. S. Gold et al., "Supplement to the Carcinogemic Potency Database (CPDB): Results of Animal Bioassays Published in the General Literature in 1993–1994 and by the National Toxi-

centage? In standard cancer tests, rodents are given a near-toxic dose of the test substance over their lifetime, the maximum tolerated dose (MTD), to maximize the chance of detecting any carcinogenicity. Evidence is accumulating that cell division caused by the high dose itself, rather than the chemical per se, contributes to cancer in these tests.[3]

High doses can cause chronic wounding of tissues, cell death, and consequent chronic cell division of neighboring cells, which would otherwise not divide. Cell division is a risk factor for cancer because there is some probability that a mutation will occur each time DNA is replicated, and some of those mutations can lead to cancer. A high proportion (41 percent) of chemicals that are carcinogens in rodent tests are not mutagenic, and their carcinogenicity may result from cell killing and consequent division at the high doses tested. Such increased cell division does not occur at the low levels of synthetic chemicals to which humans are usually exposed.

Defenders of rodent tests argue that the high rate of positive tests results from selecting more suspicious chemicals to test, and this seems a likely bias because cancer testing is both expensive and time-consuming, making it prudent to test suspicious compounds. One argument against such a selection bias is the high rate of positive tests for drugs (Table 1) because drug development favors chemicals that are not mutagens or expected carcinogens.[4]

---

cology Program in 1995–1996," *Environ. Health Perspect.* 107 (Suppl. 4, 1999): 527–600.

3. B. N. Ames and L. S. Gold, "Chemical Carcinogenesis: Too Many Rodent Carcinogens," *Proc. Natl. Acad. Sci. U.S.A.* 87 (1990): 7772–76; S. M. Cohen, "Cell Proliferation and Carcinogenesis," *Drug Metab. Rev.* 30 (1998): 339–57.

4. See L. S. Gold, T. H. Slone, and B. N. Ames, "What Do Animal Cancer Tests Tell Us About Human Cancer Risk?: Overview of Analyses of the Carcinogenic Potency Database," *Drug Metab. Rev.* 30 (1998): 359–404.

A second argument against selection bias is that the knowledge needed to predict carcinogenicity in rodent tests is highly imperfect, even now, after decades of test results have become available on which to base predictions. For example, in 1990, there was wide disagreement among experts about which chemicals would be carcinogenic when subsequently tested by the National Toxicology Program.[5] Moreover, if the primary basis for selection of chemicals to test were suspicion of carcinogenicity, selection would focus on mutagens (80 percent are carcinogenic compared to 50 percent of nonmutagens). In fact, a majority of tested chemicals, 55 percent, are nonmutagens.

It seems likely that a high proportion of all chemicals, whether synthetic or natural, would be "carcinogens" if administered in the standard rodent bioassay at the MTD, primarily because of the effects of high doses on cell death and division and DNA damage and repair.[6] Without additional data about how a chemical causes cancer, the interpretation of a positive result in a rodent bioassay is highly uncertain. The induction of cancer could be the result of the high doses tested and have no predictive value about what might occur at lower doses.

The processes of mutagenesis and carcinogenesis are complicated because of many factors, which are dose-dependent.[7] For instance, normal cells contain an appreciable level of DNA lesions, and they contain enzymes that repair the lesions with high

5. G. S. Omenn, S. Stuebbe, and L. B. Lave, "Predictions of Rodent Carcinogenicity Testing Results: Interpretation in Light of the Lave-Omenn Value-of-Information Model," *Mol. Carcinog.* 14 (1995): 37–45.

6. B. Butterworth, R. Conolly, and K. Morgan, "A Strategy for Establishing Mode of Action of Chemical Carcinogens as a Guide for Approaches to Risk Assessment," *Cancer Lett.* 93 (1995): 129–46.

7. J. G. Christensen, T. L. Goldsworthy, and R. C. Cattley, "Dysregulation of Apoptosis by C-myc in Transgenic Hepatocytes and Effects of Growth Factors and Nongenotoxic Carcinogens," *Mol. Carcinog.* 25 (1999): 273–84.

efficiency.[8] The number of those lesions increases in tissues injured by high doses of chemicals[9] and may overwhelm the capacity of the repair enzymes. The far lower levels of chemicals to which humans are exposed through water pollution or synthetic pesticide residues on food are not sufficient to increase the number of DNA lesions in any appreciable way and may pose no or minimal cancer risks.

Regulatory agencies do not consider the great uncertainties in extrapolating from the effects observed in high-dose rodent tests to predictions of possible effects in humans at far lower doses. Instead, they assume that the effects are directly proportional to dose—that there is a linear relationship between dose and cancer—and they calculate the "virtually safe dose" (VSD), which corresponds to a maximum, hypothetical risk of one additional cancer in a million exposed people, and set the VSD as the acceptable exposure level. To the extent that high doses of nonmutagens are the cause of carcinogenicity in rodent bioassays, the linear model is inappropriate.[10] Linearity of dose response seems unlikely in any case even for chemicals that are mutagens because of the inducibility of the numerous defense enzymes that deal with the thousands of exogenous chemicals that we encounter in our diets (see below), and protect us against the natural world of mutagens as well as the small amounts of synthetic chemicals.[11]

---

8. H. J. Helbock et al., "DNA Oxidation Matters: The HPLC-EC Assay of 8-oxo-deoxyguanosine and 8-oxo-guanine," *Proc. Natl. Acad. Sci. U.S.A.* 95 (1998): 288–93.

9. D. L. Laskin and K. J. Pendino, "Macrophages and Inflammatory Mediators in Tissue Injury," *Annu. Rev. Pharmacol. Toxicol.* 35 (1995): 655–77.

10. D. W. Gaylor and L. S. Gold, "Regulatory Cancer Risk Assessment Based on a Quick Estimate of a Benchmark Dose Derived from the Maximum Tolerated Dose," *Regul. Toxicol. Pharmacol.* 28 (1998): 222–25.

11. T. D. Luckey, "Nurture with Ionizing Radiation: A Provocative Hypothesis," *Nutr. Cancer* 34 (1999): 1–11; Ames and Gold, "Paracelsus to Parascience."

Regulatory agencies are moving to take nonlinearity and questions about mechanisms of carcinogenicity into account; for example, the U.S. Environmental Protection Agency (EPA) recently concluded that chloroform (a by-product of disinfecting water with chlorine) was not likely to be carcinogenic to humans unless the exposures were high enough to cause cell toxicity and increased cell division. The chloroform levels in drinking water are low and do not produce such effects.[12]

Even Rachel Carson Was Made of Chemicals: Natural vs. Synthetic Chemicals

About 99.9 percent of the chemicals humans ingest are natural, and the amounts of synthetic pesticide residues in foods are insignificant compared to the amount of natural pesticides that are always in our diet because of the plants we eat.[13] Of all dietary pesticides that humans eat, 99.99 percent are natural chemicals produced by plants to defend themselves against fungi, insects, and other animal predators. The natural pesticides come in great variety because each plant produces a different array of such chemicals.

We have estimated that on average Americans ingest roughly 5,000 to 10,000 different natural pesticides and their breakdown

---

12. U.S. Environmental Protection Agency, "Integrated Risk Information System (IRIS)" (Cincinnati: Office of Health and Environmental Assessment, Environmental Criteria and Assessment Office, 2002).

13. B. N. Ames, M. Profet, and L. S. Gold, "Nature's Chemicals and Synthetic Chemicals: Comparative Toxicology," *Proc. Natl. Acad. Sci. U.S.A.* 87 (1990): 7782–86; B. N. Ames, M. Profet, and L. S. Gold, "Dietary Pesticides 99.99 Percent All Natural," ibid., 7777–81; L. S. Gold, T. H. Slone, and B. N. Ames, "Prioritization of Possible Carcinogenic Hazards in Food," in D. Tennant, ed., *Food Chemical Risk Analysis* (London: Chapman & Hall, 1997), pp. 267–95.

products. Each day, the average American eats about 1,500 milligrams (mg = 1/1000th of a gram) of natural pesticides, which is about 10,000 times more than the 0.09 mg they consume of synthetic pesticide residues.[14]

Only a small proportion of natural pesticides have been tested for carcinogenicity, but 38 of the 72 tested are rodent carcinogens. As shown in Table 2, naturally occurring pesticides that are rodent carcinogens are ubiquitous in common fruits, vegetables, herbs, and spices. The widespread distribution of such chemicals means that no diet can be free of natural chemicals that are rodent carcinogens.

The average American eats about 2,000 mg of burnt material, which is produced in usual cooking practices, each day. That burnt material contains many rodent carcinogens and mutagens, swamping, again, the 0.09 mg of 200 synthetic chemicals, primarily synthetic pesticides, that are ingested each day and that are classified as rodent carcinogens.

The natural chemicals that are known rodent carcinogens in a single cup of coffee are about equal in weight to a year's worth of ingested synthetic pesticide residues that are rodent carcinogens. This is so, even though only 3 percent of the natural chemicals in roasted coffee have been adequately tested for carcinogenicity (Table 3). This does not mean that coffee or natural pesticides are dangerous; rather, assumptions about high-dose animal cancer tests for assessing human risk at low doses need reexamination.

14. E. L. Gunderson, "Chemical Contaminants Monitoring: FDA Total Diet Study, April 1982–April 1984, Dietary Intakes of Pesticides, Selected Elements, and Other Chemicals," *J. Assoc. Off. Anal. Chem.* 71 (1988):1200–9.

Table 2. Carcinogenicity Status of Natural Pesticides Tested in Rodents

Occurrence: *Natural pesticides that are rodent carcinogens occur in:* absinthe, allspice, anise, apple, apricot, banana, basil, beet, broccoli, Brussels sprouts, cabbage, cantaloupe, caraway, cardamom, carrot, cauliflower, celery, cherries, chili pepper, chocolate, cinnamon, citronella, cloves, coffee, collard greens, comfrey herb tea, corn, coriander, currants, dill, eggplant, endive, fennel, garlic, grapefruit, grapes, guava, honey, honeydew melon, horseradish, kale, lemon, lentils, lettuce, licorice, lime, mace, mango, marjoram, mint, mushrooms, mustard, nutmeg, onion, orange, oregano, paprika, parsley, parsnip, peach, pear, peas, black pepper, pineapple, plum, potato, radish, raspberries, rhubarb, rosemary, rutabaga, sage, savory, sesame seeds, soybean, star anise, tarragon, tea, thyme, tomato, turmeric, and turnip.

Carcinogens and Noncarcinogens among Tested Natural Pesticides:

Carcinogens: acetaldehyde methylformylhydrazone, allyl isothiocyanate, N=38 arecoline.HCl, benzaldehyde, benzyl acetate, caffeic acid, capsaicin, catechol, clivorine, coumarin, crotonaldehyde, 3,4-dihydrocoumarin, estragole, ethyl acrylate, $N2$-λ-glutamyl-p-hydrazinobenzoic acid, hexanal methylformylhydrazine, p-hydrazinobenzoic acid.HCl, hydroquinone, 1-hydroxyanthraquinone, lasicarpine, d-limonene, 3-methoxycatechol, 8-methoxypsoralen, N-methyl-N-formylhydrazine, α-methylbenzyl alcohol, 3-methylbutanal methylformylhydrazone, 4-methylcatechol, methyl eugenol, methylhydrazine, monocrotaline, pentanal methylformylhydrazone, petasitenine, quercetin, reserpine, safrole, senkirkine, sesamol, symphytine

Noncarcinogens: atropine, benzyl alcohol, benzyl isothiocyanate, benzyl N=34 thiocyanate, biphenyl, d-carvone, codeine, deserpidine, disodium glycyrrhizinate, ephedrine sulphate, epigallocatechin, eucalyptol, eugenol, gallic acid, geranyl acetate, β-N-[β-l(+)-glutamyl]-4-hydroxymethylphenylhydrazine, glycyrrhetinic acid, p-hydrazinobenzoic acid, isosafrole, kaempferol, dl-menthol, nicotine, norharman, phenethyl isothiocyanate, pilocarpine, piperidine, protocatechuic acid, rotenone, rutin sulfate, sodium benzoate, tannic acid, 1-trans-δ^9-tetrahydrocannabinol, turmeric oleoresin, vinblastine

Source: Carcinogenic Potency Database (http://potency.berkeley.edu); Gold and Zeiger, *Handbook of Carincogenic Potency.*

Table 3. Rodent Carcinogens in the Natural Chemicals Present in Roasted Coffee

---

Carcinogens: acetaldehyde, benzaldehyde, benzene, benzofuran,
N=21   benzo(a)pyrene, caffeic acid, catechol, 1,2,5,6-
                 dibenzanthracene, ethanol, ethylbenzene, formaldehyde, furan,
                 furfural, hydrogen peroxide, hydroquinone, isoprene, limonene,
                 4-methylcatechol, styrene, toluene, xylene

Noncarcinogens: acrolein, biphenyl, choline, eugenol, nicotinamide, nicotinic acid,
N=8   phenol, piperidine

Uncertain: caffeine

Yet to test: ~1,000 chemicals

Source: Carcinogenic Potency Database (http://potency.berkeley.edu); Gold and Zieger, *Handbook of Carcinogenic Potency.*

Ranking Risks

Gaining a broad perspective about the vast number of chemicals to which humans are exposed can be helpful when setting research and regulatory priorities. Rodent cancer tests by themselves provide little information about how a chemical causes cancer or about low-dose risk. The assumption that synthetic chemicals are hazardous has led to a bias in testing, and such chemicals account for 76 percent (451 of 590) of the chemicals tested chronically in both rats and mice (Table 1). The world of natural chemicals has never been tested systematically.

One reasonable strategy to use the available information about cancer risk is to construct an index to compare and rank possible carcinogenic hazards from a wide variety of chemical exposures at levels typically experienced by humans, and then to focus research and regulatory efforts on those that rank highest.[15]

---

15. L. S. Gold et al., *Misconceptions About the Causes of Cancer;* B. N. Ames,

Although one cannot say whether the ranked chemical exposures are likely to be of major or minor importance in human cancer, it is not prudent to focus attention on risks at the bottom of a ranking if the same methodology identifies numerous, common human exposures that pose much greater possible risks. Our rankings are based on the human exposure/rodent potency (HERP) index, which is the ratio between the average human exposure to a chemical and the dose that caused cancer in 50 percent of exposed rodents.

Overall, our analyses have shown that HERP values for some historically high exposures in the workplace—to butadiene and tetrachloroethylene—and to some pharmaceuticals—clofibrate —rank high, and that there is an enormous background of naturally occurring rodent carcinogens in typical portions of common foods. The background of natural exposures casts doubt on the relative importance of low-dose exposures to residues of synthetic chemicals such as pesticides. (A committee of the National Research Council of the National Academy of Sciences reached similar conclusions about natural vs. synthetic chemicals in the diet, and called for further research on natural chemicals.)[16]

The possible carcinogenic hazards from synthetic pesticides are minimal compared to the background of nature's pesticides, though neither may be a hazard at the low doses consumed. Analysis also indicates that many ordinary foods would not pass the regulatory criteria used for synthetic chemicals. Caution is necessary in drawing conclusions about the occurrence in the diet of natural chemicals that are rodent carcinogens. These di-

---

R. Magaw, and L. S. Gold, "Ranking Possible Carcinogenic Hazards," *Science* 236 (1987): 271–80.

16. National Research Council, *Carcinogens and Anticarcinogens in the Human Diet: A Comparison of Naturally Occurring and Synthetic Substances* (Washington, D.C.: National Academy Press, 1996).

etary exposures are not necessarily of much relevance to human cancer. The data call for a reevaluation of the utility of animal cancer tests in protecting the public against minor hypothetical risks without understanding how the chemical causes tumors.

Cellular Defenses Against Chemical Carcinogens Work Against Natural and Synthetic Chemicals

It is often assumed that because natural chemicals are part of human evolutionary history, whereas synthetic chemicals are recent, the mechanisms evolved in animals to cope with the toxicity of natural chemicals will fail to protect against synthetic chemicals. This assumption is flawed for several reasons.

1. Human defenses to ward off effects of exposures to toxins are usually general, directed at classes of similar chemicals, rather than tailored for specific chemicals, and they work against both natural and synthetic chemicals.[17] Examples of general defenses include the continuous shedding of cells exposed to toxins. The surface layers of the mouth, esophagus, stomach, intestine, colon, skin, and lungs are discarded every few days; DNA repair enzymes repair DNA damage regardless of the source of the damage. Detoxification enzymes of the liver and other organs generally react with classes of chemicals rather than individual chemicals.

General defense mechanisms make good evolutionary sense for animals, such as humans, which eat plants and encounter a diverse and ever-changing array of plant toxins in an evolving world. A herbivore that had defenses against only a specific set of toxins would be at great disadvantage in obtaining new food when favored foods became scarce or evolved new chemical defenses.

17. Ames, Profet, and Gold, "Nature's Chemicals and Synthetic Chemicals."

2. Various natural toxins, which have been present through-out vertebrate evolutionary history, nevertheless cause cancer in vertebrates. Mold toxins, such as aflatoxin, have been shown to cause cancer in rodents (Table 1) and other species including humans. Many common elements are carcinogenic to humans at high doses—for example, salts of cadmium, beryllium, nickel, chromium, and arsenic, despite their presence throughout evo-lution. Furthermore, epidemiological studies from various parts of the world show that certain ingested natural substances may be carcinogenic risks to humans. Naturally occurring arsenic in drinking water causes cancer of the lung, bladder, and skin,[18] and the chewing of betel nut with tobacco causes oral cancer.

3. Humans have not had time to evolve a "toxic harmony" with all of their dietary plants. The human diet has changed mark-edly in the last few thousand years. Indeed, very few of the plants that humans eat today, such as coffee, cocoa, tea, potatoes, toma-toes, corn, avocados, mangoes, olives, and kiwi fruit, would have been present in a hunter-gatherer's diet. Natural selection works far too slowly for humans to have evolved specific resistance to the food toxins in these newly introduced plants.

4. DDT is often viewed as the typically dangerous synthetic pesticide because it concentrates in adipose tissues and persists for years. DDT, the first synthetic pesticide, eradicated malaria from many parts of the world, including the United States. It was effective against many vectors of disease such as mosquitoes, tsetse flies, lice, ticks, and fleas and against many crop pests, significantly increasing the supply and lowering the cost of food, making fresh, nutritious foods more accessible to poor people. DDT was also of low toxicity to humans. DDT prevented many

18. National Research Council, *Arsenic in Drinking Water: 2001 Update* (Washington, D.C.: National Academy Press, 2001).

millions of deaths due to malaria.[19] (See also Bate chapter, this volume.)

There is no convincing epidemiological evidence,[20] nor is there much toxicological plausibility, that the levels of DDT normally found in the environment or in human tissues are likely to be a significant contributor to cancer. Two chemical properties of DDT were important in focusing attention on it. DDT, once ingested, is stored in fatty tissues, and the DDT in an insect, when eaten by a small bird, will be concentrated and stored in the bird's fat. If a larger bird, such as an eagle, eats the small bird, it will ingest the concentrated DDT and each additional meal of DDT-containing prey will increase the concentration. The chlorine components (substituents) of DDT cause it to be resistant to degradation in nature, and, as a result, it persists longer than most chemicals. Few synthetic chemicals share these properties.

These properties are not unique to synthetic chemicals. Many thousands of chlorinated chemicals are produced in nature,[21] and natural pesticides can bioconcentrate if they are fat-soluble. Potatoes, for example, contain solanine and chaconine, which are fat-soluble, neurotoxic, natural pesticides that can be detected in the blood of all potato eaters. High levels of these potato neurotoxins have been shown to cause birth defects in rodents,[22] though they have not been tested for carcinogenicity.

5. Because no plot of land is immune to attack by insects,

19. National Academy of Sciences, U.S.A., *The Life Sciences: Recent Progress and Application to Human Affairs, the World of Biological Research, Requirement for the Future* (Washington, D.C.: Committee on Research in the Life Sciences, 1970).

20. T. Key and G. Reeves, "Organochlorines in the Environment and Breast Cancer," *Br. Med. J.* 308 (1994): 1520–21.

21. G. W. Gribble, "The Diversity of Natural Organochlorines in Living Organisms," *Pure Appl. Chem.* 68 (1996): 1699–1712.

22. Ames, Profet, and Gold, "Nature's Chemicals and Synthetic Chemicals."

plants need chemical defenses—either natural or synthetic—to survive, and trade-offs between naturally occurring and synthetic pesticides are possible. One consequence of disproportionate concern about synthetic pesticide residues is that some plant breeders develop plants to be more insect-resistant, which sometimes increases their levels of natural pesticides, which can bring its own hazards. When a major grower introduced a new variety of highly insect-resistant celery into commerce, people who handled the celery developed rashes when they went out into the sunlight. Some detective work found that the pest-resistant celery contained 6,200 parts per billion (ppb) of carcinogenic (and mutagenic) psoralens instead of the 800 ppb present in common celery.[23]

Errors of Omission

High consumption of fruits and vegetables is associated with a lowered risk of degenerative diseases including cancer, cardiovascular disease, cataracts and brain dysfunction.[24] More than 200 studies in the epidemiological literature show, with consistency, an association between low consumption of fruits and vegetables and high cancer incidence (Table 4). The evidence of a protective effect of fruits and vegetables is most convincing for cancers of the oral cavity, esophagus, stomach, and lung. The median relative risk of cancer of the lung, larynx, oral cavity, esophagus, stomach, bladder, pancreas, and cervix was about double for the quarter of the population with the lowest dietary intake of fruits

23. S. F. Berkley et al., "Dermatitis in Grocery Workers Associated with High Natural Concentrations of Furanocoumarins in Celery," *Ann. Intern. Med.* 105 (1986): 351–55.

24. B. N. Ames, L. S. Gold, and W. C. Willett, "The Causes and Prevention of Cancer," *Proc. Natl. Acad. Sci. U.S.A.* 92 (1995): 5258–65; B. N. Ames, M. K. Shigenaga, and T. M. Hagen, "Oxidants, Anti-Oxidants, and the Degenerative Diseases of Aging," ibid. 90 (1993): 7915–22.

Table 4. Review of Epidemiological Studies on Association Between Fruit and Vegetable Consumption and Cancer Risk at Various Sites

Cancer site	Proportion of Studies with Statistically Significant Protective Effect of Fruits and/or Vegetables[a]	Percent of Studies with Protective Effect
Larynx	6/6	100
Stomach	28/30	93
Mouth, oral cavity, and pharynx	13/15	87
Bladder	6/7	86
Lung	11/13	85
Esophagus	15/18	83
Pancreas	9/11	82
Cervix	4/5	80
Endometrium	4/5	80
Rectum	8/10	80
Colon	15/19	79
Colon/rectum	3/5	60
Breast	8/12	67
Thyroid	3/5	60
Kidney	3/5	60
Prostate	1/6	17
Nasal and nasopharynx	2/4	—[b]
Ovary	3/4	—
Skin	2/2	—
Vulva	1/1	—
Mesothelium	0/1	—
TOTAL	144/183	79

Notes: a. Based on standard statistical tests; see the source publication for further information.

b. — = fewer than 5 studies; no percent was calculated.

Source: World Cancer Research Fund (1997). *Food, Nutrition and the Prevention of Cancer: A Global Perspective* (Washington, D.C.: American Institute for Cancer Research, 1997).

and vegetables when compared to the quarter with the highest intake.[25] The median relative risk, although elevated, was not as

25. G. Block, B. Patterson, and A. Subar, "Fruit, Vegetables, and Cancer Prevention: A Review of the Epidemiologic Evidence," *Nutr. Cancer* 18 (1992): 1–29.

high for the hormonally related cancers of breast, prostate, and ovary, or for the colon.

Inadequate diets, with too few fruits and vegetables, are a cancer risk, and they are common. Fully 80 percent of children and adolescents[26] and 68 percent of adults[27] do not eat the five servings of fruits and vegetables per day recommended by the National Cancer Institute and the National Research Council. Publicity about hundreds of minor hypothetical risks, such as pesticide residues, can cause a loss of perspective about what is important. In a survey, half the U.S. public did not name fruit and vegetable consumption as protective against cancer.[28]

Fascination with the hypothetical risks from pesticides may increase cancer risks. Fruits and vegetables are of major importance for reducing cancer; if they become more expensive because of reduced use of synthetic pesticides then consumption is likely to decline and cancer to increase. The effects of such policies will be most notable on people with low incomes who must spend a higher percentage of their income on food, and who already eat fewer fruits and vegetables.

Laboratory studies of vitamin and mineral inadequacy associate such deficiencies with DNA damage, which indicates that the vitamin and mineral content of fruits and vegetables may explain the observed association between fruit and vegetable intake and cancer risk. Antioxidants such as vitamin C (whose dietary source is fruits and vegetables), vitamin E, and selenium

26. S. M. Krebs-Smith et al., "Fruit and Vegetable Intakes of Children and Adolescents in the United States," *Arch. Pediatr.* 150 (1996): 81–86.

27. S. M. Krebs-Smith et al., "U.S. Adults" Fruit and Vegetable Intakes, 1989 to 1991: A Revised Baseline for the Healthy People 2000 Objective," *Am. J. Public Health* 85 (1995): 1623–29.

28. National Cancer Institute Graphic, "Why Eat Five?" *J. Natl. Cancer Inst.* 88 (1996): 1314.

protect against oxidative damage caused by normal metabolism,[29] smoking,[30] and inflammation.[31]

Laboratory evidence ranging from likely to compelling indicates that deficiency of some vitamins and minerals—folic acid, vitamins B_{12}, B_6, C, and E, niacin, iron, and zinc—causes damage to DNA that mimics the damage caused by radiation.[32] In the United States, the percentage of the population that consumes less than half the Recommended Daily Allowance (RDA) in the diet (that is, ignoring supplement use) for five of these eight vitamins or minerals is estimated to be: zinc (10 percent of women/men older than 50), iron (25 percent of menstruating women, and 5 percent of women over 50), vitamin C (25 percent of women/ men), folate (50 percent of women; 25 percent of men), vitamin B_6 (10 percent of women/men), vitamin B_{12} (10 percent of women; 5 percent of men). These deficiencies may constitute a considerable percentage to the cancer risk of the United States population.[33]

Folic acid (or folate) deficiency, one of the most common vitamin deficiencies in the population consuming few dietary fruits and vegetables, causes chromosome breaks in humans,[34] analogous to those caused by radiation. Folate supplementation above

29. H. J. Helbock et al., "DNA Oxidation Matters: The HPLC-Electrochemical Detection Assay of 8-oxo-deoxyguanosine and 8-oxo-guanine," *Proc. Natl. Acad. Sci. USA* 95 (1998): 288–93.

30. B. N. Ames, "Micronutrients Prevent Cancer and Delay Aging," *Toxicol. Lett.* 103 (1998): 5–18.

31. Ames, Shigenaga, and Hagen, "Oxidants, Antioxidants, and the Degenerative Diseases of Aging."

32. Ames, "Micronutrients Prevent Cancer and Delay Aging."

33. B. N. Ames and P. Wakimoto, "Are Vitamin and Mineral Deficiencies a Major Cancer Risk?" *Nature Rev. Cancer* 2 (2002): 694–704.

34. B. C. Blount et al., "Folate Deficiency Causes Uracil Misincorporation into Human DNA and Chromosome Breakage: Implications for Cancer and Neuronal Damage," *Proc. Natl. Acad. Sci. USA* 94 (1997): 3290–95.

the RDA has been shown to minimize chromosome breakage.[35] Researchers conducting a long-term study of women's health, the Nurses' Health Study, associated folate deficiency with increased risk of colon cancer.[36] They also reported that women who took a multivitamin supplement containing folate for fifteen years had a 75 percent lower risk of colon cancer.[37] Folate deficiency also damages human sperm,[38] causes neural tube defects in the fetus, and an estimated 10 percent of United States heart disease.[39]

Approximately 10 percent of the U.S. population[40] had a lower folate level than that at which chromosome breaks occur.[41] The recent decision in the United States to supplement flour, rice, pasta, and cornmeal with folate[42] may reduce the percentage of the population with the deficiency.

Other vitamins—vitamin B_6 and niacin—complement folic acid. Vitamin B_6 deficiency apparently causes chromosome breaks by the same mechanism as folate deficiency.[43] Niacin is

35. M. Fenech, C. Aitken, and J. Rinaldi, "Folate, Vitamin B12, Homocysteine Status and DNA Damage in Young Australian Adults," *Carcinogenesis* 19 (1998): 1163–71.

36. E. Giovannucci et al., "Folate, Methionine, and Alcohol Intake and Risk of Colorectal Adenoma," *J. Natl. Cancer Inst.* 85 (1993): 875–84.

37. E. Giovannucci et al., "Multivitamin Use, Folate, and Colon Cancer in Women in the Nurses' Health Study" *Ann. Intern. Med.* 129 (1998): 517–24.

38. L. M. Wallock et al., "Low Seminal Plasma Folate Concentrations Are Associated with Low Sperm Density and Count in Male Smokers and Non-smokers," *Fertil. Steril.* 75 (2001): 252–59.

39. C. J. Boushey et al., "A Quantitative Assessment of Plasma Homocysteine as a Risk Factor for Vascular Disease: Probable Benefits of Increasing Folic Acid Intakes," *J. Am. Med. Assoc.* 274 (1995): 1049–57.

40. F. R. Senti and S. M. Pilch, "Analysis of Folate Data from the Second National Health and Nutrition Examination Survey (NHANES II)" *J. Nutr.* 115 (1985): 1398–1402.

41. Blount et al., "Folate Deficiency."

42. P. F. Jacques et al., "The Effect of Folic Acid Fortification on Plasma Folate and Total Homocysteine Concentrations," *N. Engl. J. Med.* 340 (1999): 1449–54.

43. A. C. Huang, T. D. Shultz, and B. N. Ames, unpublished MS.

important to the repair of DNA strand-breaks.[44] As a result, dietary insufficiencies of niacin (15 percent of some populations are deficient),[45] folate, vitamin B_6, and antioxidants, such as vitamin C, may interact synergistically to adversely affect DNA synthesis and repair.

People with diets deficient in fruits and vegetables generally have vitamin and mineral deficiencies. The findings summarized in Table 4, which associate higher cancer rates with such diets, underline the importance of fruits and vegetables and the vitamins and minerals they contain in cancer prevention.

Vitamins and minerals, whose main dietary sources are other than fruits and vegetables, are also likely to play a significant role in the prevention and repair of DNA damage, and thus are important to the maintenance of long-term health. Vitamin B_{12} is found in animal products, and deficiencies of B_{12} cause a functional folate deficiency, accumulation of the amino acid homocysteine (a risk factor for heart disease),[46] and chromosome breaks. B_{12} supplementation above the RDA was necessary to minimize chromosome breakage.[47] Strict vegetarians are at increased risk for developing vitamin B_{12} deficiency.

Epidemiological studies of supplement usage (vitamin and mineral intake by pill) have shown at most only modest support for an association between intake of these substances and lower cancer rates. Many problems complicate those studies, including

44. J. Z. Zhang, S. M. Henning, and M. E. Swendseid, "Poly(ADP-ribose) Polymerase Activity and DNA Strand Breaks Are Affected in Tissues of Niacin-deficient Rats," *J. Nutr.* 123 (1993): 1349–55.

45. E. L. Jacobson, "Niacin Deficiency and Cancer in Women," *J. Am. Coll. Nutr.* 12 (1993): 412–16.

46. V. Herbert and L. J. Filer, Jr., "Vitamin B-12," in E. E. Ziegler, ed., *Present Knowledge in Nutrition* (Washington, D.C.: ILSI Press, 1996), pp. 191–205.

47. Fenech, Aitken, and Rinaldi, "Folate, Vitamin B12, Homocysteine Status and DNA Damage in Young Australian Adults."

the difficulty in measuring supplement use over a long period of time, and potential confounding of supplement usage with many other aspects of a healthy lifestyle that are related to it, such as more exercise, better diet, and not smoking. Clinical trials of supplements are generally too short to measure cancer risk, since cancers usually develop slowly and the risk increases with age; moreover, such trials cannot measure the potential reduction in risk if supplements are taken throughout a lifetime. Additionally, cancer risks of supplement users may be overestimated because they are more likely to undergo early screening like mammograms or tests for prostate cancer, which are associated with increased diagnosis rates, and can artificially increase the apparent incidence rate. Such confounding factors are not measured in many epidemiological studies.

The strongest effect in clinical trials was for a protective effect of vitamin E against cancers of the prostate and colon.[48] More well-done trials will increase the information about the usefulness of supplements in cancer prevention.

In the meantime, it is clear that intake of adequate amounts of vitamins and minerals may have a major effect on health, and the costs and risks of a daily multivitamin/mineral pill are low.[49] More research in this area, as well as efforts to improve diets, should be high priorities for public policy.

48. R. E. Patterson, A. R. Kristal, and M. L. Neuhouser, "Vitamin Supplements and Cancer Risk: Epidemiologic Research and Recommendations," in A. Bendich and R. J. Deckelbau, eds., *Primary and Secondary Preventive Nutrition* (Totowa, N.J.: Humana Press, 2001), pp. 21–43.
49. Ames and Wakimoto, "Are Vitamin and Mineral Deficiencies a Major Cancer Risk?"

Damage by Distraction:
Regulating Low Hypothetical Risks

Synthetic chemicals that mimic hormones—"environmental estrogens" or "endocrine disruptors"—arose as a major environmental issue in the 1990s. Environmental concerns have focused on exposures to estrogenic organochlorine residues (largely plastics and pesticides) that are tiny compared to the normal dietary intake of naturally occurring endocrine-active chemicals in fruits and vegetables.[50] These low levels of human exposure to the synthetic chemicals seem toxicologically implausible as a significant cause of cancer or of reproductive abnormalities.

Recent epidemiological studies have found no association between organochlorine pesticides and breast cancer, including one in which DDT, DDE, dieldrin, and chlordane were measured in blood of women on Long Island.[51] Synthetic hormone mimics have been proposed as a cause of declining sperm counts, even though it has not been shown that sperm counts are declining.[52] An analysis of U.S. data about sperm counts found distinct geographical differences, with the highest concentrations in New

50. S. H. Safe, "Endocrine Disruptors and Human Health—Is There a Problem? An Update," *Environ. Health Perspect.* 108 (2000): 487–93.

51. M. D. Gammon et al., "Environmental Toxins and Breast Cancer on Long Island. II. Organochlorine Compound Levels in Blood," *Cancer Epidemiol. Biomarkers Prev.* 11 (2002): 686–97.

52. S. Becker and K. Berhane, "A Meta-analysis of 61 Sperm Count Studies Revisited," *Fertil. Steril.* 67 (1997): 1103–8; J. Gyllenborg et al., "Secular and Seasonal Changes in Semen Quality Among Young Danish Men: A Statistical Analysis of Semen Samples from 1927 Donor Candidates During 1977–1995," *Int. J. Androl.* 22 (1999): 28–36; National Research Council, *Hormonally Active Agents in the Environment* (Washington, D.C.: National Academy Press, 1999); J. A. Saidi et al., "Declining Sperm Counts in the United States? A Critical Review," *J. Urol.* 161 (1999): 460–62; S. H. Swan, E. P. Elkin, and L. Fenster, "Have Sperm Densities Declined? A Reanalysis of Global Trend Data," *Environ. Health Perspect.* 105 (1997):1228–32.

York City.[53] When geographic differences were taken into account, there was no significant change in sperm counts for the past fifty years. Even if sperm counts were declining, there are many more likely causes, such as smoking and diet.

Some recent studies have compared estrogenic equivalents (EQ) of dietary intake of synthetic chemicals vs. phytoestrogens (estrogens of plant origin) in the normal diet, by considering both the amounts consumed by humans and estrogenic potency. Results support the idea that synthetic residues are orders of magnitude lower in EQ and are generally weaker in potency. Scientists using a series of *in vitro* assays calculated the EQs in 200 ml. of Cabernet Sauvignon wine and the EQs from average daily intake of organochlorine pesticides.[54] EQs in a single glass of wine were about 1,000 times higher. (Safe's chapter, this volume, and a National Academy of Sciences report[55] provide additional information about endocrine disruptors.)

Conclusions

Because there is no risk-free world and resources are limited, society must set priorities based on cost-effectiveness in order to save the most lives.[56] The EPA projected in 1991 that the cost to society of U.S. environmental regulations in 1997 would be about US$140 billion per year (about 2.6 percent of gross national prod-

53. Saidi et al., "Declining Sperm Counts in the United States?"

54. K. Gaido et al., "Comparative Estrogenic Activity of Wine Extracts and Organochlorine Pesticide Residues in Food," *Environ. Health Perspect.* 106 (Suppl. 6, 1998): 1347–51.

55. National Research Council, *Hormonally Active Agents in the Environment* (Washington, D.C.: National Academy Press, 1999).

56. R. W. Hahn, *Risks, Costs, and Lives Saved: Getting Better Results from Regulation* (New York: Oxford University Press and Washington, D.C.: AEI Press, 1996); J. Graham and J. Wiener, eds., *Risk versus Risk: Tradeoffs in Protecting Health and the Environment* (Cambridge, Mass.: Harvard University Press, 1995).

uct).[57] Most of this cost is borne by the private sector, which passes much of it along to consumers in higher prices.

Several economic analyses have concluded that current expenditures are not cost-effective; that is, resources are not used so as to save the most lives per dollar. One estimate is that the United States could prevent 60,000 deaths per year by redirecting the same dollar resources to more cost-effective programs.[58] For example, the median toxin control program, such as those administered by EPA, costs 146 times more per year of life saved than the median medical intervention program. The true difference is likely to be greater, because cancer risk estimates for toxin-control programs are worst-case, hypothetical estimates, and there may be no risk at low dose. Rules on air and water pollution are necessary (e.g., it was a public health advance to phase lead out of gasoline), and clearly, cancer prevention is not the only reason for regulations.

The many worst-case assumptions built into cancer risk assessments are there because of policy decisions, not because of scientific ones, and they confuse attempts to allocate money effectively for public health. For example, EPA estimates of synthetic pesticide residues in the diet have used the theoretical maximum human residue that is anticipated under the most severe field application conditions, which is often a large overestimate compared to the measured residues in food. Despite the EPA's estimated high risks from exposures to several pesticides, the U.S. Food and Drug Administration detected no residues of those pesticides in the food samples in its Total Diet Study.[59]

57. U.S. Environmental Protection Agency, *Environmental Investments: The Cost of a Clean Environment* (Washington, D.C.: Office of the Administrator, 1991).

58. T. O. Tengs et al., "Five Hundred Life-saving Interventions and Their Cost-effectiveness," *Risk Anal. Prod. Safe Food* 15 (1995): 369–89.

59. L. S. Gold et al., "Pesticide Residues in Food: Investigation of Dispar-

Regulatory efforts to reduce low-level human exposures to synthetic chemicals because they are rodent carcinogens are expensive, can do nothing but reduce already minuscule chemical concentrations, and are unlikely to have any effect on cancer rates. Moreover, they distract from the major task of improving public health through increasing scientific understanding about how to prevent cancer (e.g., what aspects of diet are important), increasing public understanding of how lifestyle influences health, and improving our ability to help individuals alter their lifestyles.

Why has the government focused on minor hypothetical risks at huge cost? A recent article in *The Economist* had a fairly harsh judgment:

> Predictions of ecological doom, including recent ones, have such a terrible track record that people should take them with pinches of salt instead of lapping them up with relish. For reasons of their own, pressure groups, journalists and fame-seekers will no doubt continue to peddle ecological catastrophes at an undiminishing speed.... Environmentalists are quick to accuse their opponents in business of having vested interests. But their own incomes, their fame and their very existence can depend on supporting the most alarming versions of every environmental scare.[60]

---

ities in Cancer Risk Estimates," *Cancer Lett.* 117 (1997): 195–207; L. S. Gold et al., "Pesticide Residues in Food and Cancer Risk: A Critical Analysis," in *Handbook of Pesticide Toxicology*, 2d ed., ed. R. Krieger (San Diego: Academic Press, 2001), pp. 799–842.

60. "Plenty of Gloom: Environmental Scares—Forecasters of Scarcity and Doom Are Not Only Invariably Wrong, They Think that Being Wrong Proves them Right," *The Economist*, December 20, 1997–January 3, 1998, pp. 19–21.

SIX

Nuclear Power

BERNARD L. COHEN

Industries and the products they produce are the backbone of our economy and the principal support for our high standard of living. Historically, inventors and entrepreneurs developed them, motivated largely by incentives for profits, with little or no attention to subtle environmental or public health impacts. When large fossil-fueled electric power plants were first built in the late nineteenth century and the automobile became the dominant mode of transportation in the early twentieth century, no one worried about the air pollution they caused, and there were few such concerns, largely unexpressed until long after the public became irreversibly dependent on these technologies. By that time, abandoning them was completely out of the question, and only incremental improvements could be introduced to lessen their impacts.

The Original Plan for Development

The nuclear power industry was intended to be very different. It was conceived and developed by idealistic scientists, with the backing of a powerful congressional committee providing generous funding, and had the goal of providing the blessings of unlimited low-cost energy to mankind. The nuclear scientists' and engineers' high-minded idealism led them to place heavy emphasis on environmental and health impacts. In fact, one of the major motivations of the program was to eliminate the environmental degradation associated with fossil fuel burning. Nuclear scientists were instrumental in establishing very large basic research programs (that continue to this day) to investigate the health impacts of radiation. These programs heavily emphasized safety issues and elevated the science of risk analysis to unprecedented heights.

All this research, of course, led to a very extensive scientific literature that described and projected health effects of radiation, imagined potential accident scenarios, and estimated numbers of deaths from these combinations.[1] The scientists and engineers who carried out the research gave no consideration to the fact that the public was not ready to understand the concept of a technology potentially killing people, and in any case, this literature was intended for the scientific community, not for the public. It was valuable for the scientists and engineers in their design efforts, guiding them to implement additional safety measures against low probability–high consequence failures. A byproduct of this work was conclusive evidence that nuclear power is en-

1. U.S. Nuclear Regulatory Commission (NRC), *Reactor Safety Study* (document NUREG-75/014) (Washington, D.C.: Nuclear Regulatory Commission, 1975).

vironmentally vastly superior to fossil fuel burning, the only real alternative.[2]

The electric utilities, led by conservative businessmen, were at first reluctant to become involved in this new technology, but congressional pressure, including threats of government programs to compete with their fossil fuel plants, got them involved. They brought nuclear experts into high positions in their organizations, and they eventually became enthusiastic. Nuclear power construction projects blossomed, reaching a peak of close to fifty new plants per year ordered in the 1973–74 time period. Then suddenly the ax fell.

The Opposition

Around 1970, the environmental movement, dealing with both technical and political aspects of various environmental problems, sprang to life in the United States. American public opinion widely supported the movement, as did I. I taught courses on environmental problems, sponsored a student environmental action club, and became involved with a local group that went out in small boats to collect samples of steel mill discharges that I analyzed pro bono in my laboratory.

Most of the groups that were active in the early days of the environmental movement consisted of enthusiastic, idealistic young people contributing their time and energy, which was enough to sustain them for a year or two. As some groups grew larger, they recruited dues-paying members from the public and began looking for larger-scale support from nonprofit foundations. They needed issues to attract public attention, and they soon found that questioning the health and environmental impacts of

2. Ibid.; B. L. Cohen, *The Nuclear Energy Option* (New York: Plenum, 1990).

nuclear power served that purpose very well. Nuclear power was a very new technology, with associations to the horrors of Hiroshima and Nagasaki, so it was not difficult to scare the public. Moreover, nuclear reactors were being constructed by large corporations that idealistic young people viewed as impersonal seekers after profits, callous to any environmental degradation and human suffering that they may cause. The environmentalists identified the nuclear power industry as their natural enemy.

To attack nuclear power, they needed ammunition, and it was readily found. They only had to go through the nuclear power risk analysis literature and pick out some of the imagined accident scenarios with the number of deaths expected from them. Of course, they ignored the very tiny probabilities of occurrence attached to these scenarios, and they never considered the fact that alternative technologies were causing far more deaths. Quoting from the published scientific analyses gave the environmentalists credibility and even made them seem like technical experts.

They also benefited from a timely lucky break. In the late 1960s, the scientific risk analysis community was focused on a potential "reactor meltdown" accident resulting from a hypothetical sudden loss of cooling water. Without cooling, the fuel would become very hot, accelerating chemical reactions that would generate still more heat, until the fuel would melt. Such a meltdown accident would release very large amounts of radioactivity, with the containment structure left as the only barrier to radioactivity getting out into the environment.

To protect against such events, reactors are fitted with a very elaborate and highly redundant emergency [reactor] core cooling system (ECCS) for rapidly injecting replacement water if the regular cooling water should be lost. When the first of this replacement water reaches the hot fuel rods, it would boil very rapidly, instantaneously building up a local region of high-pressure steam. There was some concern that this high-pressure steam might repel additional incoming cooling water, preventing it from reaching the fuel and thus failing to protect against a meltdown. To investigate this possibility, very crude small-scale mock-up experiments were performed in 1970–71, and they seemed to indicate that the ECCS might fail in this way.

Alarmed by these results, in 1972 a group of Boston-area scientists called for urgent action and formed a Union of Concerned Scientists to publicize the problem and demand action on it. Government regulators responded by introducing changes in reactor operating procedures and instigating a crash research program costing hundreds of millions of dollars to settle the unresolved questions. As more sophisticated experimental tests and computer analyses were developed, it became increasingly clear in the latter part of the 1973–78 time period that the ECCS would perform well, and in 1979 absolutely conclusive tests were completed that showed that the ECCS would work very well, even much better than had been expected. But by then, it was too late; the damage had been done.

By 1973, all but one of the original UCS scientist-founders became satisfied that their concerns were being adequately addressed, and they resigned from the organization. That one dissenter, Henry Kendall, joined by two nonscientists, continued to attack on the ECCS issue and built UCS into a powerful organization with thousands of dues-paying members and substantial support from nonprofit foundations. In 1974, Ralph Nader created his Critical Mass organization uniting dozens of environmental groups, with UCS as its technical adviser on nuclear issues. The supposed failure of the ECCS attracted very wide media coverage and became the most powerful and effective tool in the battle against nuclear power.

Eventually UCS leadership saw the handwriting on the wall and, long before the final resolution of the ECCS issue in 1979, had gone on to other issues. They (and the media) neglected to publicize the conclusive proof that the ECCS would perform very well. For many years, I often encountered enthusiastic young environmental activists who had never heard about the conclusive tests and were eager to explain in some detail why the ECCS could never work!

Two scientists provided further ammunition for the antinuclear activists. John Gofman and Arthur Tamplin, of the Livermore National Laboratory, claimed that the cancer risk from radiation was much larger than the risk accepted by the consensus of the scientific community. They never published their ideas, analyses, and conclusions in scientific journals, and their contentions were rejected by prestigious national and international scientific bodies, including the U.S. National Academy of Sciences, United Nations scientific committees, the International Commission on Radiological Protection, the U.S. National Council on Radiation Protection, and similar official advisory bodies in most technologically advanced nations. But to this day, Gofman and Tamplin remain heroes of the antinuclear activists, a status they share with a few other scientists—Alice Stewart, Karl Morgan, Rosalie Bertell, Ernest Sternglass, Thomas Mancuso, Irwin Bross —no more than a dozen in all. Each pursued a separate issue to reach the conclusion that the cancer risk from radiation was being underestimated, but with minor exceptions, no one of them openly supported any of the others. All got heavy media coverage for their claims, and they convinced Ralph Nader, who as a sworn enemy of nuclear power was more than eager to be convinced. But most important, they convinced the media and the public.

They failed to convince other scientists. A 1982 poll of scientific professionals specializing in health impacts of radiation found that 82 percent believed that television coverage substantially or grossly exaggerated the dangers of radiation, 76 percent believed the same about newspaper and magazine coverage, and

82 percent of them considered the public's fear of radiation to be substantially or grossly greater than is realistic.[3]

The antinuclear power enterprise raised several other issues. The technically trivial problem of radioactive waste disposal was elevated to an "unsolved problem," and it remained unsolved because of their efforts to block action. The solution, recognized and approved repeatedly by National Academy of Sciences committees for fifty years, is to convert the material into a rocklike form and place it in the natural habitat of rocks, deep underground. We know all about how rocks behave, and using this knowledge it is straightforward to show that the health effects of the buried waste will be negligible in comparison with those of burning coal or other fossil fuels to generate the equivalent electricity, even if these effects of nuclear waste are added up over millions of years.[4] In fact, there are several types of waste from coal burning, air pollution, carcinogenic chemicals released into the ground, and naturally radioactive precursors of radon, each of which will cause at least a thousand times as many fatalities as the buried nuclear waste.[5]

Theft of fissionable materials from nuclear plants was put forward as a method by which terrorists or rogue nations could obtain materials for the manufacture of nuclear weapons. Not only would such a theft be extremely difficult and dangerous to the perpetrators, but such material would be of little use in weapons. A bomb made with plutonium derived from the U.S. nuclear power industry would require a high degree of technical expertise to construct. It would be unreliable and give low explosive yield, and no bomb made from such material has ever been detonated.

3. B. L. Cohen, "Risk Analysis of Buried Waste from Electricity Generation," *American Journal of Physics* 54 (1986): 38ff.

4. Bernard L. Cohen, "A Poll of Radiation Health Scientists," *Health Physics* 50 (1986): 639ff.

5. Ibid.

The very real and much more potentially drastic proliferation problems resulting from the collapse of the Soviet Union and its nuclear weapons program is now given less public attention than was then accorded to the infinitely less important problems presented by nuclear power operations.

The antinuclear crusaders raised several other issues to prominence for brief periods. At one time they publicized "thermal pollution," the raising of the temperature of rivers, lakes, and near-shore ocean waters by a few degrees from the discharge of nuclear plant cooling water, as a threat to aquatic life, but it was quickly resolved by technical fixes, usually use of cooling towers. Low-level radioactive waste, suitably packaged and buried in shallow trenches, was somehow built up into a serious threat to public health, although even if it were distributed through the soil in disposal areas and picked up via plant roots by well-understood processes to get into our food, health impacts would be 50,000 times less than those of coal burning.[6] The media lavished heavy coverage on risks from emissions of radon gas from the waste piles generated by uranium ore processing, largely ignoring the fact that technical remedies were being instigated. In any case, it is questionable if any health impacts were experienced, and uranium mining in the U.S. has essentially stopped because far richer ores are available in remote regions of Canada and Australia.

The Battle

The decisive battle over nuclear power between nuclear scientists and antinuclear activists was waged in the 1973–80 time period. First, let's consider the cast of characters in the battle. The participants on the two sides were of entirely different ilks. The main interest in life for a typical antinuclear activist is political fighting,

---

6. Ibid.; Cohen, *Nuclear Energy Option.*

whereas most nuclear scientists have no interest in such political activity. Even if the scientists had the interest, they generally had little native ability and still less educational preparation for it. While a typical antinuclear activist was taking college courses in writing, debate, political science, and social psychology, the typical nuclear scientist was taking courses in advanced calculus, quantum and radiation physics, and molecular biology. After graduation, the former built on his education by participating in political campaigns, anti–Vietnam war protests during the 1960s and 1970s, and environmental activism, while the latter developed his scientific expertise working out mathematical complexities in neutron transport theories, studying the biological processes in the development of tumors, and devising solutions to technical problems in nuclear power plant design. While the former was making political contacts and learning how to secure media cooperation, the latter was absorbed in laboratory or field problems with no thought of politics or media involvement. At this juncture, the former went out looking for a new battle to fight and decided to attack the latter. It was a lion attacking a lamb.

From the beginning of the development of nuclear power, nuclear scientists had agonized about what safety measures were needed in power plants and what health impacts radioactivity releases might cause. They published their analyses and arguments for all to see, and it took little effort for the antinuclear activists to collect, organize selectively, and distort this information into ammunition for their battle. People experienced in debate and political fights are well prepared to do that.

When the antinuclear activists charged into battle wildly firing this ammunition, the nuclear scientists at first laughed at the naïveté of the arguments used, but they didn't laugh for long. The scientists could explain the scientific and technical invalidity of the attacks, but no one listened to their explanations. The phony charges of the attackers, dressed up with considerable public relations skills, sounded much better to the media and to members of the public with no scientific knowledge or experience. When people wanted to hear from scientists, the attackers supplied their own—there are always one or two eager to present any point of view—and who was to know that they represented only a minuscule minority of the scientific community with little or no credibility among their peers?

It was never even made clear to the public who the combatants were. The battle was not billed as scientifically illiterate political activists attacking the community of nuclear scientists, which was the true situation. Rather, it was represented as "environmentalists"—what a good, sweet, and pure connotation that name carried—attacking "big business" interests (the nuclear industry), who were willing to sacrifice the public's health and safety in their quest for profit. Jane Fonda, a prominent actress recruited for the antinuclear army, refused to debate with nuclear scientists. Her antagonists, she said, were the corporation executives.

When the media wanted to present both sides of an issue, they usually brought in corporation executives to present the pro-nuclear viewpoint. Not only were these executives limited in their knowledge and understanding, but the very fact that they represented a corporation trying to make profits from nuclear power substantially reduced their credibility.

The Three Mile Island accident, rated as one of the top media events of the century, was a crowning blow in the battle. The media consistently portrayed the accident as a close call on a public health disaster, and continue to do so to this day, although none of the studies done after the accident gives any reason to believe that to be the case. As demonstrated in those studies, the containment building would have prevented release of large amounts of the radioactivity regardless of what might have happened to the reactor.[7] The tiny amounts of radioactivity that were released received extensive media coverage, although the health impacts were completely negligible, perhaps a single extra cancer case among the 2 million people in the area.

The battle over nuclear power waxed hot and heavy for several years, swaying back and forth as incidents unfolded. The publication of the government-sponsored Reactor Safety Study in 1975, which showed that there would be very modest consequences from nearly all reactor accidents, was a positive event. The report concluded that the average number of fatalities from a meltdown would be about 400 and that there might be one meltdown in every 20,000 years of plant operation, or 0.02 deaths per year versus about 25 deaths per year due to air pollution from a coal-burning plant.[8] It received little notice outside the scientific community. The movie *The China Syndrome* (released in 1979), which implied that a reactor meltdown accident would have—not possibly might have—very horrible consequences, was an important negative event.

The Role of the Media

The antinuclear activists won a complete victory. That was no surprise; the nuclear scientists were seldom allowed on the battlefield. The battlefield here was the media, which alone has the power to influence public opinion.

Many nuclear scientists tried hard to engage in the battle. For

7. *United States President's Commission on the Accident at Three Mile Island* (Washington, D.C: U.S. Government Printing Office, 1979).; U.S. Nuclear Regulatory Commission, M. Rogovin (director), *Three Mile Island: A Report to the Commissioners and to the Public* (Washington, D.C.: Nuclear Regulatory Commission, 1980).

8. NRC, 1975.

a while I was averaging forty public lectures per year, talking to any audience that invited me. In these forty lectures, I reached perhaps 3,000 people per year, but a single TV program, produced by professionals skilled at gripping an audience, with large budgets, plentiful personnel, and excellent facilities, may reach 30 million, ten thousand times as many.

A prominent media tactic was gross overcoverage of radiation, giving the public the impression that its dangers are important and omnipresent. Using the New York Times Information Bank, which is an index to the news covered in that paper, I compared the number of times various types of accidents were covered in the newspaper with the number of deaths per year from those accidents in the U.S. I examined the years 1974–1978 so as not to include the extraordinary coverage of the 1979 Three Mile Island accident. On average, there were

- 120 entries per year on motor vehicle accidents which were killing 50,000,

- 50 entries per year on industrial accidents which were killing 12,000,

- 20 entries per year on asphyxiation accidents that were killing 4,500.

Note that the amount of coverage was roughly proportional to the number of deaths they were causing.

In contrast, for accidents involving radiation, there were

- 200 entries per year, despite the fact that there had not been a single death from such accidents, and not even an exposure that might eventually cause a cancer, during the previous fifteen years.

Not only was radiation overcovered, it was linked with inflammatory words like "deadly radiation" or "lethal radioactivity."

The media never talked about "lethal electricity," although 1,200 Americans die annually from electrocution, or about "deadly natural gas," which kills 500 per year from asphyxiation and hundreds more from fires and explosions. A nuclear waste repository is a carefully researched, highly engineered facility for the disposal of packages of radioactive waste deep underground at a cost of $5 million per truckload, but the media constantly refer to it as a "waste dump," conjuring up a picture of a truck simply tilting back to let its contents slide down into a hole in the ground. Is that a $5 million operation?

The overcoverage was heavily unbalanced. For example, Tom Najarian, a Boston physician, got the impression from talking to patients that there were excess leukemias among workers in the Portsmouth, New Hampshire, naval shipyard that services nuclear-powered submarines. Newspapers picked up the story and it soon became a national issue, with congressional hearings, government agency investigations, media debates on action alternatives, and so on. Eventually, in accordance with congressional edict, the Centers for Disease Control (CDC) did a two-year, million-dollar study. The CDC scientists concluded that there was no excess of leukemias or any other cancers among the shipyard workers

The *New York Times* ran fourteen articles, most of them on page 1, covering the original claims and reiterating assertions of large excesses of leukemias among the workers, but it covered the CDC study, which settled the issue, with a single story on page 37 of a weekday edition. The first 16 lines of the story were introductory, reviewing the original claims; then there were 9 lines on the CDC million-dollar study stating its negative findings, and the story concluded with 15 lines casting doubt on these findings by quoting reactions from antinuclear activists. Incidentally, a follow-up $10 million study of shipyard workers by CDC found fewer leukemias and other cancers among those involved with nuclear-powered ships than among those with nonnuclear ships.[9] The statistical accuracy of that conclusion was indisputable, but the *New York Times* published not a word about it.

Emotion, freely used in media coverage, had no balancing rational analysis. For example, a TV special featured beautiful twin baby girls afflicted with Hurler's syndrome, a devastating genetic disease. All sorts of details of the horrors were described —they will be blind and deaf by the time they are five years old, and then suffer from problems with their hearts, lungs, livers, and kidneys before they die at about age ten. Their father, who had worked with radiation for a short time, told the audience that he was sure that his occupational radiation exposure was the cause of this tragedy. There was no mention of the fact that his total occupational radiation exposure up to the time of conception was less than half of his exposure to natural radiation, or that a simple calculation indicates that there is only one chance in a thousand that the problem was caused by his job-related exposure. The *New York Times* ran a feature story about these babies, complete with pictures, giving the reader every reason to believe that the problem was caused by the father's occupational exposure. No evidence to the contrary was even hinted at; such evidence was presumably not part of "all the news that's fit to print."

I will never forget the TV evening news program where the lead story was the conclusion by a government agency that there might some day be a single, unrecognizable cancer death among the millions of people exposed to radioactivity released in the Three Mile Island accident. This was followed by interviews with citizens expressing great anguish over the possibility that one of

9. U.S. Department of Energy, G. M. Matanoski (director of the study), *Health Effects of Low-Level Radiation in Shipyard Workers* (Report no. DOE DE-AC02-79 EV 100995) (Washington, D.C.: Department of Energy, 1991), see tables 3.6B and 3.6D.

their loved ones might be that single victim. There was no mention of all the other industries and diverse human activities that will cause tens of thousands of cancer deaths among these same people.

Perhaps the most important problem in media coverage was (and still is) failure to quantify. For example, a minor accident in a Rochester, New York, nuclear plant that led to a small release of radioactivity was the lead story on most TV network evening news programs for two days. I can understand that it could be too technical for public consumption to state the radiation doses to the public in quantitative terms, but wouldn't it have been useful to tell the public that no one received as much exposure from that accident as he gets from natural radiation every day? Scientists constantly make such comparisons with natural radiation in media interviews, information booklets, and magazine articles, but they are never put out by the mass media—it would ruin their story. In the Rochester accident, the media did everything to enhance the impression of danger, like stating the number of people living in the area (not just near the plant), with the clear implication that this was the number of people exposed to dangerous radiation.

I often ask myself why the media act that way. In the mid-1970s, when I was publishing scientific analyses of problems associated with plutonium toxicity, I read a scare story in a popular magazine about the horrible poisonous dangers of plutonium. I thought I should educate the author so I telephoned him and began to explain things, but I soon found that he was quite knowledgeable about the subject and that he knew about my analyses and did not dispute them. I finally asked him why, knowing what he did, he would write such a scare story. He replied that he was a freelance writer trying to get published. "If I had written the article your way," he asked, "do you think it would have been published?"

My crowning disillusionment along these lines came a few years later, following the Chernobyl accident. A freelance reporter with whom I thought I had a significant friendly relationship published a page 1 article in the *New York Times* making a completely false claim that the Chernobyl reactor had a protective containment structure very similar to the one enclosing U.S. reactors. I wrote to him in a goodwill effort to set him straight, but I later learned that Richard Wilson, a Harvard nuclear scientist, had spent more than an hour explaining to him the enormous difference between U.S. and Chernobyl containment structures—the latter was designed to protect only against very minor accidents while the former is designed to defend against what is almost the worst conceivable accident. But the reporter still went ahead and published his story.

Shortly thereafter the same reporter published another page 1 article in the *New York Times* stating that more radioactive cesium was released from the Chernobyl accident than from all bomb tests combined. I sent him the detailed evidence that he was wrong by an order of magnitude and chided him for misinforming the public. His response was, "I don't tell you how to do research, so you don't tell me how to do journalism." It is obviously a very important career advancement step for a freelancer to get a page 1 article in the *New York Times*.

I still thought that most media people were acting in good faith to educate the public, so I decided to try to write papers for journals serving the journalism profession, like the *Columbia Journalism Review*, explaining how they were misinforming the public about nuclear power. I submitted two such papers to three such journals in turn. Neither was published. One-sentence letters of rejection, with no explanation, arrived within a few days.

The media give widespread attention to each of the tiny handful of scientists who claim that radiation is more harmful than the consensus estimates. In one case I investigated, a single publication in a scientific journal by Thomas Mancuso making such a claim was the subject of eleven entries in the New York Times Information Bank, but there was only one entry in the Information Bank about the twenty-plus critiques of that study that appeared in the scientific literature.

On one occasion I witnessed, Mancuso gave a talk on his work at a scientific meeting. Television cameras were everywhere, recording his remarks, but by the time his critics had their turn to speak, the TV crews had packed up their equipment and left. I have seen this media behavior repeated many times on many different issues. Perhaps the most flagrant example was in government-sponsored hearings on the emergency core cooling system (ECCS), which went on for many weeks. The TV cameras were consistently turned on when Union of Concerned Scientists speakers were presenting their antinuclear case, but turned off when their opposition, or even neutral speakers, were testifying.

Mancuso's paper was first announced to the public through a press release he composed for his university public relations office. He was bombarded for many days with calls for media interviews. I happened to be publishing a paper at that time that presented data and calculations indicating that radiation is much less harmful than the consensus estimates. Since I am at the same university as Mancuso, I decided to test the system by composing a highly enthusiastic press release on my paper, and it was given the same distribution by the same university public relations office. I never got a single call from the media. The only difference media people could possibly have seen between Mancuso's work and mine was that his said that radiation was more dangerous while mine said it was less dangerous than widely accepted estimates.

At best, the media stated that the scientific community was "split down the middle" on the risks from radiation exposure. When I told interviewers that the division was completely one-sided, the common response was, "Why should I believe you?" My reply was for them to call what they consider to be first-class universities of their choice, ask for a professor who does research on radiation health effects, and ask him the question. To the best of my knowledge, no reporter ever followed that suggestion. The media rarely reported findings of National Academy of Sciences committees, or of many other national and international committees of distinguished scientists, all of which supported the consensus estimates of radiation dangers. I will never forget the reporter who told me that he didn't care about National Academy of Sciences committees and such—he had spoken to Mancuso and could tell that what he was saying was right.

The media never made an effort to educate the public on quantitative risk estimates and use these to put nuclear risks into perspective. I published papers on catalogs of risks,[10] and used them constantly in public presentations and interviews with reporters. These are easily understandable to anyone, but they were never transmitted by the media.

For example, I showed that the risks of nuclear power to the average American are equal to the risk of a regular smoker smoking one extra cigarette every fifteen years, or of an overweight person increasing his weight by 0.012 ounces, or of raising the highway speed limit from 55 miles per hour to 55.006 miles per hour, and that they are two thousand times less than the risk of buying a subcompact car rather than a mid-size car. Even if the claims of the antinuclear Union of Concerned Scientists (UCS) are accepted, the risks are equal to the risk of a regular smoker smoking one extra cigarette every three months, an overweight person gaining 0.8 ounces, or raising the highway speed limit to 55.4 miles per hour, and thirty times less than the switch to a subcom-

10. B. L. Cohen, "Catalog of Risks Extended and Updated" *Health Physics* 61 (1991): 317–35.

pact car. I showed that if a person living close to a nuclear power plant worries about the radiation risks and decides to move away, his net risk is increased (due to traffic accidents) if that move increases his daily driving by a quarter mile.

Perhaps even more to the point is that the principal alternative to nuclear power is coal burning, which causes hundreds of times as many deaths owing to its air pollution alone in generating the same amount of electricity.[11] Every time a coal-burning plant is built instead of a nuclear plant, about one thousand extra innocent people are condemned to an early death, and this estimate applies even if the nuclear risks are those proposed by the antinuclear UCS. All the calculations leading to the above conclusions were published in prestigious scientific journals and never criticized in other published scientific papers (or elsewhere as far as I know). But none of this material was ever transmitted to the public by the mass media. Likewise it was never explained to the public that radiation doses from nuclear power are very much smaller than doses from natural radioactivity to which everyone is exposed (and which varies substantially with geography), and very much smaller than doses from medical X rays.

Nuclear scientists have tried very hard to get these points to the public by submitting articles for publication in magazines. I managed to get articles in lower-tier magazines like *Family Health, Commentary, National Review, Catholic Digest, Reason, Consumer Reports, American Legion Magazine*, but all my submissions to top-tier publications were rejected. To this day, none of these risk comparisons has been presented to the vast majority of the public, and the responsibility for this educational failure lies with the media.

I could give endless examples of media one-sidedness in covering the battle over nuclear power, involving reactor accidents,

11. Cohen, *Nuclear Energy Option.*

high-level radioactive wastes, low-level radioactive wastes, proliferation of nuclear weapons, and every other issue. In my book about the battle,[12] the index has far more references to "media" than to any other topic, despite the fact that my publisher's editor was constantly pressuring me to tone down attacks on the media for fear they would result in reduced book sales.

The Battle Outcome

As the battle over nuclear power was waged, the media clearly controlled the situation, and the media establishment swallowed the attackers' story hook, line, and sinker. The one-sided propaganda slowly but surely won over the public.

The public was driven insane over fear of radiation; that is, it lost contact with reality, one of the definitions of insanity, on that issue. Polls of relatively well informed groups, college students, and members of the League of Women Voters, rating causes of their "present risk of death," rated nuclear power as number one —ahead of cigarette smoking, which kills 150,000 Americans per year, ahead of motor vehicle accidents (50,000 deaths per year at that time), ahead of alcoholic beverages (100,000 per year), and ahead of hand guns (17,000 per year). Nuclear power has never killed a single member of the American public with its highly publicized radiation dangers.

Since government regulators must be responsive to public concern, they continually tightened their safety requirements on nuclear power plants. Fulfilling these constantly upgraded requirements involved substantially increased costs, and frequently necessitated changes in design in the midst of construction, an especially expensive undertaking. These changes often doubled the construction time for a plant, leading to increased interest

12. B. L. Cohen, *Before It's Too Late* (New York: Plenum, 1982).

costs on the capital investment. Several large nuclear plants were completed in the early 1970s at a typical cost of $170 million, whereas plants of the same size, constructed by the same people, but completed in 1983 cost an average of $1,700 million, ten times as much (the Consumer Price Index increased by a factor of 2.2 during that time interval). Some plants completed in the late 1980s cost as much as $5 billion because of these problems. Utilities building these plants suffered severe financial losses. The median cost of electricity from nuclear plants, which had been very competitive with costs from coal-burning plants, became 1.6 times higher than the latter. All nuclear plants ordered after 1974 were eventually canceled, and no nuclear power plants have been ordered in the U.S. since that time.

Ironically, Ralph Nader, the leader of the antinuclear activists, stated very early in the battle that the way to stop nuclear power was to make the costs escalate to the point where utilities could not afford to build them. I must admit that he fought a better battle than we nuclear scientists, and he won, very decisively. Unfortunately, the public has been the real loser from the victory of this so-called "public advocate."

After the Battle

By about 1980, it became clear that the battle was over, and we had lost. The public seemed to be convinced that nuclear power was bad, and it was not interested in further discussion on that subject. The environmental activists turned their attention to other issues, leaving scientists no opportunities to respond. Invitations to speak or write about the subject largely disappeared.

I subdued some of my frustration by writing a book on the battle,[13] and then decided to concentrate on my scientific research,

13. Ibid.

which then involved radon in homes. I developed new and improved techniques for measuring radon levels and carried out surveys to determine the geographical distribution of radon throughout the U.S. and its variation with house characteristics, socioeconomic status of occupants, and environmental factors. I also studied methods for reducing its concentrations in homes, and became involved in estimating its health effects.

All this work was academic until radon in homes suddenly burst into national prominence with the discovery in 1986 of high radon levels in eastern Pennsylvania and in other areas soon thereafter. This led to a 1988 pronouncement by the Surgeon General's office, given heavy media coverage, that radon in homes was killing 14,000 Americans each year. The Environmental Protection Agency went all out to publicize the problem, and the National Ad Council provided frequent public service announcements on radio and TV, with the American Lung Association backing their efforts.

A huge demand arose from householders to obtain radon measurements in their homes. This led me to set up a national measurement service, providing high-quality measurements at one-fifth of what had been the going price. Many entrepreneurs visited me to learn the technology, and set up similar measurement services, causing my low price to prevail in the industry.

As a leader in the field, I received a great deal of attention from the media, getting as many as twenty calls for interviews in a single day. And this time they were on my side—what a refreshing difference! It was a good story to tell how people's lives were being threatened and what they could do about it. For me, it seemed like a golden opportunity. In every interview, I managed to work in the fact that the radiation dose from radon in their homes was a thousand-times greater than from nuclear power, that if people were worried about radiation they should do something about radon in their homes rather than oppose nuclear power, that people who live near the Three Mile Island plant get more radiation exposure from radon in their homes every day than they got in total from the 1979 accident there, and so on.

Though other parts of my interviews were widely reported, I know of no case where the comparisons between radiation from radon in homes with radiation from nuclear power were included. They certainly never got national attention. For the media, nuclear power was the most dangerous source of radiation, and there was no way they were going to report otherwise—that would be like an attack on their religion. Of course this was a simple extension of their refusal to compare radiation from nuclear power with that from natural sources and medical X rays.

I often wondered whether the reporters were afraid to include my points about nuclear power, or whether they were edited out at a higher level. In any case, the media and the public view radiation from nuclear power and from radon in homes as entirely different and unrelated subjects. I repeatedly explained to reporters that when a cell in our bodies is hit by radiation, there is no way for it to "know" whether that radiation originated from nuclear power operations or from radon, but somehow that explanation never got reported.

My research eventually convinced me (and a great many others) that radon in homes is very much less harmful than the widely publicized estimates that were based on extrapolating from the number of excess cancers seen in uranium miners who had very high radon exposures. Those estimates were (and are) based on the assumption that the cancer risk from radiation is proportional to the dose, the so-called linear–no threshold theory (LNT).

A great deal of evidence has accumulated that the LNT grossly overpredicts the adverse effects of low-level radiation.[14] Taken altogether, the data about health risks lead to the conclusion that the low-level radiation from nuclear power in nearly all situations, or from radon in nearly all homes, is harmless (and may even be beneficial).[15] If this were made known to the public, fears of radiation and of nuclear power should evaporate, but the media has given this matter essentially no coverage, and the public continues to believe what they were convinced of in the great battle of the 1970s.

It is necessary to emphasize that all the risk comparisons given above were based on the LNT. Given that the LNT overestimates the risks of low-level radiation, the risk from nuclear power probably is much less than the risk of a regular smoker smoking one extra cigarette every fifteen years, is much less than the risk of an overweight person increasing his weight by 0.012 ounces, and so on.

On this matter, there is some excuse for the media because the scientific community is still split on the issue of application of the LNT to low-level radiation risks. But as evidence accumulates, I believe there is a good chance that scientific opinions will soon consolidate in rejecting the LNT. When that happens, I hope the media will decide that a good headline would be "MOST RADIATION FOUND TO BE HARMLESS." That should attract the public attention they so crave.

In looking for new ways of fighting back, I decided that a good approach might be to speak and publish papers about understanding the risks in our society. This would seem to be a matter of interest to the public, and there is no problem with whether it is "politically correct." I always unobtrusively worked in examples,

14. B. L. Cohen, "The Cancer Risk From Low-Level Radiation," *Am. J. Roentgen.* (in press).
15. Ibid.

like those mentioned above, of risks from nuclear power and radioactive wastes, and comparisons of health effects from coal burning vs. nuclear power.

I thought I had a big-time winner when John Stossel of ABC News created and hosted a one-hour, prime-time TV special on risk. He even told me it would be a TV version of my papers. I had frequent contacts with his staff over several months as the program was being developed, responding to requests for information and calculations. When aired, the program was excellent, but it did not include any of my examples dealing with radiation or nuclear power. I later found out that the program was constantly facing stiff opposition from upper-level executives, and Stossel had to fight hard to get it through. He managed to do so only with strong sympathy and backing from his immediate superior. I could tell that it was a harrowing experience for him.

When nuclear power advocates look for reasons to be hopeful, they find some justifiable optimism. The scientific community is widely supportive. When asked whether nuclear power development should proceed, 89 percent of all scientists and 95 percent of energy experts said "yes."[16] The general public is also supportive, with various professional pollsters finding that 65 percent to 75 percent favor nuclear power.[17] But turning this support into concrete actions is very difficult because the opposition is well organized, dedicated, and very vocal.

I have tried to bring some rationality to the debate by drawing attention to the benefits the public receives from nuclear technology. Economic analyses show that various nuclear applications account for 4 percent of our national GDP, provide 3 percent

16. S. Rothman and S. R. Lichter, "The Nuclear Energy Debate: Scientists, the Media, and the Public," *Public Opinion*, August 1982, p. 47ff.

17. For examples, see Cohen, *Nuclear Energy Option.*

of all jobs, and produce $45 billion per year in tax revenues.[18] Nuclear techniques have been the source of many useful innovations, including more precise machinery that provides better efficiency in manufacturing (e.g., thickness gauges controlling steel rolling mills), improved safety devices (e.g., smoke detectors in homes), enhanced convenience (e.g., disposable needles for flu shots), and improved materials (e.g., tougher plastics). One third of all patients admitted to U.S. hospitals undergo diagnostic procedures that employ radioactivity. In addition, 100 million radioimmunoassay tests are done annually, and 60,000 patients get radiation therapy for cancer.

A typical large university has 100 research projects using radioactivity, and the work supported by 40 percent of biomedical research grants, and described in 50 percent of articles in biomedical journals, uses radioactivity. I believe that food preservation by irradiation may be about to take off, providing more wholesome, better-tasting, and better-looking foods that are bound to attract public attention. Perhaps people will wonder why the benefits of irradiated food have been denied to them for so long, and come to appreciate the irrational, destructive activities of so-called environmental and consumer advocates.

Several years go, Glenn Seaborg responded enthusiastically to my request that he be the principal author of a book that categorized and demonstrated the benefits of nuclear technology. Assured of having Seaborg's name as a selling point, a publisher I knew was more than eager to cooperate, and guaranteed me that the book would get lots of publicity. A team of excellent authors for chapters was soon organized, and we were ready to go when

---

18. Management Information Services, Inc., *The Untold Story: The Economic Benefits of Nuclear Technology* (Washington, D.C.: Management Information Services, Inc., 1997).

Seaborg suddenly died. The project then fell apart, although there are still efforts to revive it.

Counterattacks on our environmentalist opponents have often been considered as a tactic, but few have had much impact. The most successful of these, involving a chemical agent rather than radiation, followed an attack by National Resources Defense Council (NRDC) on Alar, a chemical used in apple growing. The American Council on Science and Health showed that the scientific evidence used by NRDC was highly questionable and that the entire event was staged, with the cooperation of CBS News, by a public relations firm. This counterattack got wide publicity, including an article in *Reader's Digest*.[19] Nevertheless, it is not clear that NRDC suffered as a result. Scholarly books involving years of research have been published about the irrational behavior of antinuclear environmental groups,[20] but they have received scant publicity.

Many of us nuclear scientists are still out there fighting, despite our lack of success to date. We publish papers, teach college courses, give talks to anyone who will hear us, write letters to media people explaining their errors, organize workshops for educating grade school and high school teachers, try to develop media contacts. It will take a lot more than what we are doing to turn the situation around, but if circumstances develop that present an opportunity, we will be ready. We thought that Vice President Dick Cheney's vocal support for nuclear power might be such an opportunity, but the events of September 11 seem to have pushed that out of the realm of public interest.

Nonetheless, we realize that we must not be discouraged. Ex-

19. R. Bidinotto, "The Great Apple Scare," *Reader's Digest*, October 1990, pp. 55–56.

20. See, e.g., M. A. Benarde, *You've Been Had* (New Brunswick, N.J.: Rutgers University Press, 2002).

tensive use of nuclear power would be a great benefit to mankind, solving such important human problems as global warming, air pollution, acid rain, wars over oil supplies, oil spills in the oceans, and environmental damage from coal mining. It would allow us to preserve our precious limited supplies of fossil fuels for their unique uses, such as feedstock for producing plastics and organic chemicals. It could make deserts bloom by desalting sea water. And it can provide all the energy mankind will ever need at not much above current prices.

With all this at stake, we must fight on. Readers of this chapter can help by speaking up on behalf of nuclear power and against the fear-mongering promoted by its opponents. If opponents want to debate, we will be happy and eager to debate them, but these debates must be on a scientific basis.

SEVEN

Science or Political Science?

An Assessment of the U.S. National Assessment of the Potential Consequences of Climate Variability and Change

PATRICK J. MICHAELS

What constitutes science, and where is the line that separates a politically inspired document posing as science from a legitimate scientific assessment? When does science become "junk science"?

This nebulous region, where science, politics, and agendas intersect, is exactly the territory occupied by the recent *U.S. National Assessment of the Potential Consequences of Climate Variability and Change* (hereafter the USNA).[1] In this chapter, I examine the USNA, demonstrate that the models that serve as its basis are inconsistent with observations, and conclude that it

---

1. National Assessment Synthesis Team, *Climate Change Impacts on the United States: The Potential Consequences of Climate Variability and Change* (Washington, D.C.: U.S. Global Change Research Program, 2000).

should be withdrawn from public distribution. Further, the President's Office of Science and Technology Policy, the agency that appointed the committee that produced the USNA, should appoint a new committee and undertake another analysis.

In the famous case *Daubert v. Merrell Dow,* the Supreme Court held that expert testimony relating to scientific studies must be grounded in the methods of science. The basic test for any scientific hypothesis or model is to compare its predictions against observations. Hypothesis and models that make accurate predictions are accepted as useful and "scientific," while those that fail to make adequate predictions are discarded or modified.[2]

Although "junk science" has no rigorous definition, it is characterized by one or both of two properties: (1) data that do not meet the normal criteria for being unbiased and objective, and (2) inappropriate or incomplete representations of tests of the predictive accuracy of of models that create a false impression of reliability.

By analogy to medical practice, the application of junk science in legal proceedings or government decision making is improper practice. Suppose a physician prescribed a medication knowing it would have less of an effect on a disease than a glass of water. Further assume that this doctor had been informed of this through an irrefutable clinical trial supported by an unassailable quantitative analysis. Further, to check on the validity of that analysis, the physician repeated it, confirmed the result, and still continued to prescribe the worthless medication. The self-policing agencies in the medical community would likely judge this physician's actions as inconsistent with medical ethics.

The USNA, published in October 2000, incorporated a flaw analogous to the physician's knowingly prescribing an incorrect

2. K. R. Popper, *Conjectures and Refutations: The Growth of Scientific Knowledge* (London: Routledge & Kegan Paul, 1963).

medication. USNA begat other, related documents that perpetuate and reinforce its flaw. For example, an important chapter on impacts of climate change in the Bush administration document *Climate Action Report* 2002 was, in large part, directly taken from the USNA.[3] Far from being examined on its merits by the politicians and officials who ordered it, and flawed as it is, the USNA also serves as the basis for expensive and intrusive energy legislation currently under consideration by Congress.

House of Representatives Bill HR 4, the standing version of the Senate's 2002 Energy Legislation as of this writing (October 2002), would, if it becomes law, mandate U.S. participation in international negotiations to reduce greenhouse gas emissions and that would require that 10 percent of all U.S. energy be produced from "renewables" (largely solar energy and windmills), which are prohibitively expensive. As the basis for HR 4, Congress "finds" in Section 1001, that, "In October 2000 a U.S. Government Report found that global climate change may harm the United States by altering crop yields, accelerating sea level rise, and increasing the spread of infectious tropical diseases." That document is the USNA. The climate models that serve as its base do not work. Basing energy legislation on this document will enshrine bad science in laws that cost the nation dearly.

History and Composition

The USNA had its inception in a January 1998 letter to the National Science Foundation's Global Change Research Subcommittee chair from John H. Gibbons, assistant to President William Clinton for Science and Technology (the letter is available at www.usgcrp.gov/uscrp/nacc/background/organization/

---

3. U.S. Department of State, *U.S. Climate Action Report 2002* (Washington, D.C.: U.S. Department of State, 2002).

letter.html). Gibbons was a popular speaker on the university circuit, lecturing on the evils of rapid population growth, resource depletion, environmental degradation, and, of course, global warming. His visual aids included outdated population and resource projections from Paul Ehrlich in which "affluence" was presented as the cause of environmental degradation, a notion that has been discredited for decades; after all, environmental protection and low population growth correlate highly with per capita income. Gibbons's material on climate change was also dated, assuming growth rates for carbon dioxide and other greenhouse gases that were known to many scientists to be gross overestimates at the time the USNA was in production.[4]

In his capacity as the President's science adviser, Gibbons also led the National Science and Technology Council, established by President Clinton in November 1993, which, according to the USNA, "is the principal means for the President to coordinate science, space, and technology policies across the Federal Government." The "Membership consists of the Vice President [Al Gore], the Assistant to the President for Science and Technology [Dr. Gibbons], Cabinet Secretaries and Agency Heads with significant science and technology responsibilities, and other senior White House officials." The Council is clearly a political body. "[C]oordinating... policies" is a political task, not a scientific one.

Two political appointees, D. James Baker, at that time head of the National Oceanic and Atmospheric Administration, and Rosina Bierbaum, second in line at the Office of Science and Technology Policy, were made co-chairs of the Committee on Environment and Natural Resources, one of the many constituent committees of the National Science and Technology Council. Baker, in his role as chair, directed a subcommittee of his com-

4. J. E. Hansen et al., "A Common-Sense Climate Index: Is Climate Changing Noticeably?" *Proc. Natl. Sci.* 95 (1998): 4113–20.

mittee, the Subcommittee on Global Change Research, established by Congress in 1990, "to provide for the development... of a comprehensive and integrated United States research program which will assist the Nation and the world to understand, assess, predict and respond to human-induced and natural processes of global change." The subcommittee appointed yet *another* committee, the National Assessment Working Group, which created the "National Assessment Steering Team," which produced the USNA.

This torturous bureaucracy was larded with political appointees at all levels and dictated the conclusions to be incorporated in the USNA. Gibbons's letter didn't have to state the views of Clinton or Gore on global warming; the orders passed through so many political vettings that those who finally went to work on the USNA knew full well what was expected: produce a document that pleased the Council, which was headed by the Vice President. What member of the synthesis team would not chart a course consistent with the views of the higher-ups? If such a document were proffered, what would the professional consequences be for challenging the Vice President and the President's science adviser?

As we shall see, the resultant document so intended to please that it broke the basic ethical rule of science: that hypotheses must be consistent with facts.

The USNA Steering Committee

Formation of committees to summarize the state of global warming is a standard exercise in climate change science. The composition of those committees largely determines the outcome.

Perhaps the most prominent example is the United Nations Intergovernmental Panel on Climate Change (IPCC), whose representatives are chosen by their respective governments to provide summary documents on climate change. Only about one third of the IPCC's members are climate scientists, outnumbered by far more nonclimatologist political appointees. Not surprisingly, the IPCC reports and recommendations have been predictably controversial, often omitting refereed studies or data arguing that climate change may not be such a serious issue.

A related version of this process occurred with the composition of the National Assessment Synthesis Team, which coordinated the National Assessment. Only two members of the team were credentialed climatologists, and a clear majority was not technically disposed to provide criticism of the climate models that formed the basis of the Assessment. This circumstance created the debacle described in this chapter.

The roster of the synthesis team, shown boxed, indicates backgrounds. The only member with a doctorate in climate studies is Eric Barron. On October 13, 1994, Barron chaired a similar committee, assembled to produce a document summarizing global warming science for Congressman John Dingell (D-Mich.). Barron threatened to adjourn the assessment if the two dissenting scientists present, MIT's Richard Lindzen and I, did not stop objecting to the assessment's material and methods. The senior author of that 1994 document was Robert Corell, who is also on the USNA Synthesis Team.

The Synthesis Team did not even replicate the *faux*-diversity of the Dingell Committee. It contained not one individual who has been skeptical or critical of the importance of climate change as an issue. Some observers might consider such a roster appropriate for a committee looking at potential consequences of climate change rather than examining the evidence for change. It is not. The potential consequences vary with the predictions of climate change, and of the models the team considered, it selected two that produced the most extreme changes. Perhaps if other clima-

---

The *National Assessment Synthesis Team*

Jerry Melillo (co-chair): Ph.D., Forestry and Environmental Studies, Yale University

Anthony Janetos (co-chair); Ph.D., Biology, Princeton University

Thomas Karl (co-chair): M.S., Meteorology, University of Wisconsin

Eric Barron: Ph.D., Oceanography and Climate, University of Miami

Virginia Burckett; Ph.D., Forestry, Stephen F. Austin State University

Thomas Cecich: No doctorate

Robert Corell: Ph.D., Oceanography, Case Institute of Technology

Katherine Jacobs: No doctorate

Linda Joyce: Ph.D., Range Ecology, Colorado State University

Barbara Miller: Ph.D., Engineering, University of Illinois

M. Granger Morgan: Ph.D., Applied Physics, University of California

Edward Parson: Ph.D., Public Policy, Harvard University

Richard Richels: Ph.D., Applied Sciences, Harvard University

David Schimel: Ph.D., Rangeland Ecosystem Science, Colorado State University

---

tologists or scientists skeptical or questioning about the importance of change had been included, the team would not have produced a document based upon such extreme models.

Moreover, although estimates of potential consequences are completely dependent on the climate models that are used, except for Eric Barron and Thomas Karl, all the panel members were from fields that use predicted changes from climate models to assess impact on their particular areas of interest, such as grassland or forest ecology. They were not trained to and could not be expected to focus attention on critical analysis of the climate models themselves, and that led to the problems detailed in this chapter.

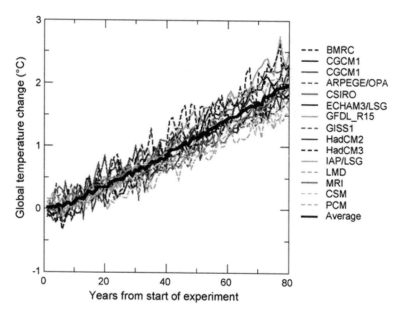

Fig. 1   Temperature changes predicted by a variety of climate models
Note: Various models (acronyms are on the right) when forced with an exponential increase (1% per year) of carbon dioxide. Most models predict a nearly linear temperature rise.
Source: Draft for Scientific Review, Intergovernmental Panel on Climate Change, *Third Assessment Report.*

The Use of Extreme Models

The synthesis team had many models from which to choose; there are literally dozens of GCMs, which are four-dimensional simulations of atmospheric behavior that calculate changes in weather and consequent climate as atmospheric composition changes. The team considered and rejected several "general circulation climate models" (GCMs) for making its predictions of future temperatures and rainfall and chose two models that predicted the most extreme climate changes. As shown on Figure 1, taken from the scientific review draft of the 2001 report of the UN Intergovernmental Panel on Climate Change (IPCC), the predictions of temperature changes from the various models are quite similar.[5]

The consensus of these models is to produce a constant (linearly increasing) rate of warming, despite the assumption of exponentially increasing concentrations of greenhouse gases, such as carbon dioxide, in the atmosphere. That is because the response of temperature to a change in concentration of a given gas is logarithmic—that is, it begins to damp off at increasing concentrations. The combination of a dampening response and an exponentially increasing concentration is a straight-line (constant) temperature increase.

The two models chosen by USNA team are clearly outliers from the family of available models. The Canadian Climate Centre model (acronymed by the USNA as CGCM1) is one of the very few that produces a substantially exponential (rather than linear) change in temperature. The other model used by the team is known as the Hadley Centre Model (acronymed by the USNA as HadCM2), developed at the United Kingdom's Meteorological Office.[6]

The CGCM1 model produces the most extreme temperature changes of *any* model that the USNA considered for inclusion, and the HadCM2 produces the most extreme precipitation changes.

- The temperature rise predicted by CGCM1—4.5°C over the U.S. between now and 2100—is more than twice the rise of 2.0°C predicted by the HadCM2, the model that predicts the second largest increase (Figure 2).

5. See Intergovernmental Panel on Climate Change (IPCC), *Climate Change 2001: The Scientific Basis. Contribution of Working Group I to the Third Assessment Report of the Intergovernmental Panel on Climate Change*, ed. J. T. Houghton et al. (Cambridge: Cambridge University Press, 2001).

6. T. C. Johns et al., "The Second Hadley Center Coupled Ocean-Atmosphere GCM: Model Description, Spinup, and Validation," *Climate Dynamics* 13 (1997): 103–34.

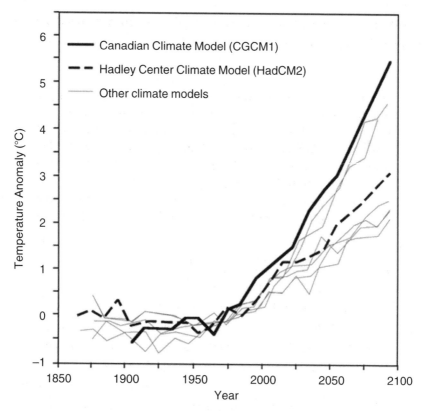

Fig. 2. Temperature increase for the United States as forecast by the climate models considered for inclusion in the United States National Assessment
Note: Notice that the Canadian Climate Model (CGCM1, heavy black line) produces the most extreme temperature rise.
Source: U.S. National Assessment of the Potential Consequences of Climate Variability and Change.

- The HadCM2 predicts more than twice the precipitation change of the next most extreme model, the CGCM1 model. The CGCM1 precipitation changes themselves are twice the average of the remaining, unselected models (Figure 3).

It is therefore clear that the Synthesis Team chose models that were far from representative of the larger population of GCMs.

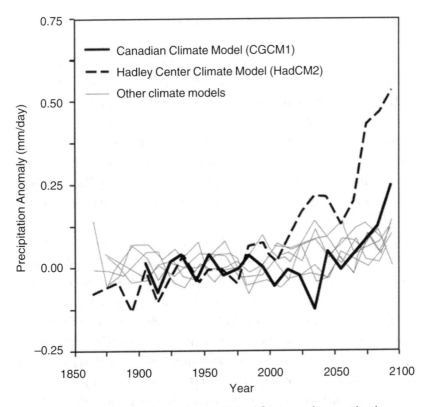

Fig. 3. The precipitation change for the United States as forecast by the climate models considered for inclusion in the United States National Assessment
Note: Notice that the Hadley Centre Climate Model (HadCM2, heavy broken line) produces the most extreme precipitation increase; the Canadian Climate Model (CGCM1, heavy black line) produces the second largest increase.
Source: U.S. National Assessment of the Potential Consequences of Climate Variability and Change.

This is profoundly different from what occurs in most other processes designed to produce scientific "consensus," which usually present the mean position plus some reasonable variation concerning a controversial issue. Moreover, the selection of models that predict the greatest changes appears to have ignored the instructions in Dr. Gibbons's request letter and the subsequent charge (www.uscrp.gov/usgcrp/nacc/background/organization/ charge-nast.html) that the team was to "take into accord the scenarios of the IPCC." The IPCC has not settled on predictions from particular models, and its scenarios for temperature changes in the next century range from 1.0 to 5.8°C.

Figure 2 presents predictions of future temperature changes from all the models considered by the Synthesis Team, and the "predictions" from each model for temperature changes over the last century and a half. The CGCM1 "predicts" that the United States should have warmed 1.5°C during the twentieth century, but observed warming, according to the most recent analysis from the National Climatic Data Center (where Thomas Karl is the director) is 0.5°C.[7] Thus CGCM1 is making a 300 percent error over the last 100 years.

Why select such an obviously inappropriate model as the CGCM1? Karl told me that the CGCM1 was chosen because it was one of only two models (along with the HadCM2) that produced separate high and low daily temperatures, and that this level of detail was required for some of the USNA's analyses.

Readers are left to consider the logic: the most extreme temperature prediction model was chosen simply because it produced day and night temperatures. That should have been a red flag. If seasonal or annual temperature predictions from a model are unreliable or extreme, then the smaller-scale values, such as daily or intra-day values, are even more unreliable. The USNA Synthesis Team should have checked predictions from its chosen

---

7. G. J. Boer et al., "A Transient Climate Change Simulation with Historical and Projected Greenhouse Gas and Aerosol Forcing: Experimental Design and Comparison with the Instrumental Record for the 20th Century," ibid. 16 (2000): 405–25.

models against recorded changes in the past before relying on those models.

Michael MacCracken, head of the National Assessment Coordination Office at the time the report was under review, supplied a different explanation for the use of the CGCM1. He said USNA wanted an example of a "plausible worst-case" scenario for change in U.S. climate. I can find nothing in Dr. Gibbons's letter or the charge to the USNA team that requested a worst-case scenario, but it is possible that the team was told that such a scenario was expected.

Whatever the reason, the Synthesis Team chose the most extreme temperature model when it chose the CGCM1. For balance, then, it could have used an analogously cold model, such as the new version from the U.S. National Center for Atmospheric Research[8] for all applications that didn't require daily data, such as mean seasonal or annual temperature or precipitation changes.

The HadCM2 forecasts of precipitation changes are as extreme as those of the CGCM1 for temperature (Figure 3). The USNA team used no other precipitation change model.

This type of model selection is prima facie evidence of Synthesis Team bias in favor of models that produced very lurid results. That no balancing models were used simply means that no balance was ever intended in the USNA, or, rather, that the USNA reflects the lack of balance evident in the Synthesis Team, itself created by a highly convoluted and clearly political chain of command.

8. B. A. Boville and P. R. Gent, "The NCAR Climate System Model, Version One," *J. Climate* 11 (1998): 1115–30; R. A. Kerr, "Model Gets It Right—Without Fudge Factors," *Science* 276 (1997): 1041.

The Failure of the USNA Models

The basic rule of science is that hypotheses must be verified by testing their predictions against observed data.[9] Hypotheses that cannot be tested can be useful, but they are not science. Hypotheses that are tested and fail must be modified and retested, or simply rejected. Science that relies upon hypotheses that have failed a comparison with reality is "junk science." A computerized climate model, however sophisticated, is indeed nothing more than a hypothesis until it is verified by testing against reality. If it fails that test, and it continues to be used for a "scientific" assessment, that assessment then falls into the "junk science" category.

Both CGCM1 and HadCM2 make predictions of U.S. climate change based upon human alterations of the atmosphere. Those alterations have been going on for well over 100 years. Do the changes those models "predicted" resemble what actually occurred in the last century?

The answer is clearly no. I compared observed U.S. annual temperature departures from the twentieth-century average with those generated by both the CGCM1 and HadCM2 models. In both cases I used ten-year running averages to minimize interannual noise. This is a simple and common test. The modeled U.S. average temperature for 1991–2000 is compared to the observed value. Then the comparison period is backed up one year, to 1990–99, and so on. This smooths out the effect of single years that are unusually warm or cold, such as occurs in a strong El Niño year (such as 1998) or after a large volcanic eruption (1992).

I then examined the differences between the modeled and

9. The Supreme Court holds this is essential in scientific testimony. In *Daubert v. Merrell Dow*, it wrote, "Many conditions will bear on the inquiry, including whether the theory or technique in question can be (and has been) tested."

observed values for both the CGCM and HadCM2, versus the result that would obtain if I simply used the average temperature for the twentieth century to predict the observed values from year to year. In fact, both models did worse than that base case. In other words, both climate models used in the USNA were worse than no model at all.

On August 11, 2000, I sent this result as a formal review comment to the USNA Synthesis Team. Specifically, I wrote:

> The essential problem with the USNA is that it is based largely on two climate models, neither one of which, when compared with the 10-year smoothed behavior of the lower 48 states (a very lenient comparison) reduces the residual variance below the raw variance of the data [this means that they did not perform better than a model that simply assumed a constant temperature]. The one that generates the most lurid warming scenarios—the Canadian Climate Centre [CGCM] Model—also has a clear warm bias. Variance reduction is a simple test of whether or not a model is valid ... and both of these models fail. All implied effects, including the large temperature rise, are therefore based upon a multiple scientific failure. The USNA's continued use of those models and that approach is a willful choice to disregard the most fundamental of scientific rules. (And that they did not find and eliminate such an egregious error is astounding.) For that reason alone, the USNA should be withdrawn from the public sphere until it becomes scientifically based.

The USNA team is required to respond to such criticism, but it chose to ignore the core argument, responding: "When the observations of the full 20th century in the U.S. are compared to the Hadley and Canadian model projections, comparable statistically significant warming is seen in all three."

This is not true. As shown earlier, the CGCM model predicts a rise of 1.5°C in U.S. temperature in the twentieth century, three times what was observed. Further, the USNA completely ignored the fact that the models were producing worse forecasts of temperature than would result from random numbers applied to the mean.

Independent Replication of the Failure

Was this the end? Was the Synthesis Team satisfied to reject my argument? No. In fact, it commissioned a special study to determine if indeed I was correct.

A member of the synthesis team was kind enough to supply the results. He or she wrote to me:

> "One has to look at the time averages. In the assessment we were most interested in, decadal to century scale trends, not annual averages [Note: As mentioned above, I used decadal (10-year) moving averages!], so [we] would not be inclined to perform the test you did. . . . Nevertheless we ran the test you did, but changed the averaging period."

Figures 4 and 5 illustrate the results from comparing variations in predicted temperature from the two GCMs with the measured variations over different time periods in the last century. The leftmost set of bars represent predicted and measured variations in temperatures over one-year periods; the other sets of bars represent variations over 5, 10, 20, and 25-year moving averages. The shaded bars (in the foreground of each figure) represent the scatter of the observed temperatures around their twentieth-century average. The lighter bars are the differences between the model-predicted and observed temperatures, or the model error. For both GCMs, at all time scales, the model errors are greater than observed temperature variations in the twentieth century. These results, generated by the Synthesis Team itself, confirmed my finding that both these models were worse than no model at all.

At all time scales averaged over the United States, both the

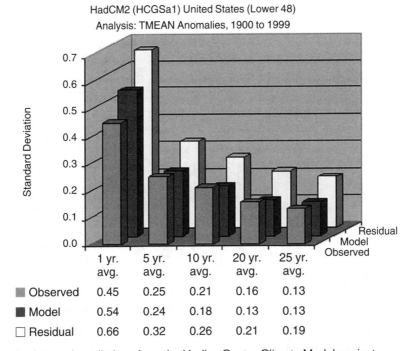

HadCM2 (HCGSa1) United States (Lower 48)
Analysis: TMEAN Anomalies, 1900 to 1999

	1 yr. avg.	5 yr. avg.	10 yr. avg.	20 yr. avg.	25 yr. avg.
Observed	0.45	0.25	0.21	0.16	0.13
Model	0.54	0.24	0.18	0.13	0.13
Residual	0.66	0.32	0.26	0.21	0.19

Fig. 4. A test of predictions from the Hadley Centre Climate Model against actual temperature variations recorded over in the United States over the twentieth century

Note: The darker bars for each time period represent the scatter of observed temperatures from the twentieth-century average. The lighter bars represent the scatter of the difference between the model-predicted temperatures and the observed temperatures. As is evident, at all time scales, the scatter of the model predictions is greater than the scatter of the observation, indicating that the model fails to account for measured temperature variations over the last century.

Source: USNA Synthesis Team member, personal communication.

HadCM2 and CGCM models fail. They failed an independent test designed to verify whether my original criticism—that the models were no better than "noise," or random numbers—was correct. So, in summary, the USNA was sufficiently concerned about my criticism that, in spite of its public brush-off, it specifically tested my hypothesis and independently verified the finding that the

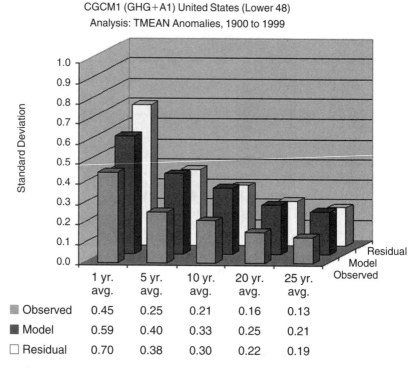

CGCM1 (GHG+A1) United States (Lower 48)
Analysis: TMEAN Anomalies, 1900 to 1999

	1 yr. avg.	5 yr. avg.	10 yr. avg.	20 yr. avg.	25 yr. avg.
▨ Observed	0.45	0.25	0.21	0.16	0.13
■ Model	0.59	0.40	0.33	0.25	0.21
☐ Residual	0.70	0.38	0.30	0.22	0.19

Fig. 5. A test of predictions from the Canadian Climate Model against actual temperature variations recorded over in the United States over the twentieth century
Source: USNA Synthesis Team member, personal communication.

models were worse than trying to predict U.S. temperatures from a table of random numbers.

Nonetheless, the Synthesis Team went through with publication of its report even after being told (and then independently verifying) that the models it relied upon could not simulate U.S. temperature on any time scale during the last 100 years. That leads to the obvious conclusion that the USNA is a politically driven polemic that merely looks scientific. It is decidedly not science by the norms of the scientific community. And it is un-

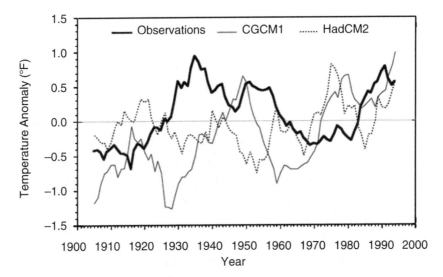

Fig. 6. The ten-year smoothed observed and predicted annual average temperature for the United States during the twentieth century by the two models used in the USNA
Source: U.S. National Assessment of the Potential Consequences of Climate Variability and Change.

likely that testimony built on it would be admissible in a court case under the standards set by the Supreme Court in *Daubert v. Merrell Dow.*

The real reason for the models' failure can be found in a simple visual comparison between U.S. annual temperature departures from the long-term mean and modeled temperatures (Figure 6). The discrepancies come about because:

1. U.S. temperatures rose rapidly—approximately 0.7°C—from about 1910 to 1930. The GCMs, which base their predictions largely on changes in atmospheric carbon dioxide, miss this warming, as the greatest changes in carbon dioxide occur after this warming.

2. U.S. temperature fell—about 0.6°C—from 1930 to 1975. That

is the period in which the climate models begin to ramp up
their warming.

3. Temperatures rose again—making up for the 0.6°C lost between 1940 and 1975—from 1975 to 2000.

The summation is that much of the warming in the U.S. record
took place before most of the greenhouse gas increases, and in
fact, nearly half of the so-called "greenhouse era" (the twentieth
century) was accompanied by falling temperatures over the U.S.
It's no wonder that no model that is fed a diet of only greenhouse
gases can get this right!

The bottom line is simple: Unless a climate model can explain
the rapid run-up in U.S. temperatures in the early twentieth century, and the subsequent temperature fall to 1975, it is not an
accurate guide to the future, because the most recent temperature
rise in U.S. temperature is not greater than the one that ended
more than seventy years ago.

The failure of the models is not surprising. Even though it,
too, suffers from considerable political overhead, the United
Nations Intergovernmental Panel on Climate Change (IPCC) has
repeatedly remarked that estimation of temperature changes over
regions, such as the continental United States, is at best problem-
atical. In the IPCC's 2001 *Third Assessment Report* (TAR), it summarized the findings of its *Second Assessment Report* (SAR) issued
five years earlier:

Overall the SAR placed low confidence in the simulation of
regional climate change produced by available modeling tools
because of three factors:

- *Errors in the reproduction of present-day regional climate characteristics* (emphasis added)

- *Wide range in the simulated regional climatic changes by different models* (emphasis added)

- The need to more comprehensively use regionalization techniques to compare the predictions made with global models to those from models that focus on smaller areas.[10]

The 2001 TAR devoted an entire chapter to regional climate projections. It says: "This chapter . . . stems from the increasing need to better understand the processes that determine regional climate. . . . To date, a relatively high level of uncertainty has characterized regional climate information." Later, in the same chapter: "Despite recent improvements and developments . . . a coherent picture of regional climate change via available regionalization techniques cannot yet be drawn. More co-ordinated efforts are thus necessary to improve the integrated hierarchy of models . . . and apply these methods to climate change research in a comprehensive strategy."

Clearly, the USNA is premised on an impossibility that is recognized by a larger community of scientists, even one as clearly politicized as the IPCC. It should therefore be no surprise that climate models fail when applied to an area as small as the lower forty-eight states. What is incomprehensible is why, then, they were used at all.

Is it scientifically proper to use models that are demonstrable failures? The answer is no. Using a model that is no better than random numbers is no better than a physician prescribing a medication that does not work.

Conclusion

It is clear that the USNA Synthesis Team crossed a clear line when it employed indefensible scientific models to generate a supposedly scientific assessment of prospective climate change in the

10. This means that current smaller-scale climate models are often not consistent with larger-scale ones.

United States. I believe this occurred because the Synthesis Team was unbalanced, containing only two climate scientists, and none who had expressed considerable skepticism about the ability of climate models to perform adequately at the level of the United States, even though the larger scientific community has expressed considerable skepticism about this ability.[11]

The result is that we now have a landmark document, the USNA, being cited as the reason for expensive and intrusive energy legislation, such as HR 4, currently before the U.S. Congress. This is a situation that needs remediation.

The nation needs a new, more scientifically based assessment of the nature and possible effects of climate change on the United States. If it is scientifically impossible to predict with any confidence, the assessment should say that. This will only occur with a more broadly based synthesis team. As it stands, the current document is clearly not science and, as a result, it falls much more in the category of a politically based polemic. The National Assessment Synthesis Team should make a very public show of withdrawing the existing Assessment and starting over.

Starting over means generating a new assessment with a team that has the diversity to withstand the political pressure—from either the left or the right—and is more consistent with normative scientific behavior. The current *U.S. National Assessment of the Potential Consequences of Climate Variability and Change* is not consistent with these norms.

---

11. See P. J. Michaels, P. C. Knappenberger, and R. E. Davis, "Integrated Projections of Future Warming Based Upon Observed Climate During the Attenuating Greenhouse Enhancement," *Proceedings of the 1st International Conference on Global Warming and the Next Ice Age*, American Meteorological Society (2001): 162–67; T. R. Karl et al., "Indices of Climate Change for the United States," *Bull. Am. Meteorological Soc.* 77 (1995): 279–92.

EIGHT

The Political Science of Agent Orange and Dioxin

MICHAEL GOUGH

Between 1961 and 1970, the United States military sprayed the herbicide Agent Orange, a mixture of two widely used agricultural chemicals, over the enemy-controlled jungles (now called "rain forests") and crop-growing regions of South Vietnam.[1] Agent Orange was shipped to Vietnam in 55-gallon drums circled by a stripe of orange paint for easy sorting from other herbicides— Agents White, Blue, Purple, and so on.

While under development in the mid-1940s, one of the chemicals in Agent Orange—*2,4-d*ichlorophenoxyacetic acid or 2,4-D

---

1. For general information about the use of Agent Orange during the Vietnam War, see M. Gough, *Dioxin, Agent Orange* (New York: Plenum, 1986), pp. 63–120, and Institute of Medicine (IOM), *Veterans and Agent Orange* (Washington, D.C.: National Academy Press, 1993), pp. 23–110.

—was used to kill dandelions in front of the Smithsonian Institution on the National Mall. It continues in worldwide use as an effective herbicide against broadleaf weeds, and it's available in every hardware and most grocery stores in "Weed-B-Gon" and other popular products. The other Agent Orange component, 2,4,5-*trichlorophenoxyacetic acid* or 2,4,5-T, was removed from markets around the world, after about thirty years of use, in the late 1970s and 1980s because of concerns that dioxin, specifically 2,3,7,8-*tetrachlorodibenzo-para-dioxin* or 2,3,7,8-TCDD or TCDD, an unavoidable contaminant of the manufacture of 2,4,5-T, was a cause of cancer and other diseases.[2]

Some $3 billion have been spent on researching possible health effects from dioxin, and the results show that the risks were overstated. Last year, the Environmental Protection Agency's Science Advisory Board concluded that the evidence that dioxin is a cause of human cancer and other diseases is unconvincing.[3] Furthermore, studies of workers exposed to the highest levels of dioxin ever experienced—levels that will never be seen again—have failed to produce any conclusive evidence of connections between dioxin and cancer[4] and the other health effects.[5]

The United States stopped using Agent Orange in Vietnam in 1970—eight years before 2,4,5-T was taken off the market in this country—because of North Vietnamese and Viet Cong charges that herbicides were a form of chemical warfare forbidden by international treaty and claims from Vietnamese, Americans, and

2. Gough, *Dioxin*, pp. 137–48.

3. U.S. Environmental Protection Agency, Science Advisory Board (SAB), *Dioxin Reassessment—An SAB Review of the Office of Research and Development's Reassessment of Dioxin* (EPA-SAB-EC-01-006) (Washington, D.C.: EPA, May 2001).

4. T. B. Starr, "Significant Shortcomings of the U.S. Environmental Protection Agency's Latest Draft Risk Characterization for Dioxin-Like Compounds," *Toxicological Sciences* 64 (2001): 7–13.

5. SAB, 2001.

others that the herbicides were causing birth defects among Vietnamese children as well as severe, perhaps irreversible, ecological damage. The most important immediate factor in the decision was laboratory tests, carried out by scientists at the Dow Chemical Company, that showed dioxin to be the most potent cause of birth defects ever tested in laboratory animals.

Veterans' Claims

By 1975, Vietnam veterans, supported by some scientists and politicians, blamed Agent Orange as the cause of their own diseases and of birth defects in their children and demanded medical treatment and monetary compensation. Their efforts received a huge boost from two television programs that associated Agent Orange with cancer in veterans and birth defects in their children.[6]

The programs found audiences ready to believe that Agent Orange caused diseases. For one thing, the United States public, long ago disenchanted with the Vietnam war and, by the late 1970s, immersed in guilt about its treatment of Vietnam veterans, willingly accepted the idea that a chemical—Agent Orange—was at the root of veterans' complaints. Moreover, environmental chemicals as the cause of human disease were staples of nightly newscasts, magazine and newspaper articles, environmental organizations' fund-raising and public-relations campaigns, lawyers looking for companies to sue, and government officials eager to increase the agencies' reach by expanding the fight against disease-causing environmental pollution. Agent Orange and dioxin became the ugly poster children for nasty environmental chemicals.

6. F. A. Wilcox, *Waiting for an Army To Die* (New York: Random House, 1983), p. 10 (of Introduction) presents a dramatic description of one of those television programs.

Through 1978, the Veterans Administration (VA) rebuffed veterans' claims for treatment and compensation for "Agent Orange diseases," saying that there was no evidence for a link between Agent Orange and the diseases for which claims were made. The veterans then took their claims to Congress.

Congress Orders Studies About Health Effects and Agent Orange Exposures

Congress could have responded to veterans' claims by directing the VA to provide medical care and to pay compensation to the veterans, in the absence of any evidence about causation, basing its decision on compassion or other policy considerations. It didn't do that. In retrospect, it would have been a clean and clearly political decision as compared to the political decisions that ushered in a series of bad scientific decisions.

The clamor for providing treatment for Agent Orange–related diseases decreased in the 1980s when the VA, with increased funding for its hospitals (Public Law 97-72, enacted in November 1981) provided treatment for "Agent Orange–related diseases." Importantly, the veteran did not have to prove exposure to Agent Orange to qualify for treatment. Instead, Congress presumed that any veteran who had served in Vietnam had been exposed and that the exposure to Agent Orange caused the veteran's illness unless a congenital condition or some other exposure was shown to be a more likely cause.[7] In practice, the law makes any disease in Vietnam veterans treatable as an Agent Orange disease because difficult, expensive, and unlikely-to-be-conclusive tests would be necessary to test the presumption.

Earlier, in 1979, Congress (Public Law 96-151) had ordered VA to plan and carry out a study of the health of Agent Orange–

7. IOM 1994, p. 50, and references there.

exposed veterans.[8] VA failed to get the study under way in a timely manner (in fairness to VA, such a study had never been done, and it was far beyond the expertise and experience of VA staff). The Centers for Disease Control (the agency is now the Centers for Disease Control and Prevention, but I'll use the old name and abbreviation "CDC," a part of the Department of Health and Human Services, DHHS) maneuvered itself into being made responsible for the study in 1982.

CDC's "Vietnam Experience Studies"

In 1982, because there was no way to determine whether an individual had been exposed to Agent Orange, CDC decided to compare the health of Vietnam veterans with the health of veterans who had not served in Vietnam in the "Vietnam experience studies."[9] The CDC found nothing to link Vietnam service with any health problems that had not been seen in veterans of other wars.

Many people who had looked for the Vietnam Experience Studies to verify that the war was causing health problems were disappointed. In particular, and with justification, they said that the effects of Agent Orange might have been overlooked because there was no way to identify veterans who had been exposed to it.

8. Ibid.; also Gough, *Dioxin*, pp. 89–103. As part of the legislation that mandated the Veterans Administration study, Congress directed the Office of Technology Assessment to review and approve the plan for the study and to monitor the conduct of the study. I was put in charge of that activity in early 1980.

9. See reports of the Centers for Disease Control Vietnam Experience Study: "Postservice Mortality Among Vietnam Veterans," *JAMA* 257 (1987): 790–95; "Health Status of Vietnam Veterans. II. Physical Health," ibid. 259 (1988): 2708–14; "Health Status of Vietnam Veterans. III. Reproductive Outcomes and Child Health," ibid. 259 (1988): 2715–19.

CDC's Measurements of
Agent Orange Exposure

After it enters the body by absorption through the skin, inhalation, or ingestion, dioxin, the toxic contaminant in Agent Orange, is deposited in the lipid (or fat) of the human body. It is only very slowly eliminated from lipid so that measuring dioxin concentrations in lipid today can provide information about exposures that happened decades ago. In the mid-1980s, CDC imported sensitive methods and instruments from Sweden that allowed scientists to determine dioxin levels in blood, which is about 4 percent lipid. The availability of the technique made it possible for CDC to do an Agent Orange study, relying on dioxin in blood measurements as an estimate of exposure.

In its Agent Orange exposure study, the CDC identified 600 Vietnam veterans who had been present at times and in areas near where the Air Force's Operation Ranch Hand had sprayed Agent Orange and compared the concentrations of dioxin in the blood lipids (these concentrations are called "body burdens") of those veterans with the concentrations in some 100 other veterans who had never served in Vietnam. The dioxin concentrations in the "exposed" and nonexposed veterans were the same, and the concentrations in both groups fell within the concentrations measured in the general population.[10]

These results were no surprise to experts in pesticide application and dispersal, who had argued all along that the concentrations of Agent Orange reaching the ground where troops might be exposed were insignificant.[11] Some veterans and some mem-

---

10. The Centers for Disease Control Vietnam Experience Study, "2,3,7,8-tetrachlorodibenzo-p-dioxin Levels in US Army Vietnam-era Veterans," ibid. 260 (1988): 1249–54.
    11. See, e.g., Gough, *Dioxin*, pp. 259–62.

bers of Congress dismissed these results, as they had dismissed the results of the Vietnam experience studies, as incompetently done or, worse, as "cover-ups."

The Ranch Hand Study

In 1982, the U.S. Air Force began a twenty-year-long study of the health of the 1,200 Ranch Hands, the Air Force personnel who sprayed 90 percent of the Agent Orange used in Vietnam, and a Comparison group of Air Force personnel who flew planes similar to those flown by Ranch Hands but did not handle herbicides. (The Ranch Hands flew C-123s; the Comparisons, C-130s.) Measurements of dioxin levels confirm that many of the Ranch Hands were exposed to Agent Orange.

The Ranch Hands and Comparisons have undergone weeklong physical and psychological examinations at five-year intervals beginning in 1982, with the last examinations begun in the fall of 2002. The examinations are carried out in civilian hospitals by physicians and technicians who are not told which men are in the Ranch Hand and which are in the Comparison group.

The Air Force scientists who direct the Ranch Hand study concluded, in 1997, that dioxin exposure is associated with increased risk of adult-onset diabetes,[12] which is the only disease that they link to dioxin. In their most recent comment on the possible dioxin-diabetes link, the Air Force scientists state that the evidence for a connection is "weaker" in the data collected in the 1997 exams than in the data from the 1992 exams.[13] I doubt that

12. G. L. Henrikson et al., "Serum Dioxin and Diabetes Mellitus in Veterans of Operation Ranch Hand," *Epidemiology* 8 (1997): 252–58.

13. J. E. Michalek and N. S. Ketchum, April 23, 2002, "Diabetes and Dioxin in Air Force Health Study Participants," typescript, 9 pp., prepared for the Department of Health and Human Services advisory committee to the Ranch Hand study.

anyone besides the Air Force investigators, who are under enormous political pressure "to find something" associated with Agent Orange, an Institute of Medicine (IOM) committee (see below), and some champions of Vietnam veterans' health claims, would interpret the available data to indicate that any connection exists.

Politics Takes Over

In 1988, congressional leaders, led by then-Representative, now-Senator Tom Daschle, who pushed the Agent Orange–causes-diseases agenda, faced a dilemma. The despised CDC studies had been negative. There was no expectation of designing a study that would differ very much from those studies or produce results that would be different.

Congress could have set aside the scientific findings and based decisions on other factors—compassion, equity, log-rolling, pork-barreling, vote-buying—or it could have sorted among competing findings and conclusions and chosen those that satisfied whatever criteria it wanted. It decided, instead, in Public Law 102-4, "The Agent Orange Act of 1991,"[14] to establish a committee in the prestigious National Academy of Sciences (NAS), to provide advice about health effects of Agent Orange.

As a result of that action, decisions about Agent Orange exist as if the CDC and Air Force studies had never been done. In late 2001, the VA was compensating 9,000 Vietnam veterans for some ten "Agent Orange–related diseases"—the number of veterans receiving compensation and the number of compensable diseases will surely increase—and it is compensating veterans' children born with a serious birth defect.

The politicians who welcome support of their preconceived

---

14. Bill Summary and Status for the 102d Congress: HR556, Public Law: 102-4 (02/06/91). http://thomas.loc.gov/cgi-bin/bdquery/D?d102:1.

opinions that Agent Orange has been a scourge among veterans, as well as citizens who receive compensation or otherwise benefit from those results, and the far larger number of citizens who see the compensation decisions as the "right thing" to do, laud the IOM committee for its "good science." In their eyes, it has extracted truth from the morass of bad experiments, bad observations, bad studies, and bad interpretations that do not support the politicians' conclusions, veterans' claims, and citizens' desires. In reality, the process has substituted an officially sanctioned, politically constrained objectivity for science at the NAS.

Congress and the Institute of Medicine

The legislation that emerged as "The Agent Orange Act of 1991" was introduced on January 17, 1991, and passed the House on January 29 by a vote of 412–0. It was sent to the Senate the next day, on January 30, where it was considered and passed by a vote of 99–0 on the same day. The legislation

> Directs the Secretary [of the Department of Veterans Affairs] to enter into an agreement with the National Academy of Sciences (NAS) under which NAS shall review and summarize the scientific evidence (and its strength) concerning the association between exposure to a herbicide agent during service in Vietnam and each disease suspected to be associated with such exposure.[15]

The text of Section 3 of the law repeats the language in the summary, and it goes on:

> For each disease reviewed, the Academy shall determine (to the extent that available scientific data permit meaningful determinations)—(A) whether a statistical association with herbicide exposure exists, taking into account the strength of

15. Ibid.

the scientific evidence and the appropriateness of the statistical and epidemiological methods used to detect the association"[16]

As we shall see, the difference between "shall review and summarize the scientific evidence," as appears in the summary and the first paragraph of Section 3, and "whether a statistical association ... exists," which appears in a subordinate paragraph of Section 3, was crucial to the NAS's discharge of its duty.

The NAS Assigns the "Veterans and Agent Orange" Program to the IOM

The NAS and its sister organizations, the National Academy of Engineering and the Institute of Medicine (IOM), are composed of about 5,000 scientists, engineers, physicians, and other experts elected to membership because of their accomplishments. According to its congressional charter, the NAS is to provide advice to Congress when requested. The usual way by which Congress obtains NAS advice is through legislation that directs an Executive Branch agency to contract with the NAS for advice. Congress directed VA to contract with the NAS, NAS assigned the Agent Orange review to the IOM, and the IOM assembled a 16-member committee whose members

> ... were selected because they are leading authorities in their scientific fields, are well-respected by their colleagues and peers, have no conflicts of interest with regard to the matters under study, and, indeed, have taken no public positions concerning the potential health effects of herbicides in Vietnam veterans or related aspects of herbicide or dioxin exposures.[17]

16. HR556, Agent Orange Act of 1991. http://thomas.loc.gov/cgi-bin/query/D?c102:1:./temp/c102dK9rK6:e7899:

17. IOM, 1994, p. vii.

Although the committee enjoys the prestige of being called an "IOM committee" (or even a "National Academy committee"), only a single member of the IOM served on the Agent Orange Committee. The other fifteen committee members were selected from universities and medical and public health schools.

Conflicts of Interest

It surprises me that IOM could find committee members who knew anything about herbicides and health but who had taken no public position on an issue that had raged for over a decade, though their not having taken a public position does not imply that they had no private position. That, however, is not the primary difficulty that arises from eliminating conflicts of interest. The primary difficulty with eliminating people who have conflicts of interest is the elimination of the people who best know the literature and research. A glance at the reference lists at the end of each chapter in the IOM 1994 report reveals hundreds of papers about the toxicology and epidemiology of herbicides. Some of those papers are good, some bad—some criminally bad. People with conflicts of interest know those papers. Without such people on the committee, the committee members are overly dependent on IOM staff or on committee members who have or develop private agendas to read, critique, and summarize the contents of the scientific literature.

There is an alternate method to deal with conflict of interest. During my tenure at the congressional Office of Technology Assessment (OTA), I put together several advisory panels and made no effort to eliminate conflicts of interest. Had I made the effort, I would have failed because I did not recognize some conflicts until a study was well under way. Instead of eliminating conflicts of interest, OTA tried to balance known conflicts of interest. Having people with conflicts of interest had the obvious advantage of bringing opinions about the scientific literature to the panel discussions, making it impossible for staff to guide the panel's deliberations.

Advisory panel members with conflicts of interest had, what was to me, an unexpected benefit. They set limits to the panel's discussion and consideration: no panel member is likely to venture beyond the speculations and conclusions of those staked-out interests. Moreover, having people with conflicts of interest is not disruptive. People on opposing sides often know each other, and if they don't, they know each other by reputation. They are polite and congenial and accommodating because of their desire to convince the other panel members of the correctness of their positions.

In its review, the IOM emphasized the subordinate clause of Section 3 of Public Law 102-4 that directed it to determine whether a "statistical association" exists between herbicide exposure and health effects. How looking for statistical associations differs from a scientific review isn't entirely clear, but the IOM points out that it did not examine the data for evidence of "causality, as is common in scientific reviews."[18]

Exposures to Environmental Chemicals and Disease

Cancer has been at center stage from the opening curtain of the Agent Orange controversy. In animal tests, dioxin is a very potent carcinogen, and it's known that dioxin is present in the environment.

For at least thirty years, the combinations of animal test results showing that a chemical causes cancer and reports that the chemical is present in the environment have been behind federal agen-

18. Ibid., p. 7.

cies' and environmental organizations' barrages of reports, allegations, and suggestions that environmental exposures are a major cause of cancer and that we are in the middle of a chemically caused cancer epidemic. The reports, allegations, and suggestions are wrong. In the early 1980s, scientists who studied cancer causation estimated that, at most, environmental exposures are associated with 2 or 3 percent of all cancers.[19] A few years later, EPA scientists and managers produced a document that agreed with that estimate.[20]

There is no cancer epidemic; cancer rates remained essentially constant (except for increases in smoking-associated cancers) from 1933, when national records were first kept, until the early 1990s, when rates began to fall.[21] The decreases that were first seen in the early 1990s have continued and deeper declines are expected.[22] (See Ames and Gold, this volume, for information about causes of cancer.)

Until "chemicals cause cancer" accusations lost their capacity to excite the public, little attention was paid to the possibility that chemicals might cause other health effects, but such possibilities are now at center stage. I will not dwell on the "chemicals cause

19. R. Doll and R. Peto, "The Causes of Cancer: Quantitative Estimates of Avoidable Risks of Cancer in the United States Today," *J. Natl. Cancer Inst.* 66 (1981), 1191–1308. And see OTA (Office of Technology Assessment), 1981, *Assessment of Technologies for Determining Cancer Risks from the Environment* (OTA2DH2D138) (Washington, D.C.: U.S. Government Printing Office), pp. 31–109.

20. M. Gough, "Estimating Cancer Mortality: Epidemiological and Toxicological Methods Produce Similar Assessments," *Environ. Sci. and Tech.* 23 (1989): 925–30.

21. P. A. Wingo et al., "Annual Report to the Nation on the Status of Cancer 1973–1996, with a Special Section on Lung Cancer and Tobacco Smoking," *J. Natl. Cancer Inst.* 91 (1999): 675–90.

22. H. L. Howe et al., "Annual Report to the Nation on the Status of Cancer (1973 Through 1998) Featuring Cancers with Recent Increasing Trends," ibid. 93 (2001): 824–42.

other health effects" accusations, but there is essentially no evidence that environmental exposures cause them.

In the absence of evidence that environmental exposures are associated with cancer or other health effects, it would be reasonable to expect IOM committee members to have been skeptical about claims of such associations. Indeed, skepticism is the hallmark of science. The IOM committee veered far away from science.

What's Risky in Herbicides?

At very high doses, such as experienced by a few chemical workers and attempted suicides, herbicides can cause symptoms of acute chemical poisoning. Environmental exposures do not cause such effects, and none was reported in the Ranch Hands.

The IOM committee failed to read or heed its own conclusions about health risks from herbicides: "In contrast to TCDD ["dioxin," as used here], there is no convincing evidence in animals of, or mechanistic basis for, carcinogenicity or other health effects of any of the herbicides, although they have not been studied as extensively as TCDD."[23]

Ignoring its own conclusion that "there is no convincing evidence in animals of, or mechanistic basis for, carcinogenicity or other health effects," the IOM committee bounded ahead to review reports of disease rates in men who were classified as exposed to "herbicides." In the vast majority of the reviewed studies there is, however, no verification of exposure.

23. IOM, 1994, p. 3.

The IOM Committee Decides About Associations of Herbicides with Diseases

The IOM committee reviewed reports about possible associations between herbicide exposures and each of thirty-two diseases and conditions and put the evidence for each association into one of four categories:

- Sufficient Evidence of an Association
- Limited/Suggestive Evidence of an Association
- Inadequate/Insufficient Evidence to Determine Whether an Association Exists
- Limited/Suggestive Evidence of *No* Association (emphasis in original)[24]

Congress had already declared that veterans who suffered from any of four diseases—chloracne, porphyria cutanea tarda, soft-tissue sarcoma, or non-Hodgkin's leukemia—were entitled to compensation. The IOM committee essentially endorsed the congressional decisions when it concluded that there was sufficient evidence for associations between herbicides and those four diseases.

The committee also decided that there was sufficient evidence for an association between herbicides and Hodgkin's disease. This addition was almost inevitable in light of IOM's evaluation of the evidence about soft-tissue sarcoma and non-Hodgkin's leukemia, for which the committee had depended on the epidemiological studies done by a group of Swedish researchers. The same researchers had published similar results from their studies of Hodgkin's disease:

24. Ibid., pp. 6–7.

When these three cancers (soft-tissue sarcoma, non-Hodg-kin's leukemia, and Hodgkin's disease) are considered as a whole, it is noteworthy that the strongest evidence for an association with exposure to phenoxy herbicides is the series of case-control studies conducted by Hardell [Lennart Hardell, a Swedish physician] and colleagues and the cohort studies of herbicide applicators and agricultural workers.[25]

Whatever Hardell and his colleagues investigated, it was not exposure to dioxin-containing herbicides. As detailed in a paper by Hardell and others in 1986, workers who had been classified as exposed to herbicides in Hardell's studies did not have elevated levels of dioxin in their bodies.[26] The IOM committee states, "Studies in other countries are sometimes positive, but not as consistently," as reported by Hardell. Indeed. Some "studies in other countries" are flatly contradictory,[27] and the ones that can be interpreted to support Hardell's findings have no verification of exposures.

The IOM committee decided to disregard the many questions and criticisms about Hardell's studies by many other reviewers. U.S. EPA, in its massive 2000 review of risks from dioxin,[28] does not rely on Hardell's studies, and the International Agency for Research on Cancer (IARC),[29] and the European Commission[30] and World Health Organization (WHO)[31] disregard them.

25. Ibid., pp. 9–10.

26. M. Nygren, C. Rappe, O. Lindstrom, M. Hansson, P.-A. Bergqvist, S. Markland, L. Domellof, L. Hardell, and M. Olsson, "Identification of 2,3,7,8-substituted Polychlorinated Dioxins and Dibenzofurans in Environmental and Human Samples," in C. Rappe, G. Choudhary, and L. H. Keith, eds., *Chlorinated Dioxins and Dibenzofurans in Perspective* (Chelsea, Mich.: Lewis, 1986), pp. 15–34.

27. M. Gough, "Human Health Effects: What the Data Indicate," *Science of the Total Environ.* 104 (1991): 129–58.

28. U.S. EPA 2001.

29. International Agency for Research on Cancer, *IARC Monographs on the Evaluation of Carcinogenic Risks to Humans: Polychlorinated Dibenzo-*

In addition to deciding that there was sufficient evidence for associations between herbicides and five diseases, the IOM committee concluded that there was "limited/suggestive" evidence for associations with respiratory cancer, prostate cancer—the two most common cancers in males—and multiple myeloma. IOM relied upon studies of chemical plant workers to decide that dioxin was associated with respiratory cancer, and in particular upon a study of U.S. chemical plant workers.[32]

The U.S. study included mortality records from twelve chemical plants. In only two of those twelve plants was there any information about smoking, and in those two plants the smoking information was collected in the 1980s. To me, it is simply unimaginable that in a study that ended up focused on respiratory cancers so little information was obtained about smoking, which is associated with some 90 percent of respiratory cancer. In particular, there is no information about the smoking rates in men who died before the 1980s, who are, after all, the source of much of the data in a mortality study.

The IOM committee's conclusions about prostate cancer and

para-*dioxins and Polychlorinated Dibenzofurans* 69 (Lyon, France: IARC, 1997). Information about this publication can be found at www.iarc.fr/ by clicking on "IARC Press" and following prompts to a listing of the Monographs and scrolling to Monograph no. 69.

30. European Commission, Scientific Committee on Food, "Opinion of the Scientific Committee on Food on the Risk Assessment of Dioxins and Dioxin-Like PCBs in Food," Adopted on May 30, 2001. http://europa.eu.int/comm/food/fs/sc/scf/out90_en.pdf.

31. Food and Agricultural Organization of the United Nations, World Health Organization, Joint FAO-WHO Expert Committee on Food Additives, 57th Meeting, Rome, June 5–14, 2001. Summary and Conclusions. Annex 4: Contaminants. 3. Polychlorinated Dibenzodioxins, Polychlorinated Dibenzofurans, and Coplanar Polychlorinated Biphenyls. http://www.who.int/pcs/jecfa/Summary57-corr.pdf. pp. 24–40.

32. M. Fingerhut et al., "Cancer Mortality in Workers Exposed to 2,3,7,8-Tetrachlorodibenzo-*p*-dioxin," *N. Engl. J. Med.* 324 (1991): 212–18.

multiple myeloma were based on studies of farmers who reported spraying herbicides. There is no information in those studies about body burdens of dioxin, and limited and inconsistent efforts were made to investigate other exposures that might have contributed to cancer rates. Neither the EPA, the European Commission, IARC, nor WHO associates herbicides or dioxin with the occurrence of prostate cancer and multiple myeloma.

Based on the IOM committee's decisions about statistical associations, the Secretary of the VA established mechanisms to pay compensation to veterans for the diseases for which the IOM committee found sufficient or limited/suggestive evidence for associations with herbicides.[33]

OTA Fails to Raise its Voice

In the 1980s, in compliance with a congressional mandate, OTA was a major player in the Agent Orange controversy. My colleague, Hellen Gelband, and I organized an advisory panel of scientists, veterans, and representatives of chemical manufacturers to review the plans and, subsequently, the results from the CDC's studies of Vietnam veterans. We prepared written reports and testified before congressional committees about OTA's conclusions and recommendations. In general, OTA agreed with CDC's conclusions that there were no significant differences between Vietnam veterans' health and the health of other veterans and that there were no measurable exposures to Agent Orange among ground-troop veterans. Somewhat remarkably, although the IOM 1994 report "was reviewed by an independent panel of

33. Information about that compensation program can be found at http://www.vba.va.gov/bln/21/benefits/Herbicide/index.htm.

distinguished experts,"[34] not a single member of OTA's advisory panel or staff was asked to participate in the review.[35]

In 1985, I left OTA, and during 1986 through 1990, I worked at a consulting firm, Environ, and a middle-of-the-road think tank, Resources for the Future. My book *Dioxin, Agent Orange* was published in 1986, and I continued to do research related to dioxin and became more and more convinced that few if any Vietnam veterans had any exposure to dioxin beyond the level common in all people, and that there was no credible evidence that environmental exposures to dioxin caused health effects.[36]

From 1987 through 1990, I chaired the VA's Advisory Committee on Health-Related Effects of Herbicides, which, despite its name, was largely responsible for addressing veterans' complaints about VA health care. The committee probably had a lot

34. IOM, 1994, p. v.

35. IOM did not publish a list of reviewers. The comment that no OTA staff or panel member participated is based on Hellen Gelband's and my personal contacts.

36. See the following articles by M. Gough: "Dioxin Exposure at Monsanto," *Nature* 318 (1985): 404 (letter); "Environmental Epidemiology: Separating Science from Politics," *Issues in Sci. and Tech.* 3 (1987): 21–30; "From Plant Hormones to Agent Orange," *ChemMatters*, February 1988; "Past War: Future Risk?" *ChemMatters*, April 1988; "The Most Potent Carcinogen?" *Resources* 92 (1988): 2–5; "Science Policy Choices and Estimation of Cancer Risk Associated with TCDD," *Risk Analysis* 8 (1988): 337–42; "The Politics of Agent Orange," in A. Young and G. Reggiani, eds., *Agent Orange and Its Associated Dioxin: Assessment of a Controversy* (New York and Amsterdam: Elsevier, 1988), pp. 181–190; "Agent Orange Studies," *Science* 245 (1989): 1031 (letter); "Human Health Effects: What the Data Indicate," *Science of the Total Environ.* 104 (1991): 129–58; "Agent Orange: Exposure and Policy," *Am. J. Public Health* 81 (1991): 289–90 (editorial); "Human Exposure from Dioxin in Soil—A Meeting Report," *J. Tox. Environ. Health* 32 (1991): 205–45; "Reevaluating the Risks from Dioxin," *J. Regulation Social Costs* 1 (1991): 5–24. Also: M. Gough and D. Turnbull, "Use of a Threshold Model for the Estimation of Risk Associated with Exposure to Chlorinated Dibenzo-p-dioxins and Dibenzofurans," in H. A. Hattemer-Frey and C. C. Travis, eds., *Health Effects of Municipal Waste Incineration* (Boca Raton, Fla.: CRS Press, 1989), pp.20131–46.

to do when it was established in 1979, but by the late 1980s, the VA had improved its medical services. In 1990, I informed the Secretary of the DVA that I was going to resign from the chairmanship. I also explained to him that the committee, so far as I could see, had largely outlived its usefulness. The Secretary decided not to appoint another chairman and to dissolve the committee.

In 1990, I returned to OTA to manage one of its nine programs, and Roger Herdman, who was a deputy director at OTA in 1990, informed me that I would have no responsibility for OTA's continuing involvement with Agent Orange because of my well-known controversial positions.[37] (I was, however, appointed to chair the DHHS committee that advises the Air Force on its study of the health of the Ranch Hands in 1990. I resigned from that committee in 1995, but accepted a reappointment from DHHS Secretary Donna Shalala in 2000, and I continue to serve on it.)

Soon after the 1992 election, John H. Gibbons, who had been its director, left OTA to become the director of the Office of Science and Technology Policy (OSTP) in the White House, and Roger Herdman became the OTA director. When the IOM report was published, Gibbons called Herdman and asked if OTA was going to respond. Gibbons, correctly, saw that the IOM report contradicted everything that OTA had said for a decade. Herdman told me that he'd decided that OTA would say nothing. At the time,

---

37. As set forth in: M. Gough, "Dioxin: Perceptions, Estimates, and Measures," in K. R. Foster, D. Bernstein, and P. Huber, eds., *Phantom Risk: Scientific Inference and the Law* (Cambridge, Mass.: MIT Press, 1993), pp. 249–278; M. Boroush and M. Gough, "Can Cohort Studies Detect Any Human Cancer Excess That May Result from Exposure to Dioxin? Maybe," *Regul. Toxicol. and Pharmacol.* 20 (1994): 198–210; J. A. Moore, R. A. Kimbrough, and M. Gough, "The Dioxin TCDD: A Selective Study of Science and Policy Interaction," in M. F. Uman, ed., *Keeping Pace with Science and Engineering: Case Studies in Environmental Regulation* (Washington, D.C.: National Academy Press, 1993), pp. 221–42.

OTA was undergoing a Herdman-initiated reorganization that would result in my program and two others being eliminated, and I was more interested in trying to fight that than taking on the IOM. I didn't advise Herdman that OTA should take a stand.

When OTA didn't speak out, no one did. Other organizations no longer had a stake in Agent Orange. CDC was no longer involved in Agent Orange research. Neither were the chemical companies after the settlement (in 1984) of a lawsuit brought by Vietnam veterans against them.[38] Veterans and members of Congress welcomed the IOM conclusions as vindication. Soon, because no one objected to them, they were being touted as good science. And, of course, they weren't science at all, as IOM had said.

Associations "Keep on Comin' ": IOM Updates, 1996, 1998, and 2000

Public Law 102-4 directs IOM to publish biannual updates, which are to include new information about conclusions already reached, as well as information that supports additional associations between herbicides and diseases. IOM has formed somewhat different committees for each update, adhering to its criterion that committee members have taken no public position on the issue of herbicides and human health. This must be an increasingly difficult task.

Update 1996—Spina Bifida in Veterans' Children

If scientists considered the IOM reports to be of scientific value, the 1996 update would be among the most frequently cited doc-

---

38. Gough, *Dioxin*, pp. 83–87. The most complete coverage is in P. Schuck, *Agent Orange on Trial* (Cambridge, Mass.: Harvard University Press, 1986).

uments in the biomedical literature.[39] Scientists don't, and the report, according to the NAS Web site (11/27/01), is no longer sold.

The IOM update committee concluded that there is limited/ suggestive evidence that a man's exposure to an herbicide is associated with an increased risk of spina bifida in his children. This conclusion flies in the face of IOM's acknowledgment that there is no known mechanism by which a father's exposures can cause birth defects.[40]

Neither dioxin nor 2,4-D nor 2,4,5-T is a mutagen; therefore none of those agents can cause a mutation in the DNA that can be transferred in sperm from a father to a child. Dioxin, which remains in a person's body years after exposure, could possibly be transferred from a man to a woman via his sperm, but sperm are so tiny that the few molecules of dioxin in a sperm would have little effect on the number already in the far-larger egg. Moreover, doses of Agent Orange large enough to cause toxic effects in male mice did not cause birth defects in mice fathered by the treated animals.[41]

In reaching its conclusion about spina bifida, the IOM committee relied primarily on the results from the Ranch Hands. There was no difference in the frequency of all birth defects in the children of Ranch Hands and Comparisons.[42] There were, however, four neural tube defects—three cases of spina bifida and one

39. Institute of Medicine, *Veterans and Agent Orange: Update 1996* (Washington, D.C.: National Academy Press, 1997).

40. IOM, 1994, pp. 593–95.

41. J. C. Lamb, J. A. Moore, and T. A. Marks, "Evaluation of 2,4-dichlorophenoxyacetic Acid (2,4-D) and 2,4,5-trichlorophenoxyacetic Acid (2,4,5-T) and 2,3,7,8-tetrachlorodibenzo-p-dioxin (TCDD) Toxicity in C57BL-6 Mice," Publication NTP-80-44 (Research Triangle Park, N.C.: National Toxicology Program, 1980).

42. W. H. Wolfe et al., "Paternal Serum Dioxin and Reproductive Outcomes Among Veterans of Operation Ranch Hand," *Epidemiology* 6 (1995): 17–22.

case of anencephaly—among the children born to Ranch Hands, and none in the children born to the Comparisons.

Chance almost certainly explains the difference in the occurrence of the neural tube defects, as it explains many other results in epidemiology. For instance, many early studies of possible effects from exposures to herbicides reported increases in cleft lip and cleft palate (none of which was considered significant)[43] among children born to exposed parents. In contrast, there were five cases of cleft lip and cleft palate among the children born to the Comparisons and none in the children born to Ranch Hands. No one would argue that Agent Orange prevents cleft lip and palate based on this observation.

Chance is a far more likely explanation for the occurrence of four cases of neural tube defects among the Ranch Hand children as compared to zero cases among the Comparison children, just as it is the most likely explanation for the occurrence of five cleft lip/cleft palate cases among the Comparison children and their absence from Ranch Hand children. The alternative explanation that herbicides cause spina bifida and prevent cleft lip/cleft palate is not at all credible.

The authors of the Ranch Hand Study, the Department of Health and Human Services committee that reviewed the study before publication,[44] the reviewers and editors of the journal *Epidemiology* that published the study, and a scientist who wrote a comment about the Ranch Hand study for *Epidemiology* found no support for an association between herbicide exposure and any birth defect. Only the IOM committee identified the biologically implausible association.

On September 19, 1996, in testimony before the Senate Committee on Veterans' Affairs, I disagreed with the IOM committee's

43. See Gough, *Dioxin*, pp. 117–20 for references.
44. I chaired that committee at that time.

interpretation of the data: "Congress asked IOM for a scientific evaluation. The IOM committee did not behave as scientists; it attached too much importance to a single finding, ignored conflicting evidence, and produced an incorrect evaluation. I believe that it is wrong and unfair to base policy on flawed science."[45]

Visibly angry, Senator Jay Rockefeller of West Virginia, a strong advocate of veterans' claims about harms from Agent Orange, questioned my scientific qualifications, my motives, and my conclusions. He invited the chairman of the IOM committee back to the witness table to respond to my comments. The chairman declined, saying he didn't want to enter into a debate. Senator Rockefeller then directed IOM to present me with a written criticism of my remarks. More than six years have passed. I've seen nothing from the IOM.

The 1996 IOM committee made findings about other two diseases. The committee downgraded IOM's evaluation of the evidence for associations between herbicide exposures and the rare metabolic disease, porphyria cutanea tarda, from sufficient to limited/suggestive. Significantly, this decision indicates that the update committees can revise earlier classifications, but it makes no difference to VA compensation decisions.

The 1996 report also added acute and subacute transient peripheral neuropathy to the list of diseases for which there is limited/suggestive evidence of an association with herbicide exposures. The committee relied upon case reports—physicians' accounts of one or a few cases of neurological problems such as tingling in hands or feet—to support its conclusions. The committee makes it clear that the case reports lacked information about such critical measures as the patients' neurological status before exposure and about other possible exposures, but decided

---

45. M. Gough, "Testimony before Committee on Veterans' Affairs," U.S. Senate, September 19, 1996.

such deficits were not enough to set aside its finding of limited/ suggestive evidence for associations. This IOM decision will not affect VA compensation policies because any transient neuropathies would have occurred long ago and would not leave a veteran disabled.

The 1998 IOM Update—No Changes

The IOM committee in 1998 made no changes to the conclusions published in the earlier volumes.[46]

The 2000 IOM Updates

IOM produced two volumes about Agent Orange in 2000. One is a special report about herbicides and diabetes. The other is an update that added a childhood cancer to the list of diseases caused by parental exposures to herbicides.

Diabetes

Like the 1996 decision about spina bifida, the IOM committee's conclusion that there is limited/suggestive evidence for an association between herbicide exposure and adult onset diabetes[47] draws upon the results from the Ranch Hand study.[48] Although the frequency of diabetes among the Ranch Hands and the Comparisons is essentially equal, in 1992, the Air Force showed a video tape to participants in the Ranch Hand health study that stated

46. Institute of Medicine, *Veterans and Agent Orange: Update 1998* (Washington, D.C.: National Academy Press, 1999).

47. Institute of Medicine, *Veterans and Agent Orange: Herbicide/Dioxin Exposure and Type 2 Diabetes* (Washington, D.C.: National Academy Press, 2000).

48. G. L. Henrikson et al., "Serum Dioxin and Diabetes Mellitus in Veterans of Operation Ranch Hand," *Epidemiology* 8 (1997): 252–58.

that an association was present between Agent Orange and diabetes.[49]

The maximum body burden of dioxin in the Comparisons is 55 ppt (parts per trillion of dioxin in fat taken from a blood sample), about ten times less than the maximum of 618 ppt in the Ranch Hands, but the incidence of diabetes is the same in both populations. The IOM 2000 committee's report about diabetes is masterful. It emphasizes every factoid that can be interpreted to support its conclusion about a limited/suggestive association and brushes aside all the contradictory information. Based on the committee's finding of a limited/suggestive association, the DVA is paying compensation to Vietnam veterans who have diabetes.

Childhood Leukemia

Making reference to a study of U.S. veterans who reported that they had served in Vietnam and to a study of Australian veterans of the Vietnam war, the IOM committee concluded that fathers' exposures could increase the occurrence of acute myelogenous leukemia in their children.[50] The IOM committee conceded that there is no information about exposure to herbicides in either study, and it ignored the data from the Ranch Hand study, which showed no excess of leukemias during the first eighteen years of the lives of Ranch Hand children.

The conclusion about acute myelogenous leukemia has the same biological implausibility as the conclusion about spina bifida. Because dioxin is not a mutagen, it is very difficult to imagine how a father's exposure to it could affect his child.

To its credit, the IOM, in 2002, reversed its decision that linked

49. I saw this videotape at the Scripps Clinic, La Jolla, California, when the 1992 medical examination was being administered.
50. Institute of Medicine, *Veterans and Agent Orange: Update 2000* (Washington, D.C.: National Academy Press, 2000).

veterans' exposures to Agent Orange with leukemia in their children because of the discovery of a computational error in one of the studies of veterans' children.[51] The IOM reversal is a welcome change because it eliminates a linkage that was drawn with no information about exposures and no hypothesis about cause and effect.

Summary of IOM Findings

The IOM committees have not provided scientific advice to Congress. Rather than looking at the data as scientists typically do to look for evidence of causality, it has picked and chosen data. A decision that limited/suggestive data for an association exists when "at least one high-quality study shows a positive association, but the results of other studies are inconsistent."[52] As I stated in my testimony before the Senate Veterans' Affairs Committee,

> ... focus on results from "one high-quality study" flies in the face of objective science that requires that all data be considered and weighed together. In fact, it literally throws out any consideration of data that do not support an association because it lets the analysts focus on a single, isolated finding as the proof of their case. Associations can arise by chance . . . [or for reasons not considered in a study], and this criterion [one high-quality study] places undue weight on them. This criterion is bad science. Congress did not, as is sometimes suggested, force it on IOM. IOM set its own criteria.

Congress asked IOM for scientific advice. It also asked for a discussion of judgments about statistical associations, but it did not preclude the IOM from behaving as scientists.

---

51. IOM, "Revised Analysis Leads to Different Conclusion About Agent Orange Exposure and Childhood Leukemia," press release, February 27, 2002. News@nas.edu.
52. IOM, 1994, p. 7.

Agent Orange and Dioxin Decisions:
Political or Scientific?

The most damning indictment of the IOM committee's deliberations and conclusions came early in March 2002, at a meeting
about Agent Orange in Hanoi. At that meeting, contrasts were
drawn between the compensation that is being paid to American
veterans and the absence of compensation for Vietnam citizens.
Christopher Portier, director of the Environmental Toxicology
Program at the National Institute of Environmental Health Sciences, dismissed U.S. decisions to compensate U.S. veterans for
"Agent Orange–related diseases" as "political."[53]

Remarkably, Portier has provided some of the risk assessments for EPA's efforts to label dioxin as a human cancer risk and
to calculate risks from environmental exposures to dioxin. I don't
know why he dismisses the IOM committee's very similar opinions about the health effects of Agent Orange as "political," but I
agree with him.

What IOM Should Do

The IOM committees are much clearer about what they don't do
than about what they do do. The 2000 *Update* says: "Consistent
with the mandate of P.L. 102-4, the distinctions between categories are based on 'statistical association,' not on causality, as is
common in scientific reviews. Thus, standard criteria used in
epidemiology for assessing causality [reference omitted] do not
strictly apply."[54] It leaves unsaid what criteria do apply.

53. "U.S. Scientists Question Vietnam Dioxin Studies," Reuters, March 4,
2002. I subsequently called Dr. Portier and asked him if he had made the
"political" remark. He confirmed that he had. Personal communication, telephone call, April 30, 2002.
54. IOM, *Update 2000*, p. 6.

IOM committees are to revisit all the IOM's earlier decisions in each of their updates. If Congress or NAS and IOM management are serious about the IOM committees' doing a scientific review of the literature about health risks from herbicides, it can insist on the committees' addressing the following issues.

Exposure

IOM should state why it does not rely on body burden measurements, which is the norm in dioxin research.[55] Short of that, IOM committees should clearly state—when referring to "exposed populations"—which exposures have been verified by body burden measurements and which have not. The reader would then be able to decide which studies discussed by the IOM committees have any validity.

What Is the Subject of the IOM Reviews?

Given the IOM's acknowledgment that there is no information that any of the herbicides used in Vietnam is a risk to human health, what is IOM examining? If the only possible culprit is dioxin, that should be stated, and IOM committees should stop talking about associations with herbicides and talk about associations with dioxin. If there is a reason—from animal studies, mechanistic (biochemical and molecular biology) studies, or epidemiology studies with careful control of other risk factors—that an herbicide should be considered risky, IOM would provide a great service by identifying it.

---

55. IOM has issued a number of contracts to develop methods to estimate exposures to Agent Orange in Vietnam. I consider all those contracts to be a waste of time and money. Enough is known about the body burdens of dioxin in veterans to conclude that few—if any—ground troops were exposed.

Cancer

IOM should re-examine its decision that there is sufficient evidence for associations between herbicides and soft-tissue sarcoma, non-Hodgkin's leukemia, and Hodgkin's disease, beginning with an examination of Hardell's exposure classification scheme. Hardell's own analysis showed that workers he had classified as exposed had the same low body burdens as found in people who were classified as unexposed. The IOM should ask experts on cancer mechanisms and cancer cause and prevention to review the Hardell and other studies about herbicides and those tumors.

IOM's conclusion about a link between herbicides and respiratory cancer depends on studies of highly exposed workers in which exposures have been verified by body burden measurements. Thomas Starr analyzed the relationships between dioxin exposures and cancer rates in those workers.[56] Although exposures varied over a 1,500-fold range, cancer rates did not increase at higher dioxin exposures, providing no support for an association.

The IOM committees should discuss all that is known about cancer rates in human populations highly exposed to dioxin and the capacity of epidemiologic studies to detect dioxin-associated cancers if they do occur. I am convinced that this task, if done with scientific objectivity, would weaken any interpretations that dioxin causes human cancers.

Spina Bifida

In my testimony before the Senate Veterans' Affairs Committee, I assumed that the IOM conclusion was correct, that the spina bifida

---

56. Starr, "Significant Shortcomings."

cases seen in the Ranch Hand children had been caused by dioxin, and that there is a relationship between dioxin exposure levels and the occurrence of spina bifida. Based on those assumptions, I calculated the number of spina bifida cases to be expected in a population of about 37,000 people in and around Seveso, Italy, who were exposed to dioxin from a 1976 chemical plant accident, and who have the highest-ever measured dioxin levels. Twelve years later, an analysis was published of 15,000 births in the Seveso area after the accident.[57] I calculated that between seven and nineteen spina bifida cases would have been expected in the 15,000 Seveso births. There was none, indicating that there is no connection between maternal or paternal exposures to dioxin and spina bifida.

Diabetes

It is clear that there is no causative association between dioxin and diabetes because very different levels of exposures to dioxin in the Comparisons and the Ranch Hands are associated with similar frequencies of diabetes. How are those data to be interpreted?

It's Not Science: What Is It?

Rather than bypass its obligation to provide the Congress with scientific advice, the IOM should seize opportunities to revisit decisions of its committees that have evaluated the evidence that Agent Orange harmed U.S. troops. The 2002 update cannot be a vehicle for a scientific evaluation; it is already complete (or nearly so). The 2004 update, which, unless Congress enacts new legislation, will be the final update, could be the vehicle for scientific

57. P. Mastroiacovo et al., "Birth Defects in the Seveso Area After TCDD Contamination," *JAMA* 259 (1988): 1668–1972.

review. Whether revisiting the decisions does or does not cause revisions, applying scientific criteria to its decisions would refurbish IOM's reputation as a scientific organization.

The Lesson To Be Drawn from Agent Orange and, Maybe, a Different Lesson To Be Drawn from Dioxin

The absence of dissent from the IOM report provides an important lesson about the power of government. When government, either Congress and its agent, the IOM, in the case of Agent Orange, or the Executive Branch, through EPA, in the case of dioxin, decides that a risk exists, it can exert and maintain continued effort to convince the public to agree with it. Year after year, the government hires additional people to work on the risk. Year after year, those people produce more and more documents. With the passage of time, organizations that might oppose the government drop out because of expense or because they move on to other things. Few people remain to dissent, to say the risk is exaggerated or, even, nonexistent.

That's the way the world is. The amazing part is that anyone tries to thwart the government's risk assessments.

Agent Orange

In the case of both Agent Orange and dioxin, the organizations that faced financial losses have gone on to other things. Agent Orange, except for probably adding more diseases to the list of diseases eligible for compensation, and certainly extending the lists of compensated veterans, is settled.

Dioxin

For about two decades, EPA has produced assessments of the risks from dioxin that claim the chemical is a cause of human cancers and other diseases and that current background exposures may be causing those effects. The EPA's Science Advisory Board (SAB) rejected key parts of EPA's 2000 dioxin reassessment.[58]

Importantly, the SAB includes members who have taken public positions on the risk or non-risk from dioxin; the SAB allows conflicts of interest. In my opinion, that's why the EPA's claims —as compared with the IOM's statements about associations between Agent Orange and diseases—have been rejected. Experts, on both sides, and experts with conflicts of interest, on both sides, produce a far more objective review of the scientific information than experts who are chosen for having no opinions.

Until recently, I thought that EPA would brush away the criticisms, say that it has the SAB's approval of all but a few details, and continue saying that dioxin in the environment causes human health effects. Now, I'm not so sure. Christopher Portier's characterization of the IOM conclusions as "political" will surely damage EPA's case because EPA depends on the same data considered by the IOM and interprets it similarly. Moreover, a new dissenting voice has arisen. The Agency for Toxic Substances and Disease Registry (ATSDR) in the Department of Health and Human Services pointedly disagrees with EPA's methods for estimating risks of cancer and other health effects from dioxin and rejects the EPA's suggestion that current exposures to dioxin may be causing adverse health effects.[59] I do not know what will result from ATSDR's disagreeing with EPA, but it may mark a crack in EPA's setting the government's dioxin agenda.

58. Science Advisory Board, Environmental Protection Agency, *Dioxin Reassessment—An SAB Review of the Office of Research and Development's Reassessment of Dioxin* (Washington, D.C.: USEPA, 2001). (EPA-SAB-EC-01-006 May 2001). Available at www.epa.gov/sab.

59. H. R. Pohl et al., "Public Health Perspectives on Dioxin Risks: Two Decades of Evaluations," *Human and Ecological Risk Assessment* 8 (2002): 233–50.

NINE

Science and Politics in the Regulation of Chemicals in Sweden

ROBERT NILSSON

After the end of World War II, science was a major organizing factor in Sweden's focusing attention on possible health and environmental risks from humans' discharge of chemicals into the environment. For many decades, Sweden has been hailed as an enviable example of how effective environmental policies based on sound expertise can be implemented to the benefit of its inhabitants, and in many respects this reputation is well deserved. For instance, it is now possible to catch salmon from bridges in Stockholm, and a steady stream of delegations from other nations has arrived to learn more about the Swedish model for environmental protection.

However, over the years, as environmentalism passed from scientists' hands to "green" nongovernmental organizations (NGOs) and to politicians eager to capture votes, impartial science of high quality became less and less important, and the Swedish regulatory machinery devoted more and more of its energy toward eliminating insignificant or hypothetical risks from chemical exposures. Basing its policies on an extreme interpretation of the precautionary principle (PP), this country has imposed some of the strictest regulations of chemicals in the world. Sweden's membership in the European Union (EU) (since 1995) has caused some changes, which may point to a more realistic assessment of chemical risks, but attempts by Swedish regulatory agencies to undercut EU regulations and directives, as well as political pressures to withdraw from the EU, threaten many of these improvements.

Many overly stringent Swedish regulations impose burdens on the country's citizens and harm the economy, while providing no or little improvement in health, safety, or the environment. Other countries, considering the possible effects of tying their policies to the PP, should study its effects in Sweden.

Science in the Emergence of Swedish Environmental Policy

The scientific community provided much of the original impetus for improved environmental protection in Sweden. Swedish scientists, for instance, focused attention on the health hazards from organic mercury compounds used in agriculture several years before the Minimata poisonings in Japan brought those problems to the attention of the rest of the world.[1] The Swedish chemist Sören Jensen was the first to describe the bioaccumulation properties of PCBs, and the pioneering radiation and biochemical re-

1. C.-G. Rosén, H. Ackefors, and R. Nilsson, "Seed Dressing Compounds Based on Organic Mercury—Economic Aspects and Health Hazards," *Svensk Kemisk Tidskrift* 78, no. 8 (1966): 8–19.

search of Lars Ehrenberg in the early 1970s opened up new approaches for quantitative determination of risk for mutations and cancer.[2]

Indeed, many scientists were closely allied with the founders of the Swedish environmental movement, and, along with the media, were instrumental in overcoming industry and government reluctance to adopt a more progressive and responsible attitude toward environmental protection. More basically, many respected scientists furnished the technical arguments that provided the foundations for improved protection of the environment.

A decade of balanced and gradual progress in reducing and regulating exposures to chemical hazards that began in the 1960s, which was largely based on scientific principles, was given additional stimulus after the Swedish producer of the sedative thalidomide (Neurosedyn), Astra, accepted responsibility for compensating for the malformations in children caused by their mothers' intake of its product.[3] The decade was not without some notable exceptions to the wise use of science, including the dioxin hysteria in the 1970s that provoked the Swedish Parliament to directly intervene, restrict, and later ban many of the chlorinated phenoxy herbicides in 1977.

In the late 1970s, there was a noticeable change in the policymakers' general attitude as questions arose about environmental causes of cancer, and the Swedish government commissioned a group of Sweden's most prominent scientists, led by the Nobel

2. S. Jensen, "Report of a New Chemical Hazard," *New Scientist* 32 (1966): 612; L. Ehrenberg et al., "Evaluation of Genetic Risks of Alkylating Agents; Tissue Doses in the Mouse from Air Contaminated with Ethylene Oxide," *Mutation Research* 24 (1974): 83–103. See also Anon., "Cover Legend on Lars Ehrenberg," *Cancer Research* 47 (September 15, 1987).

3. H. Sjöström and R. Nilsson, *Thalidomide and the Power of the Drug Companies* (London: Penguin Books, 1971).

Prize laureate in medicine, Sune Bergström, to assess the causes
of cancer among the Swedish population and to suggest preventive measures. The conclusions of the Swedish Cancer Committee,[4] in which I participated as a member of the Committee staff,
were not what the politicians had expected, and some were apparently disappointed, even dismayed by the scientists' conclusions. What activist politician could expect to win votes by revealing that sunbathing, for example, is a more significant cause
of cancer than industrial chemicals, pesticides, and air pollution?
They could publicize, of course, that smoking was bad, but they
were not eager to convey the message that diet is one of the most
important factors in developing or avoiding cancer, and that genetic susceptibility is also a major determinant of cancer risks.

Politics Takes Over

Regrettably, in spite of significant progress in toxicology and risk
assessment, science has gradually become less important in shap-
ing Swedish national policy for chemicals control. Worse still,
good science plays an ever smaller role in influencing the environmental movement, which to a large extent has been hijacked
by extremists. Many respected naturalists, instead of concentrat-
ing on the conservation of wildlife and other aspects of the natural
environment where they made major contributions, have elected
to busy themselves with complex toxicological problems for
which they have little or no training. With respect to chemical
risks, environmental pressure groups nowadays mostly preach a
primitive "eco-fundamentalism" based on ignorance of the scientific issues involved, with little understanding of the economics

4. Swedish Cancer Committee (SCC), *Cancer—Causes and Prevention,
Report to the Ministry of Social Affairs from the Cancer Committee* (Stockholm: SOU, 1984), p. 67. English translation.

of a society that provides them with all the basic conveniences and luxuries that they actively consume.

By tradition, Swedish government agencies are to act autonomously to implement the laws enacted by parliament. In recent years, however, ministers have increasingly interfered with the daily work of the agencies directly or indirectly through political appointments of managers on several levels. As a result, the central agency for chemicals control, the National Swedish Chemicals Inspectorate (KEMI), has become a powerful instrument for the promotion of the extremist green ideology favored by the Social Democrats who have been in power almost continually since World War II.

Politicians learned a lesson from the SCC report,[5] and twelve years later, in 1996, the Swedish Ministry of Environment appointed a "Chemicals Committee" chaired by the Social Democrat Kerstin Svensson to develop the basis for Sweden's chemical regulation policies. All of the committee's five delegates were politicians. Why should they bother to ask the Royal Swedish Academy of Sciences, or the world-famous Karolinska Institute, which selects nominees for the Nobel Prize in Medicine, to recommend scientists to assist in their work? Forget it! The task of assessing the *Panorama of Risks from Chemicals* was given to a consulting firm with little knowledge of toxicology.[6] Although the jumbled group of "experts" assisting the committee included some scientists, with few exceptions the scientists appeared to have been little more than hostages with limited possibilities to influence the main focus of the committee's work. Among other recommendations, the committee proposed that PVC (polyvinylchlo-

5. Ibid.
6. Statens Offentiga Utredningar (SOU), *Towards a Sustainable Chemicals Policy*, Swedish Government Public Reports Series (1997): 84, plus Annex I (in Swedish).

ride, one of the most commonly used plastics) as well as all so-called "endocrine disruptors" should be totally eliminated. The report paid no attention to the fact that oral contraceptives are the most powerful "endocrine disruptors" ever produced by industry for general use.

The Swedish Royal Academy of Sciences, the Royal Academy of Engineering Sciences, and other professional organizations scathingly criticized the committee's 1997 report *Towards a Sustainable Chemicals Policy*.[7] Expert criticism meant little to the Minister of Environment at that time (now Minister of Foreign Affairs), Anna Lindh, who, in the case of the alleged dangerous properties of PVC, declared that she had more confidence in Greenpeace than in the Academy of Sciences.

Her predecessor on the chair as Minister of Environment and Energy, Birgitta Dahl (now speaker for the Parliament), had shown the way almost a decade earlier. In April 1989, in front of an audience from the Stockholm Worker's Commune, Mrs. Dahl claimed that automobile emissions had passed cigarette smoking as the main cause of lung cancer in Sweden! The SCC appointed by Mrs. Dahl's own party comrades had found that air pollution accounted for not more than about one percent of all cancers in the Swedish population. But why should a Minister of Environment bother about checking scientific information?

The Chemical Committee's recommendations became the ideological basis for some of the most extreme chemical regulation laws in the world that culminated in the bizarre left-wing slogan "An Environment Free of Poisons" ("*En Giftfri Miljö*"). In 1999, the red-green majority of the Swedish Parliament transferred this misnomer,[8] which brings back concepts from the Mid-

---

7. Ibid.
8. Swedish Ministry of Environment, *An Environment Free of Poisons* (Government Report MJU6, 1998–99).

dle Ages, into a general political goal for the Swedish society. As pointed out centuries ago by Paracelsus in his treatise *Septem Defensiones* (written 1537–38), any chemical substance can be a poison when the dose is sufficiently high. According to the parliamentary decision of 1999, the levels of *all* anthropogenic substances in the environment "should be close to zero."

Naturally, such follies have a political background. At the level of the Swedish Parliament, the "green" block, consisting of the Environmental Party and the likewise environmentalist Center Party, exerts a substantial political influence. The Swedish "Greens" control a sufficient number of members of parliament that they can swing votes in favor either of the Social Democrats or the liberal/conservatives, endowing the Greens with clout out of all proportion to their numbers.

Reasons for Environmental Extremism in Sweden

Political influence on agency actions are part and parcel of policies in all developed nations, but the effect of environmental extremism on policy is more pronounced in Sweden than in most other countries. Why so?

Sweden has a strong tradition of cherishing unspoiled nature, based on a romanticism of the past that holds sway among prominent Swedish industrialists as well as among intellectuals, and it has promoted traditional environmental protection as well as the introduction of stringent emission controls to benefit the quality of life. However, these basically benign tendencies have been pushed to extremity by the following additional elements:

1. The high level of public concern about environmental protection, especially with regard to "environmental poisons"

2. An omnipresent, centralized, and highly politicized regula-

tory bureaucracy combined with an imbalance of power among regulators, industry, and private interests

3. Lack of coherent national technically based strategies for risk assessment coupled with regulatory emphasis on inherent properties (hazard), regardless of the probability that adverse effects will actually occur (risk level)

4. A mistaken belief that efficiency in chemicals control is proportional to the number of bans and restrictions imposed

5. A firm conviction about the unmatched excellence of the Swedish model for environmental protection, combined with a crusading spirit directed at convincing an ignorant and callous world to adopt it

In comparison with most other industrialized nations, Sweden has relatively few serious environmental problems, but I believe, as do many others,[9] that the level of risk acceptance is particularly low in large sectors of the Swedish population. Indeed, many pampered Swedish citizens, who have not experienced major natural disasters or war since Napoleonic times, appear to carry around their own personal "worry box" described by the American humorist Patrick F. McManus: "It's as though a person has a little psychic box that he feels compelled to keep filled with worries. When one worry disappears from the box, he immediately replaces it with another worry, so the box is always full. He is never short of worries."[10]

Swedish politicians more or less openly admit that the concerns of the most risk-adverse people, rather than objective measures of risk, guide their policies directed at chemicals. Such pol-

9. V. Bernson, "The Swedish Experience," *Regul. Toxicol. Pharmacol.* 17 (1993): 249–61.

10. P. F. McManus, *The Good Samaritan Strikes Again* (New York: Henry Holt, 1992), p. 1.

icy-guiding concerns are not limited to Sweden, of course. The chapters by Bruce Ames and Lois Gold and by Stephen Safe in this volume document the misguided attention focused on synthetic as opposed to natural carcinogens and on synthetic "endocrine disruptors" as opposed to natural ones in the United States.

Only a limited fraction of the total national budget is available for risk prevention, and regulatory efforts should obviously be conducted in the most cost-effective manner. However, instead of making an attempt to distinguish between significant and insignificant risks, Swedish regulators too often yield to pressures from environmental organizations, accentuating the trend toward an increasing lack of rationality in risk management to the detriment of progress in modern society. In the context of a different risk (radiation), Chauncey Starr recently aptly portrayed the possible impacts of such decisions: ". . . this example illustrates that the moral high ground assumed by well-meaning activists for single health causes may well be socially immoral, when evaluated by the welfare of the total population."[11]

Each regulatory action, based solely, or mostly, on public "concern" and ignoring actual levels of risk, strengthens the public's belief in its risk perceptions as absolute justification for political and regulatory actions. The layman critical of experts will exclaim, "You see, it was dangerous—we were right after all!"

Scientists' Responsibilities

It would be unfair to blame biased environmental policies entirely on ill-educated laymen, opportunistic bureaucrats, and politi-

---

11. C. Starr, "Hypothetical Fears and Quantitative Risk Analysis," *Risk Analysis* 21 (2001): 803–6.

cians. The scientific community shares in the responsibility, in particular when researchers with little knowledge of toxicology act far outside their own field of competence and provide fallacious interpretations of their results, while shamelessly exploiting the news media to promote their own interests. In the September 3, 2001, issue of Sweden's largest daily newspaper, *Dagens Nyheter*, four well-known scientists from the Karolinska Institute and one from the University of Lund blasted "scientists who talk rubbish" in the media so that "the legitimacy of science is abused and the general public misled."

Scientists who stop well short of talking rubbish may overextend interpretation of their own data in order to secure continued funding in certain "grant-dense" areas like health risks from chemicals. In a commentary in the U.S. journal *Science*, one scientist affiliated with the prestigious U.S. National Institute of Environmental Health Sciences bluntly stated: "Investigators who find an effect get support, and investigators who don't find an effect don't get support. When times are tough it becomes extremely difficult for investigators to be objective."[12]

The quest for funding can lead to some unholy alliances between scientists and regulators and the creation of "cash cows" for researchers. If, for example, the dioxin or the PCB issues were defused, several laboratories that for decades have specialized in dioxin and PCB-related research, successfully milking agency and other sources for support, could lose their cash cows.

An Example of Swedish Overregulation

In some important respects, the Swedish legal system differs from that found in almost all democracies. Swedish citizens do not have

12. G. Taubes, "Epidemiology Faces Its Limits," *Science* 269 (1995): 164–69.

the right to go before an independent court if they believe a new law or regulation does not conform with the provisions of the Swedish Constitution. Further, in some types of civil cases there is no possibility for private citizens or regulated industry to ask for judicial review of a government agency decision by an impartial tribunal that is independent of the government.

The absence of judicial review and of independent, external scrutiny of regulatory agencies, combined with the small size and relative political impotence of Sweden's chemical industry and the strong anti-industry sentiment in important parts of the public sector, have produced overzealous regulation of chemicals. This state of affairs is almost perfectly demonstrated in the following example.

Several years ago, Vibeke Bernson, in charge of pesticide registrations in Sweden, rejected an application for registration of a pesticide that contained a natural plant growth hormone. The hormone, marketed worldwide, is used in small quantities to stimulate root formation in cuttings of woody and ornamental plants. Mrs. Bernson rejected the application, not because of potential health and environmental hazards, but because she thought that the product was "unnecessary." From the point of view of the national economy this was certainly true. However, for a handful of farmers who had invested much of their own money in greenhouse cultivation of ornamental plants, the availability of these growth promoters was important. The sole consequence of turning down the Swedish growers' application for registration was to give the growers in other countries, especially the Netherlands, a significant competitive advantage.

Swedish Law and Civil Rights

Commenting on the Swedish nation, Charles de Gaulle is once supposed to have exclaimed, "What a wonderful people to rule!"

Looking at Sweden's state bureaucracy from his perspective, as the head of a government, I would totally agree. Housed in spacious modern offices and supported by the latest advances in information technology, Sweden's civil servants are generally efficient, much more so than in most other countries, including the United States; they are dutiful in the extreme and probably among the least corrupt (in the classical sense) in the whole world. However, there is a downside to the efficiency of the Swedish state machinery.

In most democracies, the right of citizens and industry to appeal regulatory decisions before an independent court is an important safeguard against arbitrary execution of government power. In Sweden, these rights are very much restricted. Although the Central Office for Government Auditing ("*Riksrevisionsverket*") assesses the performance of government agencies, the audits are mainly fiscal in nature, and the auditing agency's operation is not guaranteed independent from the government. Thus, there exists no professional and independent body empowered to judge agency policy or performance.

Overall, Sweden has an excellent record for most civil liberties, and the prime minister, Göran Persson, boasts of his aim to make Sweden an "ethical superpower." Sadly, however, Sweden's exemplary performance in most areas of civil rights does not extend to all aspects of the Convention on Human Rights. In particular, Sweden does not guarantee its citizens the right to a hearing of appeals to certain types of government actions.

According to Article 6 Sec.1 of *The Convention for the Protection of Human Rights and Fundamental Freedoms*, ratified by Sweden in 1950, ". . . everyone is entitled to a fair and public hearing within reasonable time by an independent and impartial tribunal established by law."

In this context, the European Court of Human Rights, which has jurisdiction over the Convention, has noted:

47. Generally speaking, the Swedish administration is not subject to supervision by the ordinary courts. Those courts hear appeals against the State only in contractual matters, on questions of extra-contractual liability and, under some statutes, in respect of administrative decisions.

48. Judicial review of the administration's acts is, therefore, primarily a matter for administrative courts. (*Sporrong and Lönnroth v. The Government of Sweden*—Case no. 1/1981/40/58-59).

Sweden's failure to have citizens' complaints judged "by an independent and impartial tribunal" has contributed to the European Court of Human Rights handing down eighteen indictments under Sec. 6-1 of the Convention against the Swedish Government. Although Austria (another European nation that has been dominated by Social Democrats since World War II) is burdened by thirty-five and Italy by twenty-seven indictments, Sweden's place as the number three offender in Europe against these basic articles of the Convention on Human Rights is not flattering for a would-be "ethical superpower."

General Legislation on Environment Protection

The fundamental goal of Sweden's *Unified Environment Code* enacted in 1999 is "to establish the prerequisites for sustainable development in society,"[13] and it applies to all human activities that have *potential* negative consequences with respect to health or the environment. The Code introduced several novel features, integrated a number of previous acts dealing with various aspects of environmental protection, including chemicals control, and calls for the Swedish Environmental Protection Agency, which is

---

13. Statens Författningssamlingar (SFS), *The Unified Environment Code* (SFS 1988:808, 1998).

responsible for implementation of the Code, to use the best available techniques for environmental protection.

The Code created separate regional Environmental Courts, and an independent Environmental Appellate Court, which can hear appeals from the Environmental Courts. The Code also allows for appeals from the Environmental Appellate Court to the Supreme Environmental Court.

For certain types of regulatory decisions—licensing emissions from industries, waste-treatment facilities, road constructions, water protection, and so on—the Code represents a marked improvement of private rights in Sweden as defined by Article 6, Sec.1 of the Convention. On the other hand, the Environmental Courts will not hear objections to restrictions issued by KEMI concerning, for instance, pesticide use, household chemicals, or other chemical products in trade. In the area of chemicals regulation, there remains no provision for taking challenges to an independent court of justice in Sweden, leaving appeals to the Court of Justice of the European Union in Luxembourg as the only option.

Swedish Precaution-Based Regulation of Chemicals

I recently asked an employee of KEMI working with the EU program charged with classifying and labeling chemical substances why Sweden always takes the most extreme position toward the harshest possible classification. The answer, "Because of the precautionary principle (PP)," made me think about the meaning of the PP. At first glance, this concept seems appealing. It makes sense to "look before you leap"; it is "better to be safe than sorry."

The prevention of the introduction of thalidomide by the U.S. Food and Drug Administration (FDA) as well as by regulators of what was then East Germany (DDR) provides an example of justifiable precautionary action. Across the world, thalidomide (trade names, Contergan, Kevadon, Distaval, Neurosedyn, etc.) caused more than 10,000 severely malformed children to be born to mothers who had used the drug during pregnancy. In both the United States and the DDR, inadequate documentation about the results of toxicological testing raised government scientists' suspicions about the safety of the drug, and on December 31, 1960, the *British Medical Journal* published an alert that thalidomide induced polyneuritis. The producers of the drug had earlier failed to make a frank disclosure about the side effect,[14] and both the U.S. and the DDR agencies had raised questions about the safety of use of thalidomide during pregnancy.[15] The U.S. and DDR decisions, based on precaution, saved thousands of babies from being born with malformations.

Sweden's restrictions on cadmium provide another example of justifiable precaution. Elevated cadmium levels in crops become a human health risk because ingested cadmium causes a progressive accumulation of the metal in the kidney cortex, eventually causing tissue damage. The success of the Swedish restrictions was measured as reversals in the progressive build-up of the metal in the environment.[16]

Well before the PP became a political slogan, government agencies and the chemical industry built precaution into risk management decisions. A decision by a chemical company not to market a potentially hazardous product is seldom if ever publicized, but the world would certainly have experienced a large number of additional severe accidents from chemicals if precaution had not prevailed among responsible industry decision mak-

---

14. Food and Drug Administration (FDA), letter, May 5, 1961.

15. Sjöström and Nilsson, *Thalidomide.*

16. R. Nilsson, *Cadmium—An Analysis of Swedish Regulatory Experience, Report to the OECD Chemicals Group and Management Committee* (Paris: January 1989).

ers. Swedish regulators rarely acknowledge such contributions to public health and safety from the chemical industry. Quite the contrary! On July 12, 2000, one of KEMI's top-ranking Social Democratic managers gave the following revealing message about his opinion of scientists associated with industry:

> It is my opinion that scientists (not scientists in general) during previous years have, to a strikingly high degree contributed to chemical uses with an impact that has completely justified many citizens' concerns. I am speaking about "scientists" who, like other lackeys, have done what their master, industry, told them to do without devoting one single thought to health and environment. I suppose that money is the driving force. I am not at all convinced that we can expect any significant initiatives from that quarter to achieve improved health and environment, rather to the contrary.[17]

According to J. Morris, German civil servants coined the term "precautionary principle" ("das Vorsorgeprinzip") in the 1970s,[18] but I have been unable to find much of a useful legal reference or definition that would be of any help to a judge in attempting to apply the PP. Indeed, the EU Commission's Economic and Social Committee noted that there are as yet few legal bases for a precautionary principle and that case law is still in its infancy.[19] Further, explicit and implicit allusion to this principle does not provide a solid base, and the Committee asked that the Commission submit a concrete and viable case soon.[20]

---

17. KEMI, Letter by e-mail from B. Lindwall to R. Nilsson, July 12, 2000. (In KEMI public record.)

18. J. Morris, *Rethinking Risk and the Precautionary Principle* (Oxford: Butterworth-Heinemann, 2000), pp. 1–21.

19. The Economic and Social Committee of the EU Commission (ESC), "Comments to the European Commission with Respect to Implementing the Precautionary Principle," *Official Journal of the European Community C 268*, 11 (September 19, 2000).

20. Ibid.

The Committee drew attention to the fact that the PP allows authorities to extend their "policing powers," and that the implementation of this concept will have major implications at the international level inasmuch as: "It enables countries to temporarily suspend their free trade commitments. The precautionary principle gives countries a sovereign right—and makes them the sole arbiter—on matters affecting the safety of their nationals. There is thus a stark contradiction with the EU Treaty."[21]

The Swedish Ministry of Environment's commentaries to the Swedish *Act on Chemical Products* of 1985 (SFS, 1985) incorporated the basic concepts of the PP into Swedish legal doctrine,[22] but it was first put forward as a legally binding doctrine in the Swedish *Unified Environmental Code* of 1998:

> 3 § Anyone who carries out, or intends to carry out, an activity or action of whatever nature shall undertake protective measures, follow restrictions and undertake such precautions in general to prevent or counteract that the activity or action in question results in damage or inconvenience with respect to human health or environment. With the same aim, any professional activity shall use the best available technique. These precautionary measures must be undertaken as soon as there is reason to believe that an activity or measure can cause harm or *inconvenience* with respect to human health or to the environment. [Emphasis added][23]

The legal text actually uses the term "inconvenience" ("*olägenhet*"), because the unified code covers everything from protecting the ozone layer to the manufacture and marketing of chemicals, the recycling of beer cans, or the building of a golf course. Recognizing that unfettered application of the law could

---

21. Ibid.
22. *Statens Författningssamlingar* (SFS), *Act on Chemical Products* (SFS 1985: 426, 1985b).
23. SFS, 1998.

result in a complete paralysis of Swedish society, many legal experts, including the government's own legal council, harshly criticized the original proposal for the new proposed Swedish legislation. As a result of the criticisms, the code that was adopted incorporates a clause calling for some kind of proportionality between action and the desired level of protection. Thus the use of the PP is to be reserved for situations "where it does not seem unreasonable to implement the same. When conducting this assessment, the benefits of the protective measures and other precautionary measures should be related to the costs for implementing the same."

However, a main defect of the Unified Environmental Code of 1998 and its accompanying explanations remains. Left unanswered is what degree of certainty (or uncertainty) is required to trigger actions based on the vague PP. Another serious shortcoming of the Swedish legislation is that it makes *anyone* who undertakes *any* action that may have a potential impact on health or the environment responsible for implementation of the PP.

The defenders of such a policy, of course, promote the argument that the "market" has to improve its (eco) toxicological competence. Wishful thinking! Even KEMI has only a handful of trained experts to perform adequate risk assessments. Delegating responsibility for implementing a poorly defined PP down to individual consumers represents a cowardly and unacceptable behavior of the Swedish state, especially in a situation when KEMI employees themselves lack clear guidelines on how to interpret and implement the PP.

The Substitution Principle

The "Substitution Principle" is a fundamental provision of the *Ordinance on Chemical Products* issued pursuant to the *Act on Chemical Products* of 1985.[24]

> If anyone uses a chemical product (or preparation as defined by 2 § of the Ordinance on Chemical Products), and in case such product (or preparation) can be replaced by a product (or preparation) that is less hazardous, but accomplishes the same or similar purpose, and does not entail an unreasonable additional cost, the more hazardous product must be avoided, i.e., it should not be used.[25]

In essence, the product substitution principle, restated in the Unified Environmental Code of 1998, means that although the use of a harmful substance or product is permitted *per se*, it must be avoided or "replaced by one that is less hazardous or completely harmless. Everyone who uses or imports a chemical product must take initiative to appraise if the same result can be achieved by using an alternative chemical product that is less hazardous or completely harmless, or in some other way."[26]

There is, of course, no such thing such as a "completely harmless" chemical product except in the imagination of politicians and the Greens. In a frightening disregard for realities, the Comments to the Unified Environmental Code extends responsibility for adhering to the substitution doctrine to everyone:

> It should be observed, that this paragraph does not only apply to professional use, but the use concept also includes the

24. Statens Författningssamlingar (SFS), *Ordinance on Chemical Products*, issued in pursuant to the *Act on Chemical Products* (SFS 1985:835, 1985b).

25. Ibid.

26. "Comments to the Unified Code," *SOU 103, Part 2* (1996), p. 29.

situation when a private person, who in his role as consumer, undertakes any kind of action . . . the purchase of a detergent may be cited as an example. When, for instance, a car owner is going to wash and clean his car and buys a detergent for this purpose, such as a degreasing agent, in a gasoline station, he must select a product that causes as little harm to the environment as possible, provided that it cleans his car.[27]

Failure to follow the substitution principle to prevent damages to humans or to the environment may carry stiff penalties. In cases of severe negligence, large fines can be levied, and violators can be subject to up to two years' imprisonment.[28]

Applying the Substitution Doctrine

Used with common sense, the substitution doctrine does not seem unreasonable. If a less hazardous chemical can do the job, why not use it? However, in practice, substitution can be required for almost any chemical product marketed in Sweden that fails to satisfy certain hazard criteria, irrespective of the actual level of risk its use carries.

Children's Sand Piles

Because very high exposures to crystalline silica can induce lung tumors in laboratory animals, the World Health Organization's (WHO) International Agency for Research on Cancer (IARC) classified it as a carcinogen.[29] Applying the Swedish interpretation of the PP, and under the criteria established by the Swedish Government's program for *An Environment Free of Poisons*, crystalline

27. Ibid.
28. SFS, 1998, 3§.
29. International Agency for Research on Cancer (IARC), "Monographs on the Evaluation of Carcinogenic Risk of Chemicals to Humans," *Silica and Some Silicates* (Lyon, France: WHO, 1987), pp. 39–143.

silica should therefore be totally eliminated from all consumer products.[30] Natural sand usually contains appreciable amounts of crystalline silica and should thus be banned for use in, for instance, sand piles for children. The lung cancer risk from silica for children playing with sand is negligible because of limited exposures, and for obvious reasons, products containing sand are, of course, not banned in Sweden. Nevertheless, the example illuminates the bizarre consequences that may result from a substitution policy that does not take actual risk into consideration.

Department Store Risk Assessment

Swedish law requires that major retailers make an assessment of potential health and environmental hazards when deciding on which products to stock and sell. As a guide to which chemicals should be avoided, KEMI has published a list of "especially hazardous chemicals" ("*OBS-listan*"). The hazard profiles of the KEMI-listed substances differ widely, from decidedly toxic compounds, like arsenic salts and benzene, to practically innocuous substances, such as metallic zinc and many zinc compounds. (Like any other chemical, including table salt, zinc and its compounds should, of course, not be dumped in rivers in large quantities, but they are perfectly safe in most other contexts.)

KEMI's list of toxics is one of the most important sources of information for retailers in deciding on their purchases. Recent versions of the KEMI list carry an explanatory section that encourages the user to make some sort of risk assessment of the listed substances rather than automatically deciding against a product because it contains one or more of the listed chemicals. However, according to information from the Swedish Chemicals Manufacturers Association, retailers' purchasing departments

---

30. Swedish Ministry of Environment, 1998–99.

can seldom undertake one.[31] Lacking the competence to do this properly, and under pressure to carry products with "green labels" (supposedly environmentally "safe"), they often refuse to buy any product that contains a chemical that is present on the KEMI list. The overall result is the promotion of a number of consumer products of inferior quality in the name of an imaginary or negligible improvement in safety. Alternatively, products are marketed that contain substances not on the list, which are less well investigated and could even be more harmful.

Reasonable and Prudent Precautionary Principle in an International Perspective

I agree that the "precautionary principle" should be given a central position in guiding legislation for the protection of man and the environment, but in a more restricted sense than it is now used in Sweden to tackle widespread "chemophobia." Not only does the Swedish interpretation of the PP open the sluices for capricious regulatory action, it also introduces a factor of arbitrariness that disrupts the functioning of a free market, inevitably inhibits sound technical development, and shifts too much responsibility for technical decisions to citizens and small businesses that are not trained to make them.

Today, reference to the PP can be found in several international agreements and declarations. However, the description of the PP that has had the greatest impact can be found in the *Rio Declaration* from the 1992 United Nations Conference on Environment and Development (UNCED) in Rio de Janeiro, and the Swedish government repeatedly referred to it when it proposed the Unified Environmental Code of 1998 to the Parliament. How-

---

31. J. Bäckström, Kemikontoret, the Swedish Chemicals Manufacturers Association (personal communication, 2002).

ever, the Swedish interpretation agrees poorly with the Declaration, where Principle 15 states that:

> In order to protect the environment, the precautionary approach shall be widely applied by States according to their capabilities. Where there are threats of serious or irreversible damage, lack of full scientific certainty shall not be used as a reason for postponing cost-effective measures to prevent environmental degradation.[32]

PP in the European Union

In 1995 Sweden became a member of EU, which, at least in some ways, has had a sobering influence on national regulatory policies. With a total population of 365 million citizens, the EU has an economy equal to that of U.S. It is a highly complex organization, and the interested reader is referred to EU (2002) for information about it.

For this discussion of the PP and regulatory policy, it is important to know that the EU Commission, the "driving force and executive body" of the EU,[33] is composed of a president and twenty independent members appointed by the Member States after approval by the European Parliament. Based in Brussels, the Commission, aided by its very large staff, proposes legislation, monitors compliance with legislation and with the treaties that govern the EU, administers common policies, and provides substantial economic support for research and development. The European Court of Justice in Luxembourg ensures that the law is observed in the process of Community integration. The EU Commission has the power to appoint expert groups to deal with general topics,

32. United Nations (UN), *Agenda 21: The UN Programme of Action from Rio* (New York: United Nations, 1992).
33. European Union (EU), "Europa. The European Union at a Glance" (http://europa.eu.int/abc-en.htm, 2002).

such as guidelines for risk assessment, classification, and labeling. The members of the expert groups, as a rule, act relatively independently of the Commission, and, above all, most have adequate scientific qualifications. The Economic and Social Committee, a source of technical analyses and opinions for the EU, is a consultative body that includes representative trade unions and social and professional groups as appropriate to the tasks assigned to it, and it has issued several documents concerning risk assessment, the PP, and regulatory policies. At the beginning of 2000, the EU Commission issued general guidelines on the use of the PP with the stated goal to "avoid unwarranted recourse to the principle as a disguised form of protectionism" and to "build a common understanding of how to assess, appraise, manage, and communicate risks that science is not yet able to fully evaluate."[34] The EU Commission makes the very important point that "the precautionary principle, which is essentially used by decision-makers in the management of risk, should not be confused with the element of caution that scientists apply in their assessment of scientific data."[35]

While the Swedish Government sees the PP as an instrument to restrict the overall use of manmade chemicals in society, the EU Commission reserves its implementation of the PP to risks that "in the event of non-action may have serious consequences." The EU Commission's statement is similar to the second sentence of Principle 15 in the Rio Declaration, which reserves the use of the PP to "threats of serious or irreversible damage." The words of the EU Commission and the Rio Declaration impose considerable restraints on when the PP should be applied, and the EU Economic

---

34. The Commission of the European Communities (CEC), *Communications from the Commission on the Precautionary Principle* (Brussels: COM, February 2, 2000).
35. Ibid.

and Social Committee underlined that the PP is to be used only for serious situations when it wrote "The contemporary risk indictor is the notion of disaster."[36]

Regulatory restraint is even more clearly spelled out for chemicals in *Agenda 21*, the program of action adopted by the UNCED Conference.[37] Under Chapter 19 of the Agenda, "banning or phasing out" by regulatory action is reserved for "toxic chemicals that pose an unreasonable *and* otherwise unmanageable risk to the environment or human health *and* those that are toxic, persistent *and* bio-accumulative *and* whose use cannot be adequately controlled."[38] [Emphases added]. In accord with industry,[39] I have no problems whatsoever with such a definition of the PP with respect to regulation of chemicals.

In summary, "risks" in the EU Commission and the Rio Declaration are on a totally different level from the risks addressed by the Swedish regulators. Swedish regulators have, for instance, banned the dry cleaning solvent trichloroethylene, barred the Swedish public from using practically all efficient pesticides, withdrawn a number of effective mosquito repellants, banned copper-based antifouling paints, and are moving to do the same with lead in ammunition, sailing boat keels, accumulators in cars, and sinkers for fishing, and to ban cadmium in recyclable accumulators, and so on. I think that Sweden has gone far beyond anything that the EU Commission had in mind for requiring application of the PP.

Unfortunately, the EU Commission is disconcertingly vague on when to act or not to act under the principle. It states that the "political decision" to rely on the principle is "a function of the

36. ESC, 2000.
37. UN, 1992.
38. Ibid.
39. The European Chemical Industry Council (CEFIC), *Position Paper: Precautionary Principle* (Brussels, Feburary 15, 1995).

risk level that is 'acceptable' to the society on which the risk is imposed." On the other hand, the EU Commission states:

> Recourse to the precautionary principle does not necessarily mean adopting final instruments designed to produce legal effects that are open to judicial review: The decision to fund a research programme or even a decision to inform the public about possible adverse effects of a product or a procedure may themselves be inspired by the precautionary principle.[40]

The EU Commission underlined that actions under the PP should be

1. proportional to the chosen level of protection
2. nondiscriminatory in their application
3. based on an examination of potential benefits and costs
4. subject to review, in the light of new data

I see little evidence that Swedish regulators consider these guidelines in their rushes to regulate.

Sweden's Application of the PP

Sweden's crusade against the use of certain heavy metals provides a recent example of a blatant failure to observe the EU Commission's first requirement of *proportionality* of measures to achieve the appropriate level of protection. Many of the proposed restrictions cannot be expected to improve human health at all, or to have significant beneficial effects on the environment. During the last decades, lead levels in the blood in the Swedish population, including children, have steadily decreased, mainly as a result of the phasing out of leaded gasoline,[41] and they are now similar to

---

40. CEC, 2000.
41. U. Strömberg, A. Schuetz, and S. Skerfving, "Substantial Decrease of Blood Lead Levels in Swedish Children 1978–94, Associated with Petrol Lead," *Occupat. Environ. Med.* 52 (1995): 764–69.

those found in totally unpolluted regions, like the Himalayas.[42] Still, Swedish regulators are resolutely determined to phase out virtually all items made of lead. In June 2001, the Swedish Government notified the EU and the World Trade Organization (WTO) of its intent to ban the use of lead in shot and buckshot, and to allow lead only in bullets that will be used on shooting ranges, and only under conditions of retrieval of the used bullets. This ban is to include Olympic competitions as well as all military purposes. Lead, when ingested, may cause severe lead poisoning in waterfowl, and existing Swedish legislation has already banned the use of lead buckshot for certain purposes. The proposed general ban on lead in other types of ammunition makes little sense.

The Swedish government's announced intentions to ban all uses of cadmium, including in recyclable accumulators, may, in fact, increase health and environmental risks. Cadmium is always present in zinc, and it is obtained from the purification of that metal. If no sensible use can be found for cadmium, the producers will simply leave it in the zinc, resulting in extensive and diffuse emission of cadmium from corroding zinc that will be impossible to control. The regulators' answers to the problems presented by cadmium-laden zinc are attempts to curb uses of zinc as well, in spite of the fact that deficiency of the essential element zinc is a public health problem.

Who Is Responsible for Application of the PP to Risk Decisions in Sweden?

The EU Economic and Social Committee underlines that the PP is the state's responsibility. Under normal circumstances, the regulators should not force the individual citizen, or even the purchasing office of a department store chain, to take on their re-

---

42. S. Piomelli et al., "Blood Lead Concentration in a Remote Himalayan Population," *Science* 210 (1980): 1135–39.

sponsibilities. The Swedish legislation observes no such restraint. It places responsibility for applying the PP on industry, businesses of all sizes, and private citizens, and it also puts the burden of proof on the manufacturer, importer, vendor, or user to demonstrate that suspicions that their product will cause a risk to man or the environment are without grounds. In other words, Sweden reverses the burden of proof, putting the burden on the organization or person wanting to sell or use the product to prove it is without risk, rather than on the government or some agent of the government to prove that it is risky. Both the EU Commission and its Economic and Social Committee reject such reversals of the burden of proof as a general principle, although reserving it for some situations.

Given the fact that the PP can be triggered under great uncertainty, the EU Commission has emphasized that measures based upon it are to be *provisional.* Not unexpectedly, Sweden has opposed this limitation.

Exporting the Precautionary Principle

Roger Bate (see his chapter in this volume) has described the usefulness of DDT in the control of malaria-bearing mosquitoes, and the resurgence of malaria in many countries after DDT use was restricted or banned. Sweden, along with several other countries, has been active in lobbying for a total ban on DDT.

I. M. Goklany, in his recent excellent monograph, discusses implementation of the PP with respect to DDT use in different countries.[43] Prudent use of the PP can justify a ban on DDT in Sweden or the U.S., where problems with malaria are limited and affordable alternatives are available. Consideration of conditions

---

43. I. M. Goklany, *The Precautionary Principle. A Critical Appraisal of Environmental Risk Assessment* (Washington, D.C.: Cato Institute, 2001).

in a country like India, where malaria is a major disease problem and alternatives to DDT are not affordable, should lead to a totally different outcome. The much more severe immediate effects of *not* using DDT should outweigh the far smaller risks that would accompany a ban. To insist that the PP should be applied the same in both kinds of countries, as Sweden has done, is unscientific as well as highly unethical.

Sweden Evades EU Legislation

The ruling Swedish political establishment is, of course, well aware that issuing restrictions based on its own extremist version of the PP may cause serious international complications. In particular, the EU Commission as well as the WTO can be expected to raise objections about Sweden introducing non-tariff barriers to trade. To head off complaints appearing before the European Court of Justice and WTO, Sweden has devised various subtle means to circumvent its international obligations under, for instance, the articles on the *Free Movement of Goods* as stipulated by the 1957 Treaty of Rome.

Defining Hazardous Substances

Pursuant to the legally binding EU Directive 67/548/EEG on *Classification, Packaging, and Labelling of Hazardous Substances,* and as a result of concerted effort, the Member Countries have classified and labeled a large number of chemicals based on degree of hazard. For certain substances, Swedish regulators have been reluctant to accept the EU evaluations, and KEMI publishes its own "particularly hazardous substances" list (*OBS-listan*) mentioned above. Referring to alleged risks to the environment based on KEMI criteria that differ from the EU regulations, Sweden promotes its own alarmist concepts about metallic copper, chromium, cobalt, nickel, and zinc and its compounds. Taking KEMI's approach to its logical ends, Swedish citizens had better get rid of all stainless steel kitchen sinks, nickel-plated faucets, zinc-plated nails, copper roof linings and gutters, and send their copper pots to a recycler of hazardous waste. Turpentine, and most kinds of commonly and widely used distilled petroleum products, should also be avoided. Other commonly used products will probably face the same fate as KEMI extends its lists.

The EU classification and labeling of a chemical as a hazard, by itself, does not translate into any regulatory action. Instead, any regulatory action is to be based on a determination of the *level* of risk associated with the particular uses of a substance. Both the EU *Directive 93/67/EEC on Risk Assessment for New Notified Substances* and the *Commission Regulation (EC) 1488/94 on Risk Assessment for Existing Chemicals* state that quantitative risk assessments are the basis for rational risk management, and that the goal of risk management is to set exposure levels sufficiently low *not* to cause harmful effects. The Swedish Ministry of Environment prefers to forget these directives, and a major part of Sweden's recent policy for chemicals regulation, based entirely on hazard with little or no consideration of exposure, is totally at odds with the basic concepts underlying risk management in the EU as well as in the U.S.

Sweden's Pesticide Regulations

Pesticide regulation is another area where Sweden wants to avoid direct confrontation with the EU Commission, while trying to evade EU regulations. Annex VI to the EU's uniform principles for evaluation and authorization of plant protection products (*Council Directive on the Placing of Plant Protection Products on the Market*, (91/414/EEC) requires that exposure assessments be conducted (Section 2.4.) as a basis for risk assessment. There are at the present no indications that the KEMI intends to comply with this aspect of the EU directive, especially when it comes to pesticide products intended for the general public.

Sweden's trick to avoid following the intentions of the directive is to classify virtually all pesticides that have previously been permitted for use by the general public as "Class II products," meaning that they can be used only by professionals. As a result, the Swedish citizen is barred from using practically all effective pesticides, including a large number of virtually safe products used by consumers worldwide.

For example, the EU recently cleared the herbicide glyphosate (Roundup), which is practically nontoxic to humans, for consumer use. Nevertheless, KEMI has notified importers and distributors that sales of glyphosate to the public will be severely restricted in the future. Faithful to its socialist traditions, the almighty Swedish State attaches no value to the billions of Swedish crowns invested by private homeowners in lawns, flowerbeds, rose gardens, and so on. An appeal to KEMI's decision will most likely be directed to the European Court of Justice.

The withdrawal of a number of copper-containing antifouling paints for pleasure boats and marine vessels in the Baltic, based on alleged minor environmental effects localized to marinas, led to a number of protests to the Swedish government. Although the government upheld the mandated withdrawals, these restrictions will likely also be appealed to the EU Commission and then further to the European Court of Justice.

Try as it will, Sweden probably cannot avoid direct confrontation with the EU Commission in some cases. Even before the EU had set up a common registration process for all active ingredients in pesticides (Council Directive 91/414/EEC), it was clear that Sweden would not be able to convince the EU of the scientific justification for its previous bans of a number of pesticides.[44] The Ministry of Environment has officially characterized this development as more or less a catastrophe for environment protection in Sweden.

This response is absolute nonsense. Sweden had banned the herbicide amitrole and several bis-dithiocarbamate fungicides because of flawed scientific evaluations that misinterpreted thyroid tumors in rodents, known to lack relevance for humans, as indicators of a human risk associated with normal usage. In contrast to Sweden's action, IARC and the U.S. Environmental Protection Agency cleared all of them of suspicions of causing cancer at current exposure levels,[45] and the EU has approved amitrole for general use. Sweden's Minister of the Environment, Kjell Larsson, has declared that Sweden will fight all the way to the European Court of Justice to stop reintroduction of these horribly dangerous pesticides.

Future Developments

My past experience in independent expert groups convened by such bodies as the Chemicals Division of the Organization for Economic Cooperation and Development (OECD), the Joint Food and Agriculture Organization/World Health Organization (FAO/WHO) Meeting on Pesticide Residues, and the International Program of Chemical Safety (IPCS) in Geneva led to high expectations for similar EU groups charged with the task of evaluating chemical risks. Although assessment of hazardous substances in EU

44. R. Nilsson, "Integrating Sweden into the European Union: Problems Concerning Chemicals Control," *The Politics of Chemical Risk—Scenarios for a Regulatory Future 9*, ed. R. Bal and Halffman (Dordrecht, Netherlands: Kluwer, 1998), pp. 159–71.

45. IARC, "Monographs on the Evaluation of Carcinogenic Risk of Chemicals to Humans," *Some Thyreotropic Agents* (Lyon, France: WHO, 2001), pp. 381–410.

may not always represent the ultimate wisdom, I expected the outcomes to be at least competitively neutral with respect to industry and trade inside the community.

However, I have been somewhat disappointed when working within the framework of the EU Existing Substances Program. Under the program, committee members from EU Member States, regulatory agencies generate comprehensive documents for individual high volume chemicals that include recommendations for classification and measures for risk reduction with far-reaching consequences for the European chemical industry. With several notable exceptions, most participants in the committees do not act as independent experts, but rather as advocates for their respective national administrations while practicing various degrees of "political toxicology." In my opinion, it seems quite clear that Sweden has had some success in exporting some of its extremist concepts to other countries in this context.

However, in 2002, as I write this, the recent swing of public opinion to the right that has toppled most of the European Social Democratic governments may herald some important changes to the EU's environmental agenda. Those changes, if they take place, may unfortunately strengthen the left-wing EU-skeptics in Sweden, and eventually result in the country's leaving the Union.

Such a move would have serious economic consequences and accelerate the ongoing marginalization of Sweden among Western nations, where an increasing part of Sweden's industry opts to move its production base outside the country. Any nation that considers incorporating the Swedish variant of the precautionary principle into major parts of its legislative framework should also consider the future competitiveness of their nation in relation to the other large economies outside the EU, primarily the U.S.A., as well as Japan, and, increasingly, China.

TEN

How Precaution Kills

The Demise of DDT and the Resurgence of Malaria

ROGER BATE

Interpretation and application of the precautionary principle by advisers and the educated elites in many developing countries are detrimental to the health and economic development in those countries. This chapter is an examination of several examples of this phenomenon, with a special focus on how unwarranted concern about adverse health and environmental impacts of DDT has caused a resurgence of malaria and deaths from that disease. Developing countries need to be very careful when employing the precautionary principle because their advisers may not appreciate the harm that can result.

Introduction

Many of our preoccupations arise from the modern paradox: although our longevity, health, and environment have never been better, we spend more time than ever worrying about all three. Concerns include both long-standing scares, such as Alar, saccharine, breast implants, passive smoking, nuclear power, pesticide residues in food, children's vaccines, and more recent scares such as mobile phone radiation, genetically modified foods, and global warming. In some cases, the concern is completely invalid, in others the scare is out of all proportion to the likely threat. For several years, my colleagues and I (at the European Science and Environment Forum www.scienceforum.net) have attempted to expose these falsehoods or exaggerations by writing in newspapers, publishing papers, and editing books. We emphasize that while the threats may be real, they are tiny. The out-of-all proportion scares they generate will, at best, divert resources and, at worst, cause significant mortality in poor countries.

This disastrous consequence comes about because intellectuals in less developed countries (LDCs), far from treating the preoccupations of the residents of economically developed countries as affectations of the very rich, adopt these same worries. Craven and Stewart provide an instructive analysis of risk issues in France and the francophone African state of Burkina Faso.[1] The medical, environmental, geographical, and political problems of Burkina Faso are radically different from those in France, but intellectuals in Burkina Faso and college students in France responded similarly to questions about risk. In fact, intellectuals in Burkina Faso had "borrowed" concerns relevant only to France, and their opinions were reflected in the national media. Thus,

---

1. R. Bate, ed., *What Risk? Science, Politics and Public Health* (Oxford: Butterworth-Heinemann, 1997).

such issues as the hypothetical threat of cancer from overhead power lines—against a background of a widespread lack of electricity for refrigeration of food and medicines or lighting for schools—are given a public airing, while serious but perennial problems such as lack of potable water, chronic infectious disease, and malnutrition are ignored.

Why this happens is not adequately established, but some factors are apparent. Media coverage in LDCs generally follows media coverage in powerful trading partners (such as the United States) or former colonial powers (such as France or Britain). Many university graduates in developing countries have been educated in the West and have likely acquired a Western worldview. When they return home, these graduates become opinion-formers in government, education, and the media. Moreover, international donor agencies frequently promote projects that reflect their priorities back home and not necessarily what is required or desirable in the LDCs. Seatbelt campaigns in countries where the only cars are those owned by the aid agencies are a good example.[2]

Even where local governments and media address local problems, the proposed solutions are often driven by Western concerns, which may be inappropriate to local conditions. Local government actions that differ from an unwritten consensus, a tacit international agreement about the "correct" way to deal with an issue, can run into a wall of criticism. Recent examples include Western criticism of South African President Thabo Mbeki's stance on AIDS, Chinese officials' refusal to sanction a UN convention on tobacco, and OPEC States' refusal to go along with the climate change consensus. In all three cases, dissidents have felt the opprobrium of the English-speaking media—conservative

---

2. R. Bate, *Life's Adventure: Virtual Risk in a Real World* (Oxford: Butterworth-Heinemann, 2000).

and liberal alike.[3] That's not to say that officials from these countries were acting in a morally correct way or in a way that will, in the long run, benefit their people, but as leaders of their nations they took actions that put their country's interests first.

Many reasons, such as the expectation of a hostile media response, local political considerations, international pressures, or even personal aggrandizement can explain why poor-country politicians do not always do what is, seemingly, best for their people.[4] There are probably thousands of examples of these decisions, such as recent rejections of well-planned, needed dam construction projects because of environmental destruction that accompanied poorly planned dams in years past. Although it's relatively easy and inexpensive to discover anecdotal examples of such decisions, few such decisions have been analyzed and documented, probably because research costs are so high. Careful, properly documented analyses are particularly rare in the environmental field.

Nevertheless, many anecdotes and the few analyses of the application of the precautionary principle (PP) in developing countries point to a pattern of decisions that harm the citizens of those countries.[5] The PP, which lacks any consistent definition, can be paraphrased (and usually is) by saying that where there is a threat of harm from a technology, lack of scientific knowledge shall not be used as a reason for postponing cost-effective measures to prevent harm. It is reasonable to everyone to "look before you leap," but the practical interpretation of the PP in many Western country policies means that only "looking" is allowed, even

3. Ibid.

4. R. Thurow, "Choice of Evils: As a Tropical Scourge Makes a Comeback, So, Too, Does DDT," *Wall Street Journal,* July 26, 2001.

5. L. Mooney and R. Bate, eds., *Environmental Health: Third World Problems, First World Preoccupations* (Oxford: Butterworth-Heinemann, 1999).

though "leaping" has been necessary for all humankind's progress beyond the cave.

Many publications have addressed this overprecautionary problem in the use of the principle in countries at all stages of economic development and provide examples of zealous promotion of the precautionary principle without due attention to the likely consequences.[6] My particular concern is how application of the principle is being exported from the rich nations to the poorest on the planet with fatal consequences.

Problems with the Precautionary Principle

The precautionary principle purports to be a rule for decision making in uncertainty. In practice, however, it is quite the opposite: a means of imposing arbitrary restrictions on the use of new technologies, be they products, processes, or services.

For example, previous risk management strategies have argued that non-proximate risk should be treated less seriously than proximate risk. But many proponents of the PP argue that remoteness of possible harm is not an excuse for inaction: the mere *possibility* that use of a particular technology *might* have an adverse consequence is sufficient for PP proponents to try to block or restrict that technology. This potential-harm argument is susceptible to the counterargument that preventing the action (technology) *might* also result in harm to human beings,[7] but it's harder to make. Proponents of new technologies are easily tarred and often dismissed with charges that they act only from self-interest.

Some interpreters of the PP demand that a technology should not be used until it has been proved to be harmless. This is im-

---

6. J. Morris, ed., *Rethinking Risk and the Precautionary Principle* (Oxford: Butterworth-Heinemann, 2001).

7. C. T. Rubin, "Asteroid Collisions and Precautionary Thinking," in ibid., pp. 105–26.

possible: it demands a level of knowledge that simply cannot be acquired. The great Aaron Wildavsky observed, "One could well ask whether any technology, including the most benign, would ever have been established if it had been forced to demonstrate that it would do no harm."[8]

The increasing use of the PP in United Nations Conventions is also proving problematic. Proponents of the PP suggest that its application must be open, informed, and democratic, and include all affected parties. Although this sounds good in principle, it can be argued that the international agreements that incorporate the PP are themselves not the products of democratic processes.[9] Furthermore, many countries, lacking the financial and human capital to evaluate the consequences of these agreements, are at a disadvantage in negotiations and may suffer in the subsequent application of the agreements.[10]

The application of the PP will prevent exposure to some new risks, but it also prevents more cost-effective reduction of exposure to existing risks. New technologies generally provide net benefits: if they did not, there would be little incentive to produce them and even less to consume them.

The Danger of Precaution
in the Developing World

Several examples illuminate the counterintuitive effects that can follow adoption of the PP in developing countries:

- Concerns about trihalomethanes (compounds created in wa-

8. A. Wildavsky, *But Is It True? A Citizen's Guide to Environmental Health and Safety Issues* (Cambridge, Mass.: Harvard University Press, 1995).

9. Morris, *Rethinking Risk.*

10. R. Tren and R. Bate, *Malaria and the DDT Story* (London: Institute of Economic Affairs, 2001).

ter chlorination, which are carcinogenic in rats) in drinking water contributed to the Peruvian government's decision to reduce the chlorination of drinking water. The resulting outbreak of cholera in Peru in 1991 killed thousands, and the disease spread across South America causing a million cases. As far as is known, trihalomethane compounds, at the low concentrations present in water, have never killed anyone. "The dose makes the poison," and trace levels in drinking water are a very different proposition from the whopping, maximum tolerated doses that caused cancer in rats.[11]

- In many poor African states there is no electricity grid or coverage is very limited, but there are often dispersed locations that could use significant amounts of energy—an aluminum smelter in Mozambique, for example. A nuclear power plant could provide electricity, but South African efforts to introduce a new small-scale technology, the Pebble Bed Modular Reactor, which is far safer than previous reactors and can be controlled and shut down remotely, are being hampered by international rejection of older nuclear technologies.[12] (See Cohen, this volume, about nuclear power science and politics in the United States.)

- At Alang in the Gulf of Cambay on India's Arabian Coast, thousands of rusting old ships are run against the beach and broken apart. Instead of using expensive dry docks, Indian entrepreneurs use a readily available natural resource, the beach, to dramatically reduce the cost of recycling and employ 40,000 men, some highly skilled and all working there by

11. E. Gersi and H. Ñaupari, "Dirty Water: Cholera in Peru," in Mooney and Bate, *Environmental Health,* pp. 17–46.

12. K. Kemm, *A New Era for Nuclear: The Development of the Pebble Bed Modular Reactor* (Cambridge: European Science and Environment Forum [ESEF], 2000). Available at www.scienceforum.net.

choice, to convert half the world's disused ships into scraps of steel to be used in Indian manufacturing. Environmentalists, instead of welcoming this approach, have pressured governments around the world to stop the practice, and the U.S. Navy no longer sends its ships to Alang. The environmentalists argue that the practice is dangerous and potentially environmentally harmful. It is dangerous for the workers, but they earn many times the income from the alternative backbreaking work in the fields and willingly make this trade-off. Similarly the localized pollution problems affect the people living and working in the region—people who are capable of making trade-offs on their own terms.[13]

My last example of disproportionate concerns making things worse involves the disease malaria, and the use of the pesticide dichlorodiphenyltrichloroethane commonly known as DDT.[14]

Malaria

Most people consider malaria to be a tropical disease, and indeed today it is, but that was not always the case. In the period called the Little Ice Age (over 300 years ago) malaria was common in England and was commonly referred to as "ague."

- William Harvey (who discovered the circulation of blood) wrote: "When insects do swarm extraordinarily and when ... agues (especially quartans) appear early as about midsummer, then autumn proves very sickly."[15]

13. W. Langeweische, "The Shipbreakers," *Atlantic Monthly*, August 2000, pp. 31–49.

14. Tren and Bate, *Malaria.*

15. P. Reiter, *From Shakespeare to Defoe: Malaria in England in the Little Ice Age* (San Juan, Puerto Rico: Centers for Disease Control and Prevention, 2000).

- The diarist Samuel Pepys suffered chronic ague. Oliver Cromwell died of the ague in a cool September 1658.

- William Shakespeare wrote about ague in eight of his plays. Most notably in *The Tempest* (act 2, scene 2), the slave Caliban curses his master Prospero, and hopes that he will be struck down by the disease: "All the infections that the sun sucks up / From bogs, fens, flats, on Prosper fall and make him / By inch-meal a disease!"

The disease is caused by parasitic single-cell protozoa—a plasmodium (such as *P. vivax* or *P. falciparum*) carried by female Anopheles mosquitoes (such as *A. atroparvus* or *A. funestus*). Malaria is characterized by bone-wracking painful periodic fevers, followed by chills, and, in some people, death.

The cure for malaria, quinine powder, was first shown to be effective against malaria as long ago as 1660; this is why we know ague was malaria, because the symptoms were the same, as was the cure. Quinine became known as Jesuit's Powder, and helped cure French King Louis XIV's son. Protestants, viewing quinine as a Catholic cure, didn't like to use it.

Even though quinine was widely used and efforts to eliminate the mosquito's habitat through better drainage (often by planting water-loving eucalyptus trees) reduced the importance of the disease, major epidemics still broke out throughout Europe during the first four decades of the twentieth century. There were epidemics in Russia as far north as Archangel on the Arctic Circle, and outbreaks in Holland, Britain, and many states in the United States. Malaria was endemic to southern U.S. states as well as to Italy and Greece. These countries completely eradicated malaria after World War II. Better access to treatment and reductions in mosquito habitats played a role in eradication, but the major change in control projects that made them successful was the use of insecticides—especially DDT.

History of DDT

DDT was first synthesized in the 1870s, but its insecticidal properties were discovered only in 1940 by the Swiss chemist Paul Muller, who won a Nobel Prize in 1948 for his work. The U.S. military had introduced DDT for control of malaria, typhus, and other insect-carried disease by 1944, and after the end of World War II, DDT was used widely around the world for vector (mosquito) control and in agriculture.

The differences between current vector control practices and past agricultural uses of DDT are important. Vector control relies on spot-spraying inside homes, shops, and other contained spaces. Agricultural use often included widespread sprayings from backpacks, trucks, or aircraft in the open environment.

Success for Some

The successful use of DDT led to enormous optimism that malaria could be eradicated from the entire globe. The reasons for this optimism were clearly apparent. DDT was, and is, highly effective in killing the malaria vector and interrupting the transfer of the malaria parasite, and it is also cheap and easy to use, putting it within reach of even the poorest countries' health budgets.

The early successes of DDT were nothing short of spectacular. In Europe and North America, DDT was widely used and malaria had been eradicated from both continents within a few years. It is thought that the transmission of malaria in Greece was halted in the course of one year. One historian even suggested that malaria eradication "was the most important single fact in the whole of modern Italian history."[16]

---

16. D. Mack-Smith, *Italy: A Modern History* (Chicago: University of Chicago Press, 1959).

Perhaps the most remarkable success story was in Sri Lanka (then Ceylon). DDT spraying began in 1946 and was an instant success with the island's death rate from malaria falling dramatically. Within ten years, DDT use had cut the prevalence of malaria from around three million cases to 7,300 and had eliminated all deaths from malaria. By 1964, the number of malaria cases had been reduced to just seventeen and at the time, it was assumed that Sri Lanka had won the war against malaria.

India also used the pesticide to great effect. When India started its malaria-control program in 1953, almost the entire country was malarial, except for the mountainous areas, and there were, and still are, six different species of Anopheline mosquito vectors. Using DDT, India managed to bring the number of cases down from an estimated 75 million in 1951 to around 50,000 in 1961 and to reduce the annual mortality from malaria from about 800,000 to a few thousand. The achievement of reducing the number of infections to this degree cannot be overstated. India's success persists today because the country continues to use DDT. Reductions in malaria in many other countries were short-lived when they discontinued its use.

No Complete Victory over Malaria

Only ten countries achieved complete eradication of malaria, four in Europe and six in the Americas and the Caribbean. A variety of reasons account for the absence of such successes elsewhere.

International malaria eradication programs got off to an optimistic beginning in the 1960s. Pushing for rapid implementation of DDT spraying to eliminate the pool of parasites in humans before mosquito-resistance to DDT developed, the World Health Assembly adopted the Global Malaria Eradication Campaign in May 1955. But a variety of failings—complacency about the level of planning necessary for successful eradication, poor training, poor DDT formulation, poor medical detection of cases, poor entomological data, and lack of political will—led to the demise of program by the mid-1960s.

Almost all the funding for the World Health Organization's (WHO) international strategy to eliminate malaria came from the United States. The U.S. contributed $17.5 million of the total $20.3 million budget of the WHO program between 1956 and 1963; all other countries combined contributed only $2.8 million. Independently of the WHO program, the U.S. Agency for International Development (USAID) spent $1.2 billion on its own malaria-control operations between 1950 and 1972.

Vector control efforts were never fully implemented in Africa, even though that continent bore the greatest burden of disease. Many African countries had neither the infrastructure nor the human capacity to carry out spraying programs systematically and effectively. However, today the infrastructure is better and eradication programs would be more likely to succeed, if they were reinstituted.

DDT was remarkably successful in almost all the countries in which it was used, but it was not a magic bullet. A number of factors, including rainfall and the migration of people, influence the spread of malaria, and building a malaria-control strategy solely reliant on vector control, and in particular on the use of one pesticide (DDT), was optimistic at best and foolish at worst. When vector control programs failed, DDT became associated with failure, although the failure was of policy, not of the chemical. In addition to the failings already listed, rapidly rising donor fatigue and some limited resistance to DDT that developed in mosquitoes contributed to the demise of DDT. Perhaps more important, environmental and health concerns about DDT (many of which have since been shown to be exaggerated) shifted the issue away from science and toward emotionalism.

Green Backlash and Its Impact Today

Perhaps the most well known attack on DDT was Rachel Carson's book *Silent Spring*, published in 1962. The book popularized DDT scares and claimed that the insecticide would have devastating impacts on bird life, particularly those higher up the food chain, such as eagles and falcons. The publisher's summary on the back of the 1972 edition of *Silent Spring* says:

> No single book did more to awaken and alarm the world than Rachel Carson's *Silent Spring*. It makes no difference that some of the fears she expressed ten years ago have proved groundless or that here and there she may have been wrong in detail. Her case still stands, sometimes with different facts to support it.

In reality her case does not stand, and as the summary states, it is largely alarmist.

Despite the fact that many of the fears surrounding DDT were unfounded and based on inadequate, unscientific studies, the U.S. Environmental Protection Agency (EPA) banned DDT in 1972. In deciding to ban, the EPA administrator, William Ruckelshaus, overturned scientific reports, including one from the U.S. National Academy of Sciences claiming that DDT had saved millions of lives, and evidence from numerous expert witnesses that firmly opposed a ban of DDT and argued in favor of its continued use. Ruckelshaus's preoccupations with potentially negative environmental and health impacts (despite all the evidence to the contrary) and his refusal to accept the offered scientific advice condemned millions to death in malarial countries by denying them access to this life-saving pesticide.[17] Without ever uttering the words "precautionary principle" and probably without ever hav-

---

17. K. Mellanby, *The DDT Story* (Farnham, Surrey, Eng.: British Crop Protection Council, 1992).

ing heard them, Ruckelshaus put the principle into operation, eliminating a proven beneficial insecticide because of perceived risks and without consideration of alternatives to banning DDT.

The green movement's attitude to DDT in disease control was (and is) nothing short of callous and couched in a neo-Malthusian idea that global populations are growing out of control and that resources are running out. Malaria is therefore bizarrely seen as a saving grace from impending environmental disaster to be brought about by overpopulation.

Critically, the EPA failed to emphasize that the amount of DDT used in vector control is tiny compared with the amount used in agriculture. There simply is no danger to the environment or human beings from using DDT in vector control, even if there was from its use in agriculture.[18]

DDT is Banned

Following the U.S. lead, most developed countries soon imposed outright bans on DDT for all uses. Some developing countries imposed a complete ban on the pesticide, as Sri Lanka did in 1964, when officials believed the malaria problem was solved. By 1969 the number of cases had risen from the low of seventeen (when DDT was used) to over a half million. Other developing countries —South Africa, for example—banned DDT for agricultural use (in 1974).

When applying pressure against the use of DDT, Western donors sometimes supported their arguments with statements that resistance was rendering it ineffective.[19] Recent evidence shows, however, that even where resistance to DDT has emerged

18. A. Attaran et al., "Balancing Risks on the Backs of the Poor," *Nature Medicine* 6 (2000): 729–731.
19. Ibid.

the "excito-repellancy" of DDT causes mosquitoes not to enter buildings that have been sprayed.[20] Simply put, mosquitoes don't like settling on areas sprayed with DDT. Hence it is unlikely that malaria rates would have increased (significantly) even if resistance became a factor.

Malaria Recovery

Malaria rates have bounced back, as explained above. Some health specialists have asserted a linkage between global warming and this resurgence.[21] But according to world expert Dr. Paul Reiter, former head of Vector Control at the U.S. Centers for Disease Control in Puerto Rico and now at Harvard University's School of Public Health:

> Increase has been attributed to population increase, forest clearance, irrigation and other agricultural activities, ecologic change, movement of people, urbanization, deterioration of public health services, resistance to insecticides and anti-malarial drugs, deterioration of vector control operations, and disruptions from war, civil strife, and natural disasters. Claims that malaria resurgence is due to climate change ignore these realities and disregard history.[22]

According to WHO (http://www.who.int/inf-pr-2000/en/pr2000-78.html), malaria kills about one million people annually, mostly children, and mainly in Africa. There are between 300 and 500 million new cases annually, meaning that between one in

---

20. J. P. Grieco et al., "A Comparison Study of House Entering and Exiting Behavior of *Anopheles vestitipennis* (Diptera: Culicidae) Using Experimental Huts Sprayed with DDT or Deltamethrin in the Southern District of Toledo, Belize, C.A," *J. Vector Ecol.* 25 (2000): 62.

21. A. J. McMichael, *Planetary Overload: Global Environmental Change and the Health of the Human Species* (Cambridge: Cambridge University Press, 1993).

22. Reiter, *From Shakespeare to Defoe.*

twenty and one in eight of all the six billion people in the world
are infected each year.

Economic Costs

Controlling malaria is obviously vital for immediate humanitar-
ian reasons, but the disease's economic burden adds to developing
countries' woes by crippling development. Professor Jeffrey Sachs
and colleagues at the Harvard University Center for International
Development analyzed the effects of malaria on twenty-seven
African economies between 1965 and 1990 and found that the
disease cut economic growth rates by one percentage point a
year.[23] The cumulative impacts are staggering. If malaria had
been eliminated in 1965, Africa's annual gross domestic product
would now be $400 billion, rather than $300 billion.

Sachs and his colleagues did more than assess only the costs
of disease treatment and losses associated with death. They also
estimated the losses from tourists and foreign investors avoiding
malaria-prone countries, the damage done by large numbers of
sick children missing school, and the increase in population and
impoverishment that ensues when parents decide to have extra
children because they know some will die. Sachs and his colleagues' study confirms research done by Richard Tren of the
NGO (nongovernmental organization) Africa Fighting Malaria,
which shows that the cost to Southern Africa is several billion
dollars a year, and that this figure was far higher in the past.[24]
(AFM is a registered NGO in South Africa, and I serve on its board
of directors.)

It is important to note that countries that have continued to

23. J. L. Gallup and J. D. Sachs, "The Economic Burden of Malaria," *Am.
J. Trop. Med. and Hyg.* 64 (2001): 85–96.
24. R. Tren, "Economic Costs of Malaria in South Africa: Malaria Control
and the DDT Issue" (1999). Available at http://www.iea.org.uk.

use DDT have lower death rates and lower economic losses than those that have tried to manage without. For example, Ecuador increased its use of DDT after 1993 and during the next six years saw a 60 percent decline in new malaria cases. By contrast, Bolivia, Paraguay, and Peru, which stopped spraying DDT altogether in 1993, saw new cases rise by 90 percent over the same period.[25]

Indeed, some developing countries, including South Africa, Botswana, Ecuador, Indonesia, and India, have quietly used DDT for the past three decades, without exciting much comment. In 1997, however, the United Nations Environment Program (UNEP) decided to promote a treaty—a framework convention—that would ban twelve persistent organic pollutants (POPs), including DDT, in all countries.

Rise of Conventions—the International Environmental Community Has Its Way

A UN Framework Convention sets the ground rules and tone of UN treaty processes. It usually establishes conditions that the parties can readily agree on. In the POPs treaty process (as in all UNEP treaties), the developed world, mainly European and American interests, are promoting the agenda and draft text. Because these countries do not produce any of the twelve targeted chemicals, it was easy for them to promote a total ban (and a PP approach) and for Green groups and politicians to claim an important victory, showing that they were changing the world—and, they didn't say, helping them to raise revenue and attract voters.

Three factors account for language of the convention not being so completely prohibitionist as it appeared in early drafts.

- Western industries argued that the earlier language would

25. Mooney and Bate, *Environmental Health.*

have opened the door to pressures from environmental organizations and the treaty secretariat on chemicals that are
produced and used in the West.

- Officials from developing countries that produce and use
  some of the twelve chemicals argued for exceptions for certain
  uses of those chemicals.

- Pressure from two or three pro-DDT anti-malaria groups who
  are concerned about the fate of DDT.

The Malaria Foundation and the Malaria Project coordinated
a pro-DDT letter signed by over 400 malaria specialists around
the world, including three Nobel laureates, which received publicity in the *New York Times* and other important media outlets.
Africa Fighting Malaria maintained a media campaign in South
Africa to remind politicians of the importance of DDT and the
potential harm of the POPs Convention. AFM brought some of the
world's foremost malaria specialists to a meeting in Johannes-
burg and hosted a press conference about the meeting. The experts bolstered the position taken by the host nation in favor of
DDT use and they isolated the environmentalists opposed to DDT
use, who eventually dropped their demands for a global DDT ban
by 2007.

The Status of DDT Under the Convention

In May 2001 in Stockholm, ninety-one countries signed the United
Nations Persistent Organic Pollutants Convention to ban twelve
organic chemicals over the next decade. Most of the chemicals
will be phased out relatively quickly, but DDT has been reprieved
for use in controlling malaria for the foreseeable future.

Malthusian environmentalists may be privately relieved to
know that the reprieve is not really working. Even though DDT
use is accepted, both under the treaty and by the World Health

Organization, the insecticide is becoming harder to procure. Simply listing DDT under the treaty has been sufficient to discourage its production and use in malarial countries, and mistaken concerns about DDT are depriving residents of LDCs, especially countries in Africa, of safer and longer lives.

DDT was probably harmful to wildlife when used in massive doses on cotton farms in the 1950s in America (although not so harmful as Carson and her followers made out), but it has never been proved to harm humans except those who tried to commit suicide with it. In any event, any harm to wildlife in America and Europe has been reversed. In contrast to its agricultural use, malaria control requires only that the insides of houses be sprayed; used properly, little DDT is released into the environment. Yet myths persist about the harms it causes. Many Zambians think it causes male impotence. Most Westerners think it causes cancer. Nearly everyone forgets that only in massive doses can DDT cause problems.

Why Countries Do Not Act in Their Own Interests

The several reasons that developing countries are not doing the best they can to fight malaria are interrelated.

1. Western Green pressure groups have maintained a PP campaign for thirty years against DDT.

2. Aid agencies, staffed by environmentalists who accept the PP arguments, have not approved funds in recent years for procurement of DDT. Indeed, some agencies, such as USAID, have even pressured countries (notably Bolivia) not to use it.[26]

3. Governments of the developed world, and increasingly of poor countries, stopped producing DDT, so that only India

26. Attaran et al., "Balancing Risks."

and China currently produce it in any quantities.[27] No private companies still produce DDT. Some former producing companies, such as Montrose Chemical of California, are still in court fighting charges about the alleged affects of DDT production, but Montrose has not produced DDT since the 1980s and it's a shell of a company compared to what it was.

4. Countries, such as Botswana in 1998, switched to other pesticides when they could not procure any DDT from dwindling world markets, even though this meant buying less of a more expensive alternative.

5. The elites in even the poorest countries, such as Mozambique, think it almost unseemly to use a pesticide that has been banned in the North and is due for elimination under the POPs treaty.[28]

6. Most people cannot believe that DDT is still the best pesticide to control malaria vectors, even though its use began nearly sixty years ago.

Only countries with political clout and political sense about DDT, notably South Africa, China, and India, still use it. South Africa had stopped using DDT in 1996 under pressure to join the world's Green community and switched to the next best alternative, the synthetic pyrethroids, which are three times the price and are effective over a shorter time span. Four years later, in 2000, South Africa decided to resume DDT spraying after malaria cases jumped by 1,000 percent because of mosquito resistance to the synthetic pyrethroids.

The only real hope for expanded use of DDT comes from some companies operating in countries that allow DDT to be used. The

27. Tren and Bate, *Malaria.*
28. R. Bate, "DDT Saves Lives," www.TechCentralStation.com, February 14, 2002.

malaria-control programs run by the metals company Billiton, in Richard's Bay, South Africa, and by various mining companies in Zambia provide examples of the continuing efficacy of DDT. In all places where DDT is being used, malaria rates are falling back to the low levels not seen for over a decade. It is possible that current supplies of DDT will run out and that manufacturers will not produce any more. Should that happen, the excellent operations that now use DDT will be forced to switch to the more expensive and less effective alternatives. This will mean that fewer lives may be protected in the future.

While the delegates of the countries who signed the POPs treaty think they have been magnanimous in exempting DDT from an immediate ban, they have unwittingly consigned many children to death in Africa. Simply listing DDT in the treaty has been sufficient for that.

Conclusion

The increasing use of the precautionary principle is stifling development in Europe and to a lesser, but increasing, extent in America and around the world.[29] In rich countries, the precautionary principle costs money, and because of its inflexible application, it is unlikely to provide benefits. In poorer countries, it is likely to be harmful, sometimes causing catastrophic effects on human health. Concerns about chlorination and the push for a DDT ban are the most obvious examples of this phenomenon.

In my opinion, the PP should rarely be used to make decisions, and never by Western advisers to LDCs. If the PP is to be adopted more broadly, decisions about adoption must genuinely be made by those worst affected by its implementation, with full accounting of cost-benefit and risk-risk trade-offs.

29. Morris, *Rethinking Risk.*

Making such changes is easier said than done. The initial reason for using the PP was to enable decisions to be made when there was considerable uncertainty about the impact of a technology. As use of the PP expands, attempts to be rational, to use the best science available, and to balance the possible outcomes are essential.

It is far from certain who will do the job of being rational, using the best science, and balancing the outcomes. It is fairly obvious that Western multinational companies, which have much to gain from the use of sound science in the developing world, will not be the vehicle to promote science as the basis of policy because they are easy targets for discrediting by environmental organizations and the media. Neither can it be expected that Western NGOs or governments, which have staked their policies on regulation of new technologies, will be prepared to question the application of the PP.

The most likely promoters of sound science and opposers of the PP will be pro-growth activists and scientists from the developing world. For example, pro-biotech female Kenyan scientists make a far more compelling case for the benefits of the technology to the world's media than do white male directors of Monsanto. Similarly, media-aware rural doctors' groups in India, demanding the use of DDT to prevent malaria, are more effective than predominantly white pro-market people like me.

The organized self-interest of the poor is the best hope against the widespread use of the PP. It is essential for those who value the use of science in policy to help these interests organize: the pro-DDT campaign is perhaps something of a template.

ELEVEN

The Revelle-Gore Story

Attempted Political Suppression of Science

S. FRED SINGER

This is a personal account linking efforts to suppress scientific publication about climate science and policy by then-Senator (later vice president) Al Gore and his staff.[1] In those efforts, an individual working closely with Senator Gore and his staff made false and damaging statements about my behavior as a scientist. I filed a libel suit against the individual. The suit was settled when he issued a retraction and apology to me that included a statement that members of Senator Gore's staff had made "similar statements and insinuations" to those that he retracted.

Vice President Al Gore also tried to influence at least one TV

---

1. Candace Crandall played a pivotal role in the author's lawsuit against Dr. Justin Lancaster and its resolution, and she contributed to the drafting of this chapter.

news anchor to carry out an investigation designed to discredit those who disagreed with his personal views about climate change. His effort failed because of the newsman's integrity.

Our country's laws provide protection from libelous statements, and I was able to defend myself through the legal process. The free press and a newsman's integrity saved a number of scientists, including me, from a public attack intended to discredit them. In my case, "the system worked," but it cost my legal representatives and me money and time to defend against attacks launched from one of the most powerful politicians of the time.

Background

Dr. Roger Revelle was one of the outstanding oceanographers of the twentieth-century. My acquaintance with him goes back to the International Geophysical Year (IGY) of 1957, which was a major undertaking of the world's geophysicists to conduct measurements of the Earth and its environment. As part of the IGY, Dr. Revelle started the groundbreaking measurements of atmospheric carbon dioxide that led him and colleagues at the Scripps Institute of Oceanography in La Jolla, California, to conclude that not all carbon dioxide emitted from the burning of fossil fuels would be quickly transferred into the ocean and some might accumulate in the atmosphere. And indeed, as the measurements soon showed, atmospheric CO_2 was increasing steadily, with only about half absorbed in the ocean.

Revelle and I intersected again a decade later. He had served as science adviser in the Department of Interior, and I followed him in a similar position. In 1968, as a deputy assistant secretary of Interior, I organized a symposium under the auspices of the American Association for the Advancement of Science (AAAS) on the global effects of environmental pollution. Dr. Revelle participated as a panelist and discussed the possible effects of increasing

CO_2 on global climate. He considered the possibility that human-caused modification of atmospheric composition might affect climate to be a "grand geophysical experiment," and he didn't express any particular concerns about possible negative impacts from global warming.

Dr. Revelle and I continued to have professional interactions in the 1970s. He invited me to spend a few months as his guest at the Center for Population Studies at Harvard where he was a visiting professor, and Al Gore was to be one of his students. While his wife was traveling, I stayed in his house, and we lived as bachelors for a couple of weeks.

I later served on an AAAS committee that he chaired. After Dr. Revelle's return to California, whenever I visited the Scripps Institution, I would stop by to talk to him about ongoing work and the state of the world.

The *Cosmos* Article

In February 1990, at the annual meeting of the AAAS in New Orleans, Dr. Revelle presented an invited paper on ocean fertilization. He discussed the idea that adding nutrients like iron, which are present in only very low concentrations in seawater, would stimulate the production of plankton and thereby accelerate the absorption of CO_2 from the atmosphere into the ocean. By that time, the idea had begun to take hold that greenhouse warming from increased CO_2 presented an important environmental problem, and ocean fertilization ("ocean farming," as it is sometimes called) seemed a possible mitigation scheme. I was quite taken by the approach and arranged to discuss it with him the following morning over breakfast at the Hilton Hotel where we were both staying. At that meeting we agreed to write an article about greenhouse warming. As the junior member, I undertook to write a first draft that included ideas about ocean fertilization from Dr. Revelle's AAAS paper.

While we were working on the article, Dr. Revelle and I decided to invite Dr. Chauncey Starr to join us as a coauthor because of his expertise about energy research and policy and because we had made extensive use of his ideas and quoted from his work in the first draft. Dr. Starr, who holds the National Medal of Technology, is a member of the National Academy of Engineering, and was then the director of the Electric Power Research Institute in Palo Alto, California. After Dr. Starr joined us, I agreed to prepare an expanded draft, and in the following weeks I sent three successive versions to my coauthors and to other scientists, receiving comments and completing a near-final draft in late 1990.

We decided to submit the article to the Cosmos Club of Washington, D.C., for publication in the inaugural issue of the *Cosmos* journal. The circulation of the *Cosmos* journal is small, going to approximately 3,000 members of the club. Although the club was founded for "the advancement of its members in science, literature, and art," and "their mutual improvement by social intercourse,"[2] few members have a deep interest in the subject of climate change, and *Cosmos* is not the sort of journal read by Washington policy wonks.

The *Cosmos* editors accepted the article and sent me galley proofs in January 1991. I took the galleys with me when I attended a climate workshop at the Scripps Institution in February and discussed final corrections with Drs. Starr and Revelle who also attended the workshop.

Dr. Starr offered only minor changes, having made his main contributions in the earlier drafts. Dr. Revelle offered to meet with me after the final session of the workshop to discuss suggested

2. Cosmos Club, "The Cosmos Club," http://www.cosmos-club.org/main.html (undated).

changes, which he had marked in his copy of the galleys. On February 6, we met for roughly two hours in his office to go over the changes, which involved spirited discussions of, among other things, the value of mathematical climate models. Dr. Revelle was quite skeptical about the models, but I persuaded him that they might be substantially improved within a decade. Our discussion is preserved in scribbles made on the galleys, which I saved in my files together with the earlier drafts. When we were satisified with the galleys, we went to his house for cocktails, followed by dinner in a restaurant with his wife Ellen, and several of his friends.

Our *Cosmos* article, "What to Do About Greenhouse Warming: Look Before You Leap," appeared in April 1991.[3] Our main conclusion was a simple message: "*The scientific base for a greenhouse warming is too uncertain to justify drastic action at this time.*" It echoes almost precisely Dr. Revelle's words in letters to members of Congress following hearings in the (very hot) summer of 1988, in which concerns about global warming were raised. One of his letters went to then-Congressman Tim Wirth, who chose not to heed Revelle's advice and, as Under Secretary of State for Global Affairs, became a close ally of Vice President Gore in promoting the drastic restrictions on fossil fuel use embodied in the 1997 Kyoto Protocol to the 1992 Rio Climate Treaty.

Drs. Starr, Revelle, and I each received reprints of the *Cosmos* article, which we sent to colleagues, as is the usual custom. In addition, my organization, the Science and Environmental Policy Project (SEPP), sent reprints to its media contacts. Our article and conclusions created no stir of any kind.

Dr. Revelle died three months later, in July 1991. A remarkable

---

3. S. F. Singer, C. Starr, and R. Revelle, "What To Do About Greenhouse Warming: Look Before You Leap," *Cosmos* 1 (1991): 28–33.

man and scientist, he remained professionally active right to the end, traveling and lecturing throughout the United States.

The *Cosmos* article seemed forgotten. But late in 1991, Dr. Richard Geyer of Texas A & M University contacted me about writing a chapter for an edited book, *A Global Warming Forum: Scientific, Economic, and Legal Overview.*[4] Being inundated with other projects, I suggested that he contact the editor of *Cosmos* for permission to reprint the article I had coauthored with Drs. Revelle and Starr. Professor Geyer agreed.

The Lancaster Flap

More than a year after our article appeared in *Cosmos,* journalist Gregg Easterbrook, a contributing editor to *Newsweek,* referred to it in a piece entitled "Green Cassandras" in the July 6, 1992, issue of the *New Republic* and gave it a political slant.[5] He wrote that Al Gore in his book *Earth in the Balance*[6] had claimed that Dr. Revelle, as his mentor at Harvard, had introduced him to the problem of climate change. In his article, Mr. Easterbrook wrote: "*Earth in the Balance* does not mention that before his death last year, Revelle published a paper that concludes, 'The scientific base for greenhouse warming is too uncertain to justify drastic action at this time. There is little risk in delaying policy responses.'"[7]

Following Mr. Easterbrook's piece, other columnists and editorial page editors, including George Will, picked up on the subject. The contradiction between what Senator Gore wrote about what he had learned from Dr. Revelle and what Dr. Revelle had

4. R. Geyer, ed., *A Global Warming Forum: Scientific, Economic, and Legal Overview* (Boca Raton, Fla.: CRC Press, 1993).
5. G. Easterbrook, "Green Cassandras," *New Republic,* July 6, 1992, pp. 23–25.
6. A. Gore, *Earth in the Balance* (New York: Plume, 1992).
7. Easterbrook, "Green Cassandras."

written in the *Cosmos* article embarrassed Senator Gore, who had become the leading candidate for the vice presidential slot of the Democratic Party. When the difference between Senator Gore's book and Dr. Revelle's article was raised during the 1992 vice presidential debate, Senator Gore deflected it, sputtering that Dr. Revelle's views had been "taken completely out of context."

I was unaware of these developments until I received a telephone call on July 20, 1992, from Dr. Justin Lancaster at the Environmental Science and Policy Institute, Harvard University, who introduced himself as a former associate of Dr. Revelle. In our conversation, Lancaster first requested and then demanded that I remove Revelle's name from the article to be reprinted in the Geyer volume. I was taken aback by such an unusual request and asked Lancaster to write me a letter, which he did on the same day. I replied, saying that I could not remove Revelle's name since he was a coauthor and could not give his permission as he had died. In any case the copyright for the article resided with the *Cosmos* journal.

When I refused his request, Dr. Lancaster stepped up the pressure on me. First at a memorial symposium for Dr. Revelle at Harvard in the fall of 1992 and in a lengthy footnote to his written remarks at that event, he suggested that Dr. Revelle had not really been a coauthor and made the ludicrous claim that I had put his name on the paper as a coauthor "over his objections." He later added the charge that I had pressured an aging and sick colleague, suggesting that Dr. Revelle's mental capacities were failing at the time.[8] Subsequently, Dr. Anthony D. Socci, a member of Senator Gore's staff, made similar outrageous accusations in a lengthy letter to the publishers of the Geyer volume, requesting that the

---

8. J. Lancaster, letter to Dr. Richard Geyer, Bryan, Tex., August 17, 1992; J. Lancaster, letter to Ms. Helen Linna and Ms. Barbara Caras, CRC Press, October 20, 1992.

Cosmos article be dropped.[9] Neither the editors nor the publishers consented to the requests (near demands) of Lancaster and Socci.

My repeated requests to Dr. Lancaster that he cease his defamation and retract his false accusations failed to get an acceptable response. Only then and encouraged by my wife, Candace Crandall, did I file a libel suit against Dr. Lancaster.

The Libel Suit Against Dr. Lancaster

The Center for Individual Rights of Washington, D.C., filed the libel suit on my behalf in April 1993, with the Washington law firm of Kirkland and Ellis serving as pro bono counsel. Dr. Lancaster, an attorney, first handled his own defense but later was represented pro bono by the Boston law firm of Goodwin Procter and Hoar.

The discovery process for the suit produced a number of revelations about Dr. Lancaster's interactions with Senator Gore and the senator's staff (including Dr. Socci) and about the senator and his staff's intentions. According to Dr. Lancaster's deposition, Senator Gore called him after the Easterbrook article appeared. During the phone call, the senator asked Dr. Lancaster about Dr. Revelle's mental capacity in the months before his death and whether the article accurately reflected his views.

In a draft for a letter in reply to the senator's questions, Dr. Lancaster completely undermined the claims that he later made against me, stating Dr. Revelle was "mentally sharp to the end" and that he was "not casual about his integrity," Dr. Lancaster also wrote that Dr. Revelle had shown the *Cosmos* manuscript to him before it was published, with the comment that he "felt it was honest to admit the uncertainties about greenhouse warming, including the idea that our ignorance could be hiding benefits as

9. A. D. Socci, letter to Mr. Robert Grant, CRC Press, October 27, 1992.

well as catastrophes." Most important, Dr. Lancaster stated that he and Dr. Revelle "agreed that there did not seem to be anything in the article that was not true" and that "Roger thought about and probably agreed with the overall thrust of the article, i.e., look before you leap."[10]

In the discovery process, we also learned that Dr. Lancaster had been an advisory editor for the Geyer volume but had not objected to the *Cosmos* article's carrying Dr. Revelle's name until after Gregg Easterbrook's piece in the *New Republic* had caused embarrassment to Al Gore. We also found much additional evidence linking Senator Gore to Dr. Lancaster. Dr. Lancaster prepared seven drafts for a reply to the *New Republic* in response to Mr. Easterbrook's article and ran them by the senator's staff. On one fax, he asked, "Is this close to what the Senator had in mind?"[11] In faxes to Dr. Lancaster, Gore's staff director Katie McGinty sensibly admonished him to stop denying Dr. Revelle's coauthorship —because, after all, "Revelle's name is on the paper."[12] She suggested adding, "a concluding sentence such as, 'Senator Gore was right in relying on and praising [in his book] Revelle's contributions' would also be effective."[13]

Facts That Became Clear During the Discovery Process

1. Dr. Lancaster's many written statements and correspondence indicate that he was aware that Dr. Revelle had fully collaborated on the *Cosmos* article and indeed that the article incorporated the paper that Dr. Revelle had presented at the February 1990 AAAS

10. J. Lancaster, draft letter to Senator Albert Gore, July 20, 2002, found on a computer disk of Dr. Lancaster during the discovery process.

11. J. Lancaster, Fax cover sheet to draft letter from Dr. Lancaster and two others objecting to G. Easterbrook's article in the *New Republic* ("Sent 7/10/92" handwritten on cover sheet).

12. K. McGinty, Faxed memorandum to J. Lancaster, July 10, 1992.

13. K. McGinty, Fax to J. Lancaster, July 21, 1992.

meeting. Only two years after the article appeared and Al Gore had become a vice presidential candidate did Lancaster raise any questions about the *Cosmos* article.

2. From the beginning of this controversy, Dr. Lancaster had been aware that I still had the galley proofs of the *Cosmos* article, with Dr. Revelle's handwritten corrections and annotations in the margin, demonstrating his active participation in the preparation of the article.

3. Dr. Revelle's calendar, as we learned from his secretary, showed a full schedule of speaking engagements, conferences, and travel for that period and after. One would not expect such a schedule if Dr. Revelle was an invalid and becoming senile as Dr. Lancaster later claimed.

4. Contrary to statements made by Dr. Lancaster, no member of Dr. Revelle's family or his scientific colleagues expressed complaints, second thoughts, or any other negative views about the article, and no member of the family ever requested that Dr. Revelle's name be taken off the *Cosmos* article.

5. Moreover, Dr. Revelle's daughter wrote a letter in response to George Will's column, published in the *Washington Post*, that affirmed Dr. Revelle's coauthorship and restated many points made in the *Cosmos* article.[14]

6. Rather than attempt to obtain information about the writing of the article from another source, according to Dr. Lancaster's deposition, he never bothered to contact Chauncey Starr, the third coauthor of the *Cosmos* article. Apparently, Senator Gore's office focused his attention on me, probably because of my public skepticism about the magnitude of the effects of global warming.

7. Like Senator Gore, Dr. Lancaster seemed to be under the impression that scientists who question the basis for a global

---

14. C. R. Hufbauer, "Global Warming: What My Father Really Said," *Washington Post*, op-ed, September 13, 1992.

warming catastrophe, such as Robert Balling, John Christy, Hugh Ellsaesser, William Happer, Sherwood Idso, Richard Lindzen, Patrick Michaels, William Nierenberg (Revelle's successor as director of the Scripps Institution), Chauncey Starr, Roy Spencer, and many others are part of some sort of energy-industry conspiracy. The facts don't bear that out, at least in my case, although some of the others may have received support from the energy industry. So far as Dr. Lancaster's funding was concerned, a December 27, 1993, *Boston Globe* article revealed that he received financial support from the Natural Resources Defense Council and the Environmental Defense Fund, two organizations actively promoting the idea of a climate emergency.

Victory

A public relations campaign by Dr. Lancaster in late 1993 in the Boston area failed to elicit any local or national attention for his side of the case. More spectacularly, an attempt by Vice President Gore and his staff to get the case aired on ABC News *Nightline* and to besmirch the reputations of some scientists who disagreed with the senator about global warming not only failed; it backfired.

On February 24, 1994, Ted Koppel revealed on his *Nightline* program that Vice President Gore had called him and suggested that Mr. Koppel investigate the political and economic forces behind the "antienvironmental" movement. In particular, Vice President Gore had urged Mr. Koppel to expose as fact that several U.S. scientists who had voiced skeptical views about greenhouse warming were receiving financial support from the coal industry and/or groups such as the Lyndon Larouche organization or Reverend Moon's Unification Church.

Mr. Koppel didn't do the vice president's bidding and asked rhetorically, "Is this a case of industry supporting scientists who happen to hold sympathetic views, or scientists adapting their views to accommodate industry?" He closed the show by chastising Gore for trying to use the media to discredit skeptical scientists:

> There is some irony in the fact that Vice President Gore—one of the most scientifically literate men to sit in the White House in this century—[is] resorting to political means to achieve what should ultimately be resolved on a purely scientific basis. The measure of good science is neither the politics of the scientist nor the people with whom the scientist associates. It is the immersion of hypotheses into the acid of truth. That's the hard way to do it, but it's the only way that works.

The attempt to use Mr. Koppel to tar the reputations of his opponents brought criticism down on the vice president, and I learned of rumors that the Clinton White House had become nervous about the issue, and perhaps Vice President Gore himself was becoming nervous. In any case, on April 29, 1994, Dr. Lancaster's attorneys indicated they were ready to have him sign a retraction and apology.[15]

In its press release celebrating the victory, the Center for Individual Rights stated:

> Any attempt to alter or suppress a scientist's published views after his death cannot be tolerated. This retraction is an important victory for science. Politics too often takes precedence over scientific evidence. Had Dr. Singer not taken action against Lancaster's false and defamatory claims, it would have had a chilling effect on all scientists now confronting political correctness on environmental issues.[16]

15. J. Lancaster, "Statement by Justin Lancaster" to settle libel suit brought by F. Singer, April 29, 1994. (See also Addendum.)

16. Center for Individual Rights, "'Global Warming' Libel Suit Reaches Settlement," press release, May 24, 1994.

Final Reflections

To me, Mr. Gore's involvement in this case as a senator and then as vice president was surprising and intimidating. It demonstrated his willingness to use the power of public office in attempts to undermine the reputation of those who disagree with him and to win by smearing them rather than relying on the strengths of his arguments

Although Mr. Gore does not hold office as I write this in 2002, it is almost certain that he will be involved in electoral politics for many years to come. I have two major concerns about Mr. Gore and his position (or perhaps "posturing" is a better word) on global climate change and scientists who disagree with him.

1. He appears to believe that those who disagree with him are part of some vast industry-led conspiracy, and his ego will not entertain the thought that his opposition really is just a group of individuals and small organizations led by people whose motivation is something other than financial gain. Some scientists who oppose him do receive funding from organizations and companies that have earned Mr. Gore's ire, and he has tried, as he did with Ted Koppel, to smear those scientists with guilt by association. Ironically, I think that Mr. Gore would be first in line to defend people who are besmirched that way by others, even if he disagreed with their opinions.

2. As his own aides have reportedly said, Gore has "a long memory." Like Richard Nixon, it is said that he's a "don't get mad, get even"[17] kind of guy—witness the many scientists who have been harassed and bullied (see chapter by Happer, this volume) and the journalists who have been frozen out or fired.

17. B. Zelnick, *Gore: A Political Life* (Washington, D.C.: Regnery, 1999).

More generally, Mr. Gore's actions show some ways in which a powerful politician can attack his enemies. Even in my case, where I "won," his attacks, through Dr. Lancaster, diverted me from other work, caused me to incur court costs, and reduced the time I could spend on running SEPP. Such a victory is very costly. Mr. Gore, on the other hand, risked only exposure of his methods.

More positively, my experience shows that an individual scientist depending on the due process of the country's legal system and the independence of the news media (or at least some of its members) can oppose the politically powerful. And my victory in the libel suit may inhibit other politicians from attempting to discredit those scientists who disagree with them, or, perhaps more likely, discourage individuals, such as Dr. Lancaster, from engaging in such activities to further political goals.

Addendum

Statement by Justin Lancaster

The late Professor Roger Revelle was a true and voluntary coauthor of the article entitled "What To Do About Greenhouse Warming: Look Before You Leap," along with Professor S. Fred Singer and Chauncey Starr, Ph.D. The article was published in April 1991 in the inaugural issue of *Cosmos*, the journal of the Cosmos Club of Washington, D.C.

I retract as being unwarranted any and all statements, oral or written, I have made which state or imply that Professor Revelle was not a true and voluntary coauthor of the *Cosmos* article, or which in any other way impugn or malign the conduct or motives of Professor Singer with regard to the *Cosmos* article (including but not limited to its drafting, editing, publication, republication, and circulation). I agree not to make any such statements in future. I fully and unequivocally retract and disclaim those statements and their implications about the conduct, character, and ethics of Professor Singer, and I apologize to Professor Singer for the pain my conduct has caused him and for any damage that I may have caused to his reputation. To the extent that others, including Anthony D. Socci, Ph.D., Edward A. Frieman, Ph.D., and Walter H. Munk, Ph.D.,[18] relied on my statements to make similar statements and insinuations, I also apologize to Professor Singer. I also regret that I have caused Professor Singer to incur litigation costs to resolve this matter.

/s/ Justin Lancaster
Dated April 29th, 1994.

18. Socci was on Gore's senate staff. Frieman and Munk were scientists at the Scripps Institute of Oceanography, whom Lancaster knew well; they were all politically active in the Gore campaign of 1992.

Index